ADVANCED
QuickBASIC

ADVANCED
QuickBASIC

Don Inman
Bob Albrecht
Arne Jamtgaard

Osborne **McGraw-Hill**

Berkeley New York St. Louis San Francisco Auckland Bogotá
Hamburg London Madrid Mexico City Milan Montreal New Delhi
Panama City Paris São Paulo Singapore Sydney Tokyo Toronto

Osborne **McGraw-Hill**
2600 Tenth Street
Berkeley, California 94710
U.S.A.

For information on translations and book distributors outside of the U.S.A.,
please write to Osborne **McGraw-Hill** at the above address.

A complete list of trademarks appears on page 353.
Screens produced with InSet®, from Inset Systems, Inc.

Advanced QuickBASIC

1234567890 DOCDOC 898

ISBN 0-07-881361-1

CONTENTS

PREFACE

BASIC is the most commonly used language for personal programming. Some dialect of BASIC is included with the purchase of most personal computers, and many personal computer users program in BASIC because it is easy to learn and use.

QuickBASIC from Microsoft takes a giant leap beyond yesterday's BASIC. Since it has its roots in earlier versions of Microsoft BASIC, it is still easy to learn and use. Although most of your own BASICA or GW-BASIC programs can be run from QuickBASIC, you will soon be rewriting old BASIC programs to take advantage of QuickBASIC's advanced features.

QuickBASIC Version 4.5 takes another leap beyond earlier versions. It is designed to be used at two levels, one for the beginner and one for the advanced programmer. Whichever level you use, you can edit, compile, run, and debug programs within a single environment. All of QuickBASIC's programming tools are contained in one integrated package, ready for use at any time.

ABOUT THIS BOOK

This book has been written for, and developed using, QuickBASIC Version 4.5. It is assumed that you have previously programmed in some version of BASIC. If you have used some form of Microsoft BASIC or an earlier version of QuickBASIC, you are ready to move right into QuickBASIC Version 4.5. A knowledge of MS-DOS (the Microsoft Disk Operating System) is also assumed.

This book offers a different point of view and a different approach to learning how to use the massive amount of information available from the Microsoft manuals and disks. A background is laid in early chapters to provide a common base for the material that follows. The book contains many demonstration examples and programs to simplify the use of QuickBASIC procedures, statements, functions, and programming methods. Screen displays show what is happening at critical stages in the development of demonstrations and in program use. As you work through *Advanced QuickBASIC*, you'll find it helpful to sit down at your computer and run the examples and demonstration programs.

Although we describe specific steps in a given operation, it is not practical to describe the steps for every conceivable computer configuration. Some demonstrations use a minimal, two floppy-disk system for operational steps. If you are using a hard disk drive, the steps will be different, but less involved, than those used with a floppy drive system. It is much easier to transfer such information from a small system to a large system than vice versa.

The same logic is used in the chapters describing the use of graphics. The book limits discussions to screen modes for text (SCREEN 0), four-color graphics (SCREEN 1), and two-color graphics (SCREEN 2). These are the screen modes usually available in a minimal system. If you use other modes, the techniques described can easily be altered to fit them.

A consistent style of programming has been used in this book. Programs are easy to read and understand. Programming "tricks" and shortcuts that would detract from learning have been avoided. The nomenclature and syntax of QuickBASIC features are as close as possible to those used in the Microsoft manuals.

The first three chapters provide background information on QuickBASIC. Chapter 1 describes and reviews QuickBASIC. Chapter 2 discusses the conventions and programming style used in this book and then compares QuickBASIC Version 4.5 with earlier QuickBASIC versions. Chapter 3 explains the advantages and uses of Quick libraries and shows how to create a library of three subprograms step by step.

Chapters 4 through 7 are devoted to the development of graphics techniques. In Chapter 4, the discussion of text mode graphics, often used in business applications, explains the creation and use of pull-down windows. Since different numbering systems are used to display text and graphics, the chapter discusses the relationship between text and graphics screen positions. The relationship is used to correlate the placement of mixed text/graphics screen displays.

Chapter 5 presents tiling patterns as an alternative to solid-colored shapes. Chapter 6, on sprites and animation, presents some practical applications and techniques used in a lighter vein. Chapter 7 discusses the transformation of two-dimensional objects on the screen by the use of WINDOW and VIEW statements, as well as by the use of matrix multiplication.

Chapters 8 through 11 describe the creation and use of several kinds of data files. Chapter 8 discusses sorting and searching methods using files stored in arrays. The same methods are demonstrated using disk files in the remaining chapters. A large medical information program is slowly developed by adding sections to a small original program. You learn how to enter patient data and add information as additional patient visits are made. Indexed, keyed, relational, and unstructured files are discussed.

Microsoft QuickBASIC Version 4.5 is an extremely powerful language that contains rich and elegant features. While it is impossible to cover all of its capabilities in a book this size, we present a variety of advanced features and techniques to provide a background for further exploration in your own areas of interest. Programming skills are developed through use. You are encouraged to use what you learn from this book for such exploration and development.

Don Inman
Bob Albrecht
Arne Jamtgaard

ADVANCED QuickBASIC
CONVENIENCE Disk

You may wish to order a disk containing all programs discussed in *Advanced QuickBASIC*. All files are in ASCII format.

Advanced QuickBASIC disk: $10.00 (check or money order)

Name: _____

Address: _____

City, State, ZIP: _____

Send to:

Different Worlds Publications
2814 19th Street
San Francisco, CA 94110

California residents, please add applicable sales tax.

Allow 4-6 weeks for delivery.

1

A COMMON
STARTING POINT

Since readers of this book have a wide variety of computer experience, the authors made some assumptions to arrive at a useful common starting point for those readers. This book assumes that you have been using and so have considerable knowledge of earlier versions of QuickBASIC, preferably QuickBASIC Version 4.0. A working knowledge of Turbo Basic, MBASIC, ZBASIC, True BASIC, or some other version of the ever-popular BASIC language would also provide you with the necessary background.

If you have not had such experience, the authors recommend that you read and use a beginning QuickBASIC 4.5 book, such as *QuickBASIC Made Easy* by Bob Albrecht, Wenden Wiegand, and Dean Brown (Osborne/McGraw-Hill, 1989). Or you could choose an intermediate QuickBASIC 4.0 book such as *Using QuickBASIC*, by Don Inman and Bob Albrecht (Osborne/McGraw-Hill, 1988).

A BIT ABOUT QuickBASIC

Any authors' attempt to classify a discussion as beginning, intermediate, or advanced is subject to the interpretation of the reader. Therefore, this chapter presents a common starting point for this advanced presentation.

1

QuickBASIC 4.5 is the latest version of QuickBASIC from Microsoft Corporation. It runs much more quickly than interpreted BASIC versions and still retains the interactive qualities of the language. It combines the interactive strength of interpreted BASIC with the speed of a compiler and the functions of structured, modular languages.

QuickBASIC 4.5 functions like QuickBASIC 4.0, except that a number of changes have been made to make it easier to use for beginning programmers. For example, the setup procedure now provides a simpler and more comprehensive SETUP program with tree-structured menus. With this program you can make your configuration choices before you begin to actually install QuickBASIC 4.5. These choices are saved in the QB.INI file so that SETUP can remember and display all your configuration choices when it is run again.

QuickBASIC provides the following two levels of menus:

- **EasyMenus**   These provide the simplest user interface. Items that provide advanced or redundant features have been removed from the full menus. Also, unnecessary items that might confuse the beginner have been removed, and some dialog boxes have been simplified.

- **Full Menus**   These provide all the features that are used by advanced programmers.

The SETUP program allows the following two levels of installation:

- **Level 1**   This level is used with EasyMenus. Use the default settings of the SETUP program. You can change the options whenever you wish from the Options menu.

- **Level 2**   This level provides all the features needed for advanced programming.

Since this book is intended for advanced programmers, Easy Menus and the Level 1 SETUP are ignored except where a distinction is necessary.

QuickBASIC includes the following features:

- Compatibility with BASICA and GW-BASIC
- A built-in, full-featured editor, compiler, and debugger
- Pull-down menus, dialog boxes, and on-line help
- Commands selected from menus by keyboard or mouse
- Compiles in memory to save time
- Checks syntax as program lines are entered
- Supports structured programming with alphanumeric labels, structured logic statements, subprograms, and multi-line functions
- Supports libraries of program modules
- Supports the creation of .EXE files
- Supports graphics, BLOAD, BSAVE, sound, music, and event trapping

As you can see, QuickBASIC employs the same powerful yet friendly and easy-to-use language environment that is characteristic of other versions of Microsoft BASIC.

QuickBASIC has many advanced features, yet it is compatible with IBM's Advanced BASIC (BASICA) and Microsoft's GW-BASIC which run on many IBM PC compatible computers. QuickBASIC is intended for users who know these interpreted versions of Microsoft BASIC. Of course, if you have used earlier versions of QuickBASIC, this latest version will seem familiar.

The features added to QuickBASIC 4.5 allow you to make an easier transition from GW-BASIC and other languages to Quick-

BASIC. You can now progress smoothly from a beginning level to the more advanced features of QuickBASIC. When you become advanced enough, you may want to move on to the powerful features of Microsoft's BASIC Compiler.

USE OF BASIC RESERVED WORDS

A good starting point for an advanced presentation is to discuss which BASIC statements and functions to use and which not to use. Many of you have probably programmed in BASICA or GW-BASIC. Since Microsoft's QuickBASIC 4.5 is compatible with BASICA and GW-BASIC, many ASCII-saved BASICA or GW-BASIC programs can be loaded, compiled, and run by Quick-BASIC. However, some BASICA and GW-BASIC statements and functions cannot be used, some require modification, and some are carry-overs from earlier versions of Microsoft BASIC. The following section discusses such statements and functions.

Unusable Reserved Words

The BASICA and GW-BASIC statements and functions in the following list cannot be used in a QuickBASIC 4.5 program because they perform editing operations on the source file, interfere with program execution, refer to a cassette device, or duplicate support provided by the QuickBASIC environment:

AUTO	DELETE	LLIST	MOTOR	SAVE
CONT	EDIT	LOAD	NEW	USR
DEF USR	LIST	MERGE	RENUM	

No statement or function in this list is used in this book.

Modifiable Reserved Words

BASICA and GW-BASIC programs that contain the following statements may require modification before they can be compiled and run by QuickBASIC 4.5. See the *Programming in BASIC* manual that came with your QuickBASIC package for a detailed description of how these statements are used by QuickBASIC 4.5.

BLOAD	CHAIN	DIM	RESUME
BSAVE	COMMON	DRAW	RUN
CALL	DEF	PLAY	

This book assumes you are aware of the necessary modifications. It discusses and uses the statements in this list as they are described in the *Programming in BASIC* manual.

Appendix A gives a complete list of QuickBASIC 4.5 reserved words. This book may use any reserved words in that list, except for the statements listed here.

OTHER PREPARATORY CONSIDERATIONS

You should know how to use all menus and their associated dialog boxes. QuickBASIC lets you use both the mouse and keyboard for menu and dialog box selection. The *Learning to Use QuickBASIC* manual explains how to move around between menus and dialog boxes, with both keyboard and mouse. Therefore, this book assumes that you know how to use the method appropriate for your system. This book does not give detailed information on how to select menu items or dialog box responses.

You should also have some knowledge and experience in using the QuickBASIC editor and the debugging tools. You should be familiar with most of the QuickBASIC keywords of Version 4.5.

This book discusses new QuickBASIC 4.5 keywords when they are introduced.

This chapter includes a quick review of intermediate level topics with which you should be familiar. If any of the material in the rest of this chapter is unfamiliar to you, you should consult your QuickBASIC manuals or read through a beginning or an intermediate level book such as those referred to earlier.

QuickBASIC REVIEW

To understand QuickBASIC terminology, you need to have a clear concept of the unit called a module. A module is an individual file containing QuickBASIC statements. A module can be a self-contained program, or it can be a file containing one or more SUB or FUNCTION procedures that are invoked from other modules. Programs that contain more than one module are called multi-module programs. When you save a multi-module program, each module is saved in a separate file.

Every QuickBASIC program has a main module. In a multi-module program, the main module contains the first statement to be executed when the program is run. A module can be a part of many different programs. However, a module can be the main module of only one program (the program that bears the module's name). In a single module program, the program, including any SUB and FUNCTION procedures, is the main module.

The procedures SUB...END SUB and FUNCTION...END FUNCTION are particularly important to QuickBASIC programs. These procedures are similar to subroutines and DEF FN statements, but they have distinct advantages over the older structures. The three major benefits of programming with these procedures are as follows:

- They allow you to break your programs into discrete logical units. Each unit can be tested and corrected more easily than programs that do not contain such units.

- Once procedures have been debugged, they can be used as building blocks in the same or other programs.

- They are generally more reliable because they have only one entry point and because any variables declared inside them are, by default, local to that procedure.

User-Defined Functions

You can use the DEF FN statement to name and define your own functions. You can use either a single-line function definition as in GW-BASIC and BASICA, or you can use the powerful multi-line function definition that is not available in GW-BASIC and BAS-ICA. You can only use DEF FN functions in the module in which they are defined.

Program 1-1 uses the following three single-line function definitions:

DEF FNcent#   Rounds a double precision number to two places

DEF FNmin!   Finds the minimum of two single precision numbers

DEF FNsrch%   Searches a string for a substring

Notice that DEF FN functions must be defined before the function is used. That is, you must position the function definition ahead of any statement in the source text that refers to the DEF FN. You may want to group function definitions together early in the program, before any of them are used.

When you run Program 1-1, it first asks you to enter two double precision numbers. The numbers you enter are assigned to the variables *first#* and *secnd#*. These variables are used in DEF FNcent# to round the numbers to two decimal places.

Next, Program 1-1 asks you to enter two single precision values. The values you enter are assigned to *n1!* and *n2!* respec-

```
REM ** DEMONSTRATION OF DEF FN **
' Program 1-1   File: PR00101.BAS

REM ** Define Function FNcent# **
' Rounds a double precision number to two places
DEF FNcent# (mn#) = SGN(mn#) * INT(100 * ABS(mn#) + .5) / 100

REM ** Define Function FNmin! **
' Finds the minimum of two single precision numbers
DEF FNmin! (n1!, n2!) = n1! * ABS(n1! <= n2!) + n2! * ABS(n1! > n2!)

REM ** Define Function FNsrch% **
' Searches a string for a substring
DEF FNsrch% (st$, sbst$) = INSTR(UCASE$(st$), UCASE$(sbst$))

REM ** Input Numbers **
DEFINT A-Z: CLS
INPUT "First double precision number, please "; first#
INPUT "Second double precision number, please "; secnd#
PRINT : INPUT "First single precision number, please "; n1!
INPUT "Second single precision number, please "; n2!
PRINT

REM ** Call Numeric Functions and Print Results **
PRINT "Rounded value of first number is "; FNcent#(first#)
PRINT "Rounded value of second number is "; FNcent#(secnd#)
PRINT
PRINT "Minimum of single precision numbers is "; FNmin!(n1!, n2!)
PRINT

REM ** Input Strings, Search, and Print **
LINE INPUT "String to be searched, please? "; st$
LINE INPUT "String to search for, please? "; sbst$

REM ** Call String Function and Print Results **
PRINT : found = FNsrch%(st$, sbst$)
IF found = 0 THEN
   PRINT CHR$(34); sbst$; CHR$(34); " not found in the string."
ELSE
   PRINT CHR$(34); sbst$; CHR$(34); " starts at position";
   PRINT found; "in the string."
END IF
END
```

Program 1-1. Demonstration of DEF FN

tively. The single precision variables *n1!* and *n2!* are used in DEF FNmin!. This function identifies the minimum of *n1!* and *n2!*, which is displayed on the screen as a single precision value, along with the rounded values of the double precision values *first#* and *secnd#*.

Finally, it asks you to enter a string and then a substring. The computer searches the entered string for the entered substring. You can enter the strings in upper case, lower case, or a mixture of upper and lower case. The search is independent of case. If the substring is not found, the computer displays this fact on the screen. If the substring is found, the computer displays the position in the string where the substring begins.

The search function is performed by DEF FNsrch% using the variable *st$* for the string and *sbst$* for the substring. The three function definitions are shown in the following listing:

```
DEF FNcent# (mn#) = SGN(mn#) * INT(100 * ABS(mn#) + .5) / 100

DEF FNmin! (n1!, n2!) = n1! * ABS(n1! <= n2!) + n2! * ABS(n1! > n2!)

DEF FNsrch% (st$, sbst$) = INSTR(UCASE$(st$), UCASE(sbst$))
```

A typical output of Program 1-1 is shown in Figure 1-1.

```
First double precision number, please ? 1234567.890123
Second double precision number, please ? 354.065123456789

First single precision number, please ? 123.4567
Second single precision number, please ? 190.1234

Rounded value of first number is  1234567.89
Rounded value of second number is  354.07

Minimum of single precision numbers is  123.4567

String to be searched, please? This is the string to be searched.
String to search for, please? Ring

"Ring" starts at position 15 in the string.




Press any key to continue
```

Figure 1-1.   Output of Program 1-1

QuickBASIC's multi-line function definition is more powerful than the single-line function definition. You can place a block of statements between the function's name and parameter list line and the end of the function as shown in the following listing. The vertical ellipses represent the block of statements that define the function.

```
DEF FNfunctionname (parameterlist)
    .
    .
    .
END DEF
```

Program 1-2 uses two multi-line functions to define more complex functions that cannot be squeezed into a single line.

Variables used within a DEF FN function definition are global to the current module by default. However, you can make a variable in a DEF FN function local by putting it in a STATIC statement. A STATIC statement is not used in the function definitions in Program 1-2. Therefore, all variables used in the definitions are global.

Function definitions often contain a parameter list in parentheses following the function's name. A parameter is a variable name that holds a place for the arguments that are passed to the function. Incoming parameters are protected from being modified in a DEF FN function. The following listing shows that the variable *strng$* is used as a parameter in Program 1-2.

```
DEF FNcount% (strng$)

DEF FNsqueeze$ (strng$)
```

The statement that calls the function contains an argument list. An argument is a constant, variable, or expression that is passed to a function when it is called. DEF FN functions are called by using them in QuickBASIC statements. Variables are passed to a DEF FN function by a value in an argument list. Technically, when you are using a DEF FN function, a temporary copy of the variable is created, and the address of the copy is then

```
REM ** WORD COUNTER & SPACE SQUEEZER **
' Program 1-2  File: PR00102.BAS

REM ** Define FUNCTIONS **

' FNcount% counts words in a string
DEF FNcount% (strng$)
  words = 0
  FOR num = 1 TO LEN(strng$)
    char$ = MID$(strng$, num, 1)
    IF char$ = " " THEN
      words = words + 1
    END IF
  NEXT num
  FNcount  = words + 1
END DEF

' FNsqueeze$ squeezes spaces from a string
DEF FNsqueeze$ (strng$)
  squeeze$ = ""
  FOR num = 1 TO LEN(strng$)
    char$ = MID$(strng$, num, 1)
    IF char$ <> " " THEN
      squeeze$ = squeeze$ + char$
    END IF
  NEXT num
  FNsqueeze$ = squeeze$
END DEF

REM ** Use the Function Definitions **
DEFINT A-Z: CLS
LOCATE 2, 10: PRINT "Type Q and press ENTER to quit."
VIEW PRINT 5 TO 24
DO
  LINE INPUT "String, please ? "; teststring$
  IF UCASE$(teststring$) = "Q" THEN
    EXIT DO
  END IF
  PRINT
  PRINT "The word count is "; FNcount%(teststring$)
  PRINT :  PRINT "Your squeezed string is"
  PRINT FNsqueeze$(teststring$)
  PRINT
LOOP
VIEW PRINT: CLS
END
```

Program 1-2.   Word Count and Space Squeezer

passed to the function. As shown in the following listing, Program 1-2 calls each DEF FN function and passes each one the value of *teststring$*, the string that you enter.

```
PRINT "The word count is "; FNcount%(teststring$)
PRINT FNsqueeze$(teststring$)
```

Notice that block IF...THEN...ELSE statements are used in Program 1-2. This format provides a clear and readable structure. In the program section called "Use the Function Definitions," an EXIT DO statement is included to allow an orderly exit from the DO...LOOP when you press the Q key. DO...LOOP statements may also use an UNTIL or WHILE clause in either the DO or the LOOP statement.

A VIEW PRINT statement is used to specify a "scrolling" area of the text screen. First the instruction "Type Q and press ENTER to quit" is printed at line 2. Then the VIEW PRINT statement specifies lines 5 to 24 as the scrolling area to be used for future printing. Therefore, the instructions do not scroll off the

```
        Type Q and press ENTER to quit.

String, please ? This is a test string to count words and squeeze spaces.

The word count is  11

Your squeezed string is
Thisisateststringtocountwordsandsqueezespaces.

String, please ?
```

Figure 1-2.   Program 1-2: first string

screen when this area fills. Just before the program ends, another VIEW PRINT statement that specifies no lines expands the scrolling area to the full screen.

Typical outputs for Program 1-2 are shown in Figure 1-2 and Figure 1-3.

FUNCTION...END
FUNCTION Procedure

The multi-line DEF FN function improves on the single line DEF FN function definition. However, the FUNCTION...END FUNCTION procedure provides the same capability with some additional advantages.

All variables used within a FUNCTION procedure are local to the procedure. However, you can use global variables with the

```
        Type Q and press ENTER to quit.

String, please ? This is a test sentence to count words and squeeze spaces.

The word count is  11

Your squeezed string is
Thisisatestsentencetocountwordsandsqueezespaces.

String, please ? Now, here is a second sentence.

The word count is  6

Your squeezed string is
Now,hereisasecondsentence.

String, please ? q
```

Figure 1-3.   Program 1-2: ready to quit

SHARED statement or the SHARED attribute of other statements.

Program 1-3 uses two FUNCTION procedures. Except for the opening and closing lines, the block of statements in the FUNC-TION are the same as those in the DEF FNSqueeze$ function definition of Program 1-2. The difference between the opening line and the two closing lines is shown in the following listing:

```
FUNCTION Squeezer$ (strng$)          DEF FNsqueeze$ (strng$)
   .                                     .
   .                                     .
   .                                     .
   Squeezer$ = squeeze$                  FNsqueeze$ = squeeze$
END FUNCTION                          END DEF
```

A FUNCTION procedure begins with the keyword FUNC-TION followed by its name (FUNCTION Squeezer$ in the previous example). The first line may also include a list of parameters containing the variables being passed to or from the FUNCTION. Only one variable, *strng$*, is passed in this example.

A FUNCTION procedure returns a single value in its name, so the name of a FUNCTION must agree with the type it returns. In the previous example, the string *Squeezer$* is returned. The value to be returned (*squeeze$*) is assigned in the next to last line in the example. The FUNCTION name (Squeezer$) must match the name of the value returned (*Squeezer$*).

The end of the FUNCTION procedure must be declared by an END FUNCTION statement.

A FUNCTION procedure is accessed by using its name in an expression. The following listing shows you three ways to access the FUNCTION named "Squeezer$" and pass the variable *Array$(num)*:

```
After$(num) = Squeezer$(Array$(num))

PRINT Squeezer$(Array$(num))

If Squeezer$(Array$(num)) = "END" THEN PRINT
```

Program 1-3 uses the first form in the previous listing to call FUNCTION Squeezer$. The value of the Squeezer$ procedure is

```
DECLARE FUNCTION Squeezer$ (strng$)
DECLARE FUNCTION Count% (strng$)
REM ** WORD COUNT & SQUEEZER WITH FUNCTIONS **
' Program 1-3  File: PR00103.BAS

REM ** Get Array Size and Dimension Array **
DEFINT A-Z: CLS
LOCATE 2, 2: INPUT "How many strings"; size
REDIM Array$(1 TO size)
REDIM After$(1 TO size)

REM ** Print Instructions, Set Viewport, Get Strings **
CLS : LOCATE 2, 10
PRINT "Type Q and press ENTER to quit."
VIEW PRINT 5 TO 24
FOR num = 1 TO UBOUND(Array$)
  LINE INPUT "String, please ? "; Array$(num)
  IF UCASE$(Array$(num)) = "Q" THEN
    EXIT FOR
  END IF
  After$(num) = Squeezer$(Array$(num))
  WordCount = Count%(Array$(num))
NEXT num
VIEW PRINT: CLS : num = num - 1
PRINT "The total word count is"; WordCount
PRINT
FOR num = 1 TO UBOUND(Array$)
  PRINT After$(num)
NEXT num
END

FUNCTION Count% (strng$) STATIC
  words = 0
  FOR num = 1 TO LEN(strng$)
    char$ = MID$(strng$, num, 1)
    IF char$ = " " THEN
      words = words + 1
    END IF
  NEXT num
  RunCnt = RunCnt + words + 1
  Count = RunCnt
END FUNCTION

FUNCTION Squeezer$ (strng$)
  squeeze$ = ""
  FOR num = 1 TO LEN(strng$)
    char$ = MID$(strng$, num, 1)
    IF char$ <> " " THEN
      squeeze$ = squeeze$ + char$
    END IF
  NEXT num
  Squeezer$ = squeeze$
END FUNCTION
```

Program 1-3.   Word Count and Space Squeezer with FUNCTIONS

assigned to the variable *After$(num)*. The value being passed to the procedure is the string *Array$(num)*, which has just been entered.

This illustrates that a DEF FN function definition and a FUNCTION procedure are implemented quite differently. You enter a DEF FN definition as a part of the main program. You enter a FUNCTION procedure as a part of the main program, but it is listed separately and viewed from the View menu.

A FUNCTION procedure is entered from the Edit menu by selecting the New FUNCTION option. A dialog box then appears where you enter the name of the FUNCTION...END FUNCTION to be used. After your entry, QuickBASIC provides part of the first line and the last line of the procedure. For the Squeezer$ FUNCTION, QuickBASIC automatically provides the following lines:

```
FUNCTION Squeezer$_
END FUNCTION
```

You then finish the first line and enter the balance of the FUNCTION procedure.

The Count% FUNCTION procedure of Program 1-3 illustrates an optional feature. Notice the word STATIC at the end of the first line of this procedure, which is shown in the following listing:

```
FUNCTION Count% (strng$) STATIC
```

This optional STATIC attribute indicates that the FUNCTION's local variables are to be saved between calls to the FUNCTION. The word count for each string is calculated in the Count% procedure and assigned to the variable *RunCnt*.

```
RunCnt = RunCnt + words + 1
```

The value of *RunCnt* is preserved between calls so that the word count of additional strings can be added to keep a running total. After the final call to the function, the value of *RunCnt* is the total word count for all the strings you entered.

The STATIC attribute is not needed in the Squeezer$ FUNC-TION. In that procedure, each string is assigned to a different variable.

The strings you entered in Program 1-3 are assigned as elements of an array (*Array$*) that is dimensioned by a REDIM statement that dynamically assigns the array's size according to your input. Another array (*After$*) is used for the final squeezed strings. The following listing shows how this array is also dynamically dimensioned:

```
REDIM Array$(1 TO size)
REDIM After$(1 TO size)
```

FOR...NEXT loops that include array statements use Quick-BASIC's UBOUND function to define the upper limit of the loop counter. An example of this is shown in the following listing:

```
FOR num = 1 to UBOUND(Array$)
```

Enter and run Program 1-3. Figure 1-4 shows an example of typical input to the program and Figure 1-5 shows the resulting output.

SUB...END SUB Procedure

A SUB procedure's opening and closing lines are similar to those of a FUNCTION procedure. The SqzCount SUB procedure used in the next program has the following opening and closing lines:

```
SUB SqzCount (Array$())
    .
    .
    .
END SUB
```

The STATIC attribute is not used in SqzCount because the SUB procedure is only called once. Thus, the word count does not have to be preserved to produce a running total of words used.

```
        Type Q and press ENTER to quit.

String, please ? This is a test demonstration of Program 1-3.
String, please ? It accepts strings entered from the keyboard.
String, please ? It counts the total number of words entered
String, please ? in the strings and prints the strings as
String, please ? squeezed strings.
```

Figure 1-4.   Five strings for Program 1-3

Be sure to consider the following points when you are deciding whether to use the STATIC option with SUB and FUNCTION procedures:

1. Variable access is much faster when STATIC is used.

2. Extra time is required to access a non-STATIC SUB or FUNCTION procedure because variable space must be allocated on the stack.

3. Large SUB and FUNCTION procedures that have many variables use a lot of stack space and often require the use of a CLEAR statement. This uses space that could otherwise be allocated to strings.

Notice that the characters are squeezed and the words are counted in the same IF...THEN...ELSE block. These two

```
The total word count is 33

Thisisatestdemonstrationof Program1-3.
Itacceptsstringsenteredfromthekeyboard.
Itcountsthetotalnumberofwordsentered
inthestringsandprintsthestringsas
squeezedstrings.
```

```
Press any key to continue
```

Figure 1-5.   Output of Program 1-3

actions were performed in separate FUNCTION procedures in Program 1-3.

Any variables or arrays in a SUB procedure are considered to be local to that subprogram, unless they are explicitly declared as shared variables in a SHARED statement. The array *After$* is declared in a SHARED statement within the subprogram. The variable *words* is declared to be shared by the SHARED attribute in a DIM statement in the main program.

```
      .
      .
      .
DIM SHARED words AS INTEGER    'in main program
      .
      .
      .
  SHARED After$()              'in SUB
```

Since both *words* and *After$()* are declared as shared, they do not have to appear in the argument of the CALL statement or the parameter list of the SUB procedure. However, the array *Array$* was not declared as shared. Therefore, it appears in both the argument list of the CALL statement and the parameter list of the SUB procedure.

Program 1-4 uses a single SUB...END SUB procedure to do the work of the two FUNCTION procedures in Program 1-3.

You can enter a SUB procedure from the Edit menu by selecting the New SUB option. A dialog box then appears where you enter the name of the SUB...END SUB to be used. QuickBASIC provides the first and last line of a new SUB procedure, as it does for FUNCTION procedures.

SUB procedures are called differently than FUNCTION procedures. You cannot call a SUB procedure by using its name within an expression; a call to a SUB is a stand-alone statement. However, there are two ways you can call a SUB procedure. The first way is to use a CALL statement that includes the name of the SUB procedure. The second way is to use the name of the SUB procedure as a statement by itself. Both ways are shown in the following listing for the SUB procedure SqzCount(Array$( )):

```
CALL SqzCount(Array$())     'Array$() enclosed in parentheses
SqzCount Array$()           'Array$() not enclosed
```

Notice that the array is not enclosed in parentheses in the second form. If you omit the CALL keyword (as in the second form) and you are not using QuickBASIC to write the program, you must declare the procedure in a DECLARE statement before you reference it in a program.

This book uses the CALL statement (the first form in the example) to show you that a SUB procedure is being called as you browse through a program listing.

You can pass simple variables, elements of arrays, complete arrays, elements of records, and complete records to procedures. You can also pass expressions involving results from operations on variables and constants to a procedure.

```
DECLARE SUB SqzCount (Array$())
REM ** WORD COUNT & SQUEEZER WITH SUB **
' Program 1-4   File: PROO104.BAS

REM ** Initialize **
DEFINT A-Z
DIM SHARED words AS INTEGER
CLS : words = 0
LOCATE 2, 2: INPUT "How many strings"; size
REDIM Array$(1 TO size)
REDIM After$(1 TO size)

REM ** Print Instructions, Set Viewport, Get Strings **
CLS : LOCATE 2, 10
PRINT "Type Q and press ENTER to quit."
VIEW PRINT 5 TO 24
FOR num = 1 TO UBOUND(Array$)
   LINE INPUT "String, please ? "; Array$(num)
   IF UCASE$(Array$(num)) = "Q" THEN
     EXIT FOR
   END IF
NEXT num
CALL SqzCount(Array$())
VIEW PRINT: CLS : num = num - 1
PRINT "The total word count is"; words
PRINT
FOR num = 1 TO UBOUND(Array$)
   PRINT After$(num)
NEXT num
END

SUB SqzCount (Array$())
   SHARED After$()
   FOR str = LBOUND(Array$) TO UBOUND(Array$)
     squeeze$ = ""
     FOR num = 1 TO LEN(Array$(str))
       char$ = MID$(Array$(str), num, 1)
       IF char$ <> " " THEN
         squeeze$ = squeeze$ + char$
       ELSE
         words = words + 1
       END IF
     NEXT num
     After$(str) = squeeze$
     words = words + 1
   NEXT str
END SUB
```

Program 1-4.   Word Count and Space Squeezer with SUB

Program 1-4 passed a complete array, *Array$*, to the SUB SqzCount. This is done by including the array's name, followed by an empty pair of parentheses, in the argument parameter list as shown in the following example:

```
CALL SqzCount(Array$())
```

As mentioned previously, if a procedure does not need an entire array, you can pass individual elements of the array instead. To pass elements to a procedure, use the array's name followed by the appropriate element subscripts in parentheses.

The LBOUND and UBOUND functions allow you to generalize an array's size when you pass an array to a procedure. LBOUND returns the smallest index value of an array subscript. UBOUND returns the largest index value of the array. Program 1-4 uses LBOUND and UBOUND in SUB SqzCount% as part of the FOR...NEXT loop that evaluates the strings in the array. The following listing shows the appropriate lines from that program:

```
      .
      .
      .
FOR str = LBOUND(Array$) TO UBOUND(Array$)
      .
      .
      .
NEXT str
```

Figure 1-6 shows a typical output of Program 1-4.

Argument Checking for Procedures

When you use the QuickBASIC editor to write and edit your programs, you will notice that QuickBASIC automatically inserts a DECLARE statement for each procedure when the program is saved. The DECLARE statement consists of the keyword

```
The total word count is 32

Thisisatestdemonstrationof Program1-4.
ItusesoneSUBtoreplacethetwoFUNCTIONs
of Program1-3.
Thewordsofallstringsarecounted,and
thestringsaresqueezed.
```

```
Press any key to continue
```

Figure 1-6.   Output of Program 1-4

DECLARE, followed by the word SUB or FUNCTION, the name of the procedure, and a set of parentheses. If the procedure has no parameters, the parentheses are empty. If it has parameters, the parentheses enclose a parameter list that specifies the number and type of arguments to be passed to the procedure. The parameter list has the same format as the parameter list in the definition line of the SUB or FUNCTION procedure.

The parameter list in DECLARE statements turns on "type checking" of arguments passed to the procedure. Every time a procedure is called with variable arguments, those variables are checked to make sure they agree with the number and type of the parameters in the DECLARE statement.

Sometimes QuickBASIC does not generate DECLARE statements in the module that calls the procedure. For instance, QuickBASIC cannot generate a DECLARE statement when your program contains a module that calls a FUNCTION procedure in

another module. In this case you must enter the DECLARE
statement at the beginning of the module where the FUNCTION
is called. Without the DECLARE statement, the call to the
FUNCTION procedure is considered a variable name. Quick-
BASIC also cannot generate a DECLARE statement for a procedure that is in a Quick Library.

If you write programs with your own text editor and then compile them outside the QuickBASIC environment, be sure to put
DECLARE statements in the necessary places. See your Microsoft manuals for a more detailed explanation.

DECLARE statements can appear only at the module level,
not within a procedure, and must be placed before any executable
statement. A DECLARE statement affects the entire module in
which it appears.

Merging Files

Sometimes you can use a previously saved module in a new program. Rather than re-entering the module manually, it would be
more efficient to load the previously saved module from the stor-
age disk. QuickBASIC lets you merge a previously saved file with
a current file.

For example, suppose that you previously saved Program 1-5
under the name PRO0105.BAS. This program contains only some
remarks and a subprogram called CreateFile, which creates an
unstructured sequential file.

Now suppose that you have entered Program 1-6.

You can merge Program 1-5 with Program 1-6 by following
these steps:

1. Place the cursor in Program 1-6 at the blank line just above
   the statement "REM ** DIM Array & CALL File Scanner **."

```
DECLARE SUB ScanFile
REM ** SCAN A FILE **
' Program 1-6  File: PRO0106.BAS

REM ** DIM Array & CALL File Scanner **
```

```
DECLARE SUB CreateFile ()
REM ** CREATE A FILE **
' Program 1-5   File: PRO0105.BAS
DIM SHARED Text(1 TO 5)   AS STRING

REM ** CALL File Creator **
CALL CreateFile

REM ** End Program **
END

SUB CreateFile
' Create NotePad.Dat file.  Each record is a string.
DEFINT A-Z

   ' Put instructions in lines 21 to 25.
   Text$(1) = STRING$(74, 196)
   Text$(2) = "Create a new file called NotePad.Dat."
   Text$(3) = "Put the data disk in drive B and press any key."
   Text$(4) = "Enter one record at the prompt (>)."
   Text$(5) = "Press ENTER with no data to end the file."
   CLS
   FOR row = 1 TO 5
     LOCATE row + 20, 3: PRINT Text$(row);
   NEXT row

   ' Wait for a keypress to begin.
   LOCATE 10, 28: PRINT "Press a key to begin."
   anykey$ = INPUT$(1)

   ' Define rows 1 to 20 as a viewport.  Used for entering records.
   VIEW PRINT 1 TO 20
   CLS 2

   ' Open the file NotePad.Dat on drive B for output as file #1.
   OPEN "B:NotePad.Dat" FOR OUTPUT AS #1

   ' Enter records from keyboard and write to file.
   DO
     LINE INPUT "> "; record$
     PRINT
     IF record$ = "" THEN EXIT DO
     PRINT #1, record$
   LOOP

   ' Close the file and end the subprogram.
   CLOSE #1
   VIEW PRINT
END SUB
```

Program 1-5.   Create a File

```
DECLARE SUB ScanFile ()
REM ** SCAN A FILE **
' Program 1-6  File: PRO0106.BAS

REM ** DIM Array & CALL File Scanner **
DIM SHARED Text(1 TO 5) AS STRING
CALL ScanFile

REM ** End Program **
END

SUB ScanFile
' Scan the NotePad.Dat File, one record at a time.
DEFINT A-Z

  ' Put instructions in lines 21 to 25.
  Text$(1) = STRING$(74, 196)
  Text$(2) = "Scan the Note Pad file, one record at a time."
  Text$(3) = "Put the data disk in drive B and press any key."
  Text$(4) = "Starts with the 1st record in the viewport."
  Text$(5) = "Press space bar to get next record, Q to quit."
  CLS
  FOR row = 1 TO 5
    LOCATE row + 20, 3: PRINT Text$(row);
  NEXT row

  ' Define rows 1 to 20 as a viewport, used for scanning records.
  VIEW PRINT 1 TO 20

  ' Wait for a key press to begin.
  LOCATE 10, 28: PRINT "Press a key to begin."
  anykey$ = INPUT$(1)
  CLS 2                                    'Clears only viewport

  ' Open the file NotePad.Dat on drive B for input as file #1.
  OPEN "B:NotePad.Dat" FOR INPUT AS #1

  ' Read one record each time a key other than Q is pressed.
  DO UNTIL EOF(1)
    LINE INPUT #1, record$
    PRINT record$
    PRINT
    nextkey$ = INPUT$(1)
    IF UCASE$(nextkey$) = "Q" THEN EXIT DO
  LOOP

  ' Close the file and end the subprogram
  CLOSE #1
END SUB
```

Program 1-6.   Scan a File

2. Access the Merge selection from the File menu.

3. Type the name of the file to be merged (PRO0105) in the dialog box.

   You have now merged Program 1-5, which is highlighted in Figure 1-7, with Program 1-6 to form a new program. Now follow these steps to delete several unnecessary lines:

1. Delete the following lines:

```
REM ** CREATE A FILE **
' Program 1-5  File: PRO0105.BAS
```

2. Also delete the two extra End Program, REM, and DIM SHARED lines.

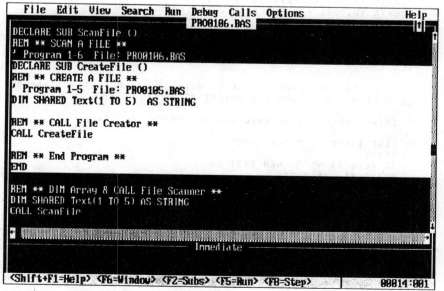

Figure 1-7.   Merged programs

```
DECLARE SUB CreateFile ()
DECLARE SUB ScanFile ()
REM ** CREATE & SCAN A FILE **
' Program 1-7   File: PRO0107.BAS
DIM SHARED Text(1 TO 5)  AS STRING

REM ** CALL File Creator & Scan File **
CALL CreateFile
CALL ScanFile

REM ** End Program **
END

SUB CreateFile
' Create NotePad.Dat file.  Each record is a string.
DEFINT A-Z

   ' Put instructions in lines 21 to 25.
   Text$(1) = STRING$(74, 196)
   Text$(2) = "Create a new file called NotePad.Dat."
   Text$(3) = "Put the data disk in drive B and press any key."
   Text$(4) = "Enter one record at the prompt (>)."
   Text$(5) = "Press ENTER with no data to end the file."
   CLS
   FOR row = 1 TO 5
     LOCATE row + 20, 3: PRINT Text$(row);
   NEXT row

   ' Wait for a keypress to begin.
   LOCATE 10, 28: PRINT "Press a key to begin."
   anykey$ = INPUT$(1)

   ' Define rows 1 to 20 as a viewport.  Used to enter records.
   VIEW PRINT 1 TO 20
   CLS 2

   ' Open the file NotePad.Dat on drive B for output as file #1.
   OPEN "B:NotePad.Dat" FOR OUTPUT AS #1

   ' Enter records from keyboard and write to file.
   DO
     LINE INPUT "> "; record$
     PRINT
     IF record$ = "" THEN EXIT DO
     PRINT #1, record$
   LOOP
```

Program 1-7.   Create and Scan a File

```
    ' Close the file and end the subprogram.
    CLOSE #1
    VIEW PRINT
END SUB


SUB ScanFile
' Scan the NotePad.Dat File, one record at a time.
DEFINT A-Z

    ' Put instructions in lines 21 to 25.
    Text$(1) = STRING$(74, 196)
    Text$(2) = "Scan the Note Pad file, one record at a time."
    Text$(3) = "Put the data disk in drive B and press any key."
    Text$(4) = "Starts with the 1st record in the viewport."
    Text$(5) = "Press space bar to get next record, Q to quit."
    CLS
    FOR row = 1 TO 5
      LOCATE row + 20, 3: PRINT Text$(row);
    NEXT row

    ' Define rows 1 to 20 as a viewport, used to scan records.
    VIEW PRINT 1 TO 20

    ' Wait for a key press to begin.
    LOCATE 10, 28: PRINT "Press a key to begin."
    anykey$ = INPUT$(1)
    CLS 2                                     'Clears only viewport

    ' Open the file NotePad.Dat on drive B for input as file #1.
    OPEN "B:NotePad.Dat" FOR INPUT AS #1

    ' Read one record each time a key other than Q is pressed.
    DO UNTIL EOF(1)
      LINE INPUT #1, record$
      PRINT record$
      PRINT
      nextkey$ = INPUT$(1)
      IF UCASE$(nextkey$) = "Q" THEN EXIT DO
    LOOP

    ' Close the file and end the subprogram
    CLOSE #1
END SUB
```

Program 1-7. Create and Scan a File (*continued*)

```
REM ** End Program **
END

REM ** Dim Array & CALL File Scanner **
DIM SHARED Text(1 TO 5) AS STRING
```

3. Move the DECLARE SUB CreateFile () statement near the top of the program.

4. Change the REM (CALL File Creator) to

```
REM ** CALL File Creator & Scan File **
```

5. Change the program's name, number, and file name as follows:

```
REM ** CREATE & SCAN A FILE **
' Program 1-7  File: PRO0107.BAS
```

After merging the programs and making these changes, you have Program 1-7. Sample notes entered in Program 1-7 are shown in Figure 1-8. The result of a complete scan of the Note Pad File is shown in Figure 1-9.

You can build up a tool box of FUNCTION and SUB procedures to use in more than one program if you save them as individual files that can be merged with other programs.

Making .EXE Files

You can create and run QuickBASIC programs in the Quick-BASIC environment. Once you have a program running in QuickBASIC, you can make a version of it that will run directly from the MS-DOS command line. This version is called an executable file and is identified by the file name extension .EXE.

Executable files can be created in two different forms. You make the choice from a dialog box when you select Make EXE File from the Run menu.

The first form is the .EXE file requiring BRUN45.EXE. As the name suggests, the QuickBASIC BRUN45.EXE file must be

```
> This is a note pad file.

> Each line entered is a record in an unstructured sequential file.

> The notes are created in a SUB named CreateFile.

> Another SUB in this program is called ScanFile.

> We will go there after we complete the file with this record.

>




────────────────────────────────────────────────────

Create a new file called NotePad.Dat.
Put the data disk in drive B and press any key.
Enter one record at the prompt (>).
Press ENTER with no data to end the file.
```

Figure 1-8.   Input to Program 1-7

present when you run a file of this type from DOS. Therefore, anyone using this type of executable file has to have QuickBASIC or at least the BRUN45.EXE file, which Microsoft allows you to distribute with your file. This type of .EXE file has some advantages. An .EXE file produced this way is much smaller than a stand-alone .EXE file. Common variables and open files are preserved when CHAIN statements are used. The BRUN45.EXE run-time module resides in memory, so it does not need to be reloaded for each program in a system of chained programs.

The second form of .EXE file is the stand-alone .EXE. A file of this type includes the support routines found in BRUN45.EXE. Therefore, this type of .EXE file requires more disk space than the first type. Common variables listed in COMMON statements are not preserved when a CHAIN statement transfers control to

```
This is a note pad file.

Each line entered is a record in an unstructured sequential file.

The notes are created in a SUB named CreateFile.

Another SUB in this program is called ScanFile.

We will go there after we complete the file with this record.




                                                                    
_____

Scan the Note Pad file, one record at a time.
Put the data disk in drive B and press any key.
Starts with the 1st record in the viewport.
Press space bar to get next record, Q to quit.
```

Figure 1-9.   Output of Program 1-7

another program. Some advantages of stand-alone .EXE files are that they may save RAM space when they are run if you have small, simple programs that do not require all the routines in the run-time module; execution does not require a run-time module on the disk. Other users do not have to have QuickBASIC or BRUN45.EXE to run stand-alone .EXE files.

This chapter has given you an idea of the knowledge you need to get the most out of this book. If necessary, browse your Quick-BASIC manuals for any references to unfamiliar topics in this chapter.

2

CONVENTIONS, STYLE, AND UPDATES

Learning to program offers you an opportunity to increase your problem solving abilities. The computer is a valuable tool for learning to think logically. Programming teaches you to break down the problem solving process into defining the problem, dividing the problem into a series of smaller subproblems, and then writing a computer program in small functional blocks to fit the subproblems. Using this process you can reach a solution logically, quickly, and reliably. During the process, you also become acutely aware of the capabilities and the limitations of the computer. You are more important in the problem solving process than the tools you use.

This chapter discusses certain conventions used to promote good programming style and structure. These conventions will introduce you to the style of programming supported by Quick-BASIC. Structure and good style are practices that you should use for all BASIC programs. Remember that the computer is a machine, but it is used by people. Therefore, people should write programs that are easy for other people to read and understand.

These conventions are used in this book to standardize the examples and to provide a learning environment that will help you switch smoothly from the version of BASIC with which you are familiar to Microsoft's QuickBASIC, Version 4.5. This chapter also discusses changes made from earlier versions of QuickBASIC.

NOTATIONAL CONVENTIONS

This book generally follows the notational conventions used in the Microsoft QuickBASIC manual. These conventions conform to those used in most BASIC reference books, with the exceptions noted in the following sections.

Ellipsis

An ellipsis consists of three horizontal dots (. . .). When it is used in this book it conveys one of the following meanings:

1. Something has been omitted.
2. An item of the same form has been repeated.

   Here are some examples:

```
IF...THEN
DATA constant1 [,constant2] ...
```

Vertical Ellipsis

A vertical ellipsis (three vertical dots) indicates that a portion of a program has been omitted. The following example shows the first and last lines of a subprogram from Program 1-7 of Chapter 1 with a vertical ellipsis indicating the missing lines.

```
SUB CreateFile
   .
   .
   .
END SUB
```

[Square Brackets]

Square brackets indicate that the information enclosed is optional. Microsoft uses double brackets in its QuickBASIC manuals for optional information.

A default value is supplied by QuickBASIC when you do not provide the optional information. For example, look at the following line:

```
FOR count = first TO last [STEP increment]
```

The square brackets around STEP increment indicate that you are not required to supply the step information. If you do not supply it, the loop increment defaults to plus 1. If you want the increment to be different, then provide a STEP value.

{Braces}

Braces indicate that you can choose from two or more entries following a BASIC keyword. A slash (/) separates choices within braces. You must choose at least one of the entries unless the entries are also enclosed in square brackets.

In the following example, you must provide either a line number or a line label after the keyword GOSUB. Line numbers are not used in this book.

```
GOSUB {linenumber/linelabel}
```

Both braces and square brackets are used in the following description of the RETURN statement.

```
RETURN [{linenumber/linelabel}]
```

In this case, the square brackets indicate that you do not need to enter anything after the RETURN statement. The braces indicate that you can enter either a line number or a line label. The line-number/linelabel option allows you to pass program control from a subroutine to a location other than the line following the GOSUB that called the subroutine. This concept is shown in the following lines:

```
RETURN

RETURN 370

RETURN backyonder
```

PROGRAMMING CONVENTIONS AND STYLE

A computer accepts information, processes that information according to specific instructions, and produces results. The primary reason for learning to program is to be able to make your computer perform these functions as flexibly as possible. Commercial programs are available for many purposes, but they are seldom written for an individual's specific needs. They are written to be used by as many different people as possible so as to increase sales. When you write your own programs, you can make the computer do exactly what you want, in just the way that you want it done.

Programming helps you develop skills useful in solving problems. You learn to define a problem and break it down into smaller, more manageable parts. Then you write a series of instructions for each part.

These parts, called blocks or modules, each solve a particular part of your original problem. The problem is solved by linking the parts together into a complete program. To create an effective program, all of your instructions to the computer must be written in a form that the computer understands. The instructions should also be easy for other people to read, understand, and use.

You may be tempted to write programs with little thought as to their logic or structure. You may intend to use the program only once, and think that no one else will use it. But you never know when you may want to use a good program again. Good programming style is a good habit, because it produces good programs.

This book presents examples that use a consistent set of programming conventions and a structured style. No matter what version of BASIC you use, you can still structure programs into functional blocks. Several elements of this structured style are shown in this chapter, and additional elements are explained in later chapters. The following sections contain the conventions and style used for all programs in this book.

REMARK Statements

Each functional block of a program begins with one or more REMARK (REM) statements that indicate the function of that part of the program. Statements that change the flow of the program (such as IF...THEN GOTO ...) should never direct execution to a line that begins with a remark.

Programs begin with a series of REM statements. The first REM states the name of the program. After the first line, the apostrophe (') is used instead of REM to denote a remark. The second line gives the program number and the file name under which the program is stored. You can enter other descriptive information in subsequent remarks in the first program block. Remember, remarks are not executed, but they supply descriptive information to your QuickBASIC source program. Remarks are not included in the compiled program. The following listing shows an example of remarks in Program 1-1.

```
REM ** DEMONSTRATION OF DEF FN **
' Program 1-1   File: PRO0101.BAS
```

This example shows the use of the apostrophe (') as an alternate way to indicate remarks. You can also use this form to provide comments at the end of some executable lines, as shown in the next example:

```
IF number = INT(number) THEN        'condition
   PRINT "Integer"                  'possible result 1
ELSE
   PRINT "Non-integer"              'possible result 2
END IF
```

You can use asterisks (**) to set off the remarks that describe the program in the first block and those that describe all other blocks. This makes it easier to browse through a program and find the REMs. The REMs provide an outline of a program, as shown in the following listing:

```
REM ** WORD COUNTER & SPACE SQUEEZER **

REM ** Define FUNCTIONs **

REM ** Use the Function Definitions **
```

When you outline a program with REM statements before you write it, you have taken the first step toward producing a structured program. The REM statements provide you with a plan. The plan may change as you write the program, but the REMs give you a place to start.

BASIC Keywords

You may enter QuickBASIC keywords in either upper or lower case. After you enter a line, QuickBASIC changes any keywords that you entered in lower case to upper case. In this book, BASIC keywords appear entirely in upper case.

Variables

QuickBASIC allows you to use unique variable names up to 40 characters long. You may enter QuickBASIC variables in either upper or lower case, and they will be listed exactly as you typed them. QuickBASIC variables will be shown in the text in lower case or in both upper and lower case.

Near the beginning of each program, the default variable type is usually set to integer by a DEFINT A-Z statement. Integer variables take up less memory space than other variable types. The explicit type identifiers $ & ! and # are used to identify string, long integer, single precision, and double precision variable types respectively. Integer variables used in this book will usually have no explicit identifier. The following listing shows some examples of this:

```
char$ = MID$(strng$, num, 1)
squeeze$ - squeeze$ + char$
RunCnt& = RunCnt& + words + 1
circum! = 2 * pi!
```

This convention makes programs easier to read. It clearly distinguishes variables from QuickBASIC keywords, which are in all upper case, and makes variable types easy to recognize.

Line Numbering

Line numbers are not required in QuickBASIC and so are not used in this book.

Punctuation Conventions (, ; :)

When a comma, semicolon, or colon is used in this book, it is always followed by a space, as shown in the following examples.

```
char$ = MID$(strng$, num, 1)

PRINT "The word count is "; FNcount%(teststring$)

PRINT : PRINT "Your squeezed string is"
```

In this example, QuickBASIC provides some systematic spacing of its own. It adds a space after the first PRINT statement in the third example.

Operation and Relational Symbols

In this book, one space is added before and after an operation symbol (+ − * / ...) or relational symbol (= < > <= >= <>). The following listing shows some examples:

```
words = words + 1

min#1 = first# * ABS(first# <= secnd#)

two = (year MOD 100 <> 0)
```

Please note that one exception to this rule does exist. When the dash (-) is used to denote a negative number, it is not followed by a space. This is shown in the next example:

```
FOR here = bottom TO top STEP -1
```

Using liberal spacing in programs makes them much easier to read. When memory was expensive, as many characters as possible were eliminated to fit programs into the memory-starved computers. This restriction is seldom necessary today. However, you will still see programs that are "crunched" in magazines and even in some books.

QuickBASIC does not allow you to crunch programs when its Syntax Checking feature is turned on. In some cases, it even provides its own formatting to ensure a uniform program appearance. However, you can turn off the Syntax Checking feature and use QuickBASIC as a text editor. Syntax Checking was on when the programs in this book were developed.

Loops

QuickBASIC has three loop structures: FOR...NEXT, WHILE...WEND, and DO...LOOP. These three loop structures use similar formatting conventions. Indentations are used to delineate the body of each loop. In this book, two spaces are used for indentations. You may want to use a different number of spaces.

QuickBASIC allows you to omit the variable following the NEXT keyword in a FOR...NEXT loop. However, this variable is included in demonstration programs to clearly show where each loop ends.

Examples of FOR...NEXT, WHILE...WEND, and DO...LOOP loops are shown in the following listing:

```
FOR num = 1 to UBOUND(Array$)
  LINE INPUT "String, please " "; Array$(num)
  IF UCASE$(Array$(num)) = "Q" THEN
    EXIT FOR
  END IF
NEXT num

WHILE UCASE$(nextkey$) <> "Q"
  nextkey$ = INPUT$(1)
WEND

DO
  LINE INPUT "> "; Note$(NoteNum): PRINT
  chars = CountChars(Note$())
  words = CountWords(Note$())
  over$ = UCASE$(Note$(NoteNum))
  NoteNum = NoteNum + 1
LOOP WHILE over$ <> "END"

DO UNTIL EOF(1)
  LINE INPUT #1, record$
  PRINT record$
  PRINT
  nextkey$ = INPUT$(1)
  IF UCASE$(nextkey$) = "Q" THEN EXIT DO
LOOP
```

Multiple Statements

Multiple statements are only used when the statements form a compound function, when they perform some related action together. When multiple statements are used on the same line, one space follows the colon separator. Multiple statements on one line are sometimes used to set an initial value for variables before the beginning of a loop. See the next listing for an example using multiple statements.

```
CLS: LOCATE 2, 10              'Clear screen and locate cursor

top = LBOUND(Array): bottom = UBOUND(Array)     'variable
DO WHILE top < bottom                           'assignment
   .
   .
   .
   top = top + 1
LOOP
```

Multiple Decision Structures

The block IF...THEN...ELSE structure expands the usefulness of the single-line IF...THEN...ELSE structure used in other BASIC dialects. It also makes the structure easier for you to read. An example from Program 1-4 is shown in the next listing:

```
IF char$ <> " " THEN
  squeeze$ = squeeze$ + char$
ELSE
  words = words + 1
END IF
```

SELECT CASE is a multiple-choice decision structure similar to a block IF...THEN...ELSE statement. However, SELECT CASE is much more flexible. An example of the conventions used for SELECT CASE is shown in the following listing:

```
SELECT CASE number
  CASE 0, 2, 4, 6, 8
    PRINT "Even decimal digit"
  CASE 1, 3, 5, 7, 9
    PRINT "Odd decimal digit"
  CASE ELSE
    PRINT "Not a decimal digit"
END SELECT
```

Procedures

The QuickBASIC procedures FUNCTION...END FUNCTION and SUB...END SUB use indentation conventions similar to those used for loops. Examples of each of these two procedures are shown in the next listing:

```
FUNCTION Squeezer$ (strng$)
  squeeze$ = ""
  FOR num = 1 to LEN(strng$)
    char$ = MID$(strng$, num, 1)
    IF char$ <> " " THEN
      squeeze$ = squeeze$ + char$
    END IF
  NEXT num
  Squeezer$ = squeeze$
END FUNCTION

SUB SqzCount (Array$())
  SHARED After$()
  FOR str = LBOUND(Array$) TO UBOUND(Array$)
    squeeze$ = ""
    FOR num = 1 to LEN(Array$(str))
      char$ = MID$(Array$(str), num, 1)
      IF char$ <> " " THEN
        squeeze$ = squeeze$ + char$
      ELSE
        words = words + 1
      END IF
    NEXT num
    After$(str) = squeeze$
    words = words + 1
  NEXT str
END SUB
```

When procedures are used in a program, each FUNCTION
...END FUNCTION and each SUB...END SUB has a corresponding DECLARE statement. The DECLARE statements of
Program 1-7 appear at the beginning of the program, as shown in
the following listing:

```
DECLARE SUB CreateFile ()
DECLARE SUB ScanFile ()
REM ** CREATE & SCAN A FILE **
    .
    .
    .
```

Other conventions will be introduced throughout the book as
they are needed.

DEMONSTRATING
CONVENTIONS

Program 2-1 demonstrates the conventions and style discussed in
this chapter. This practical application allows you to enter a series
of short notes. It then counts the characters and words you
entered, and prints the notes and the character and word counts.

The notes are assigned as elements in an array named *Note$*.
The array is dimensioned for 20 notes, but you can increase this
limit if you wish. The SHARED attribute is used in the DIM
statement so that the array may be used by the procedures
(CountChars, CountWords, and Prnt) without passing them as
parameters. The number of notes (*NoteNum*) is also shared in this
way.

When you run the program, it prints a prompt (>) and then
waits for you to enter a note. When you enter the note, it is
accepted by a LINE INPUT statement. The note is assigned as an
element of an array string (*Note$*). A sample entry of five notes is
shown in Figure 2-1.

After you have entered the last note, type **END** as a note, and
then press ENTER. This terminates the entry of notes. The END
entry is not really a note, although it is included in the array.

```
DECLARE FUNCTION CountChars (Rec$())
DECLARE FUNCTION CountWords (Rec$())
DECLARE SUB Prnt (item$())

REM ** NOTE PAD WITH COUNTERS **
' Program 2-1  File: PRO0201.BAS

REM ** Initialize **
DEFINT A-Z: CLS
DIM SHARED Note(1 TO 20) AS STRING, NoteNum AS INTEGER

REM ** Input Notes, Count Characters & Words
symb = 0: NoteNum = 1: PRINT
DO
  LINE INPUT "> "; Note$(NoteNum): PRINT
  chars = CountChars(Note$())
  words = CountWords(Note$())
  over$ = UCASE$(Note$(NoteNum))
  NoteNum = NoteNum + 1
LOOP UNTIL over$ = "END"
chars = CountChars(Note$()) - 3
words = CountWords(Note$()) - 2
CALL Prnt(Note$())
PRINT : PRINT "Number of characters in notes: "; chars
PRINT "Number of words in notes: "; words
END

FUNCTION CountChars (Rec$()) STATIC
  symb = symb + LEN(Rec$(NoteNum))
  CountChars = symb
END FUNCTION

FUNCTION CountWords (Rec$()) STATIC
  FOR symb = 1 TO LEN(Rec$(NoteNum))
    look$ = MID$(Rec$(NoteNum), symb, 1)
    IF look$ = " " THEN word = word + 1
  NEXT symb
  word = word + 1
  CountWords = word
END FUNCTION

SUB Prnt (item$())
  CLS
  FOR num = 1 TO NoteNum - 2
    PRINT item$(num)
  NEXT num
END SUB
```

Program 2-1.   Note Pad with Counters

```
> This program allows you to enter a number of short notes.

> When you have entered all the notes you want, type END to quit.

> One FUNCTION counts the number of characters in the notes.

> Another FUNCTION counts spaces to calculate the approximate word count.

> A SUB prints the notes.

> end
```

Figure 2-1.   Five notes entered in Program 2-1

As you enter the notes, one FUNCTION...END FUNCTION procedure (CountChars) counts the number of characters entered, including punctuation and spaces. Another FUNCTION...END FUNCTION procedure (CountWords) calculates the number of words by counting the spaces in each note and adding one for the last word of the note. When you type in the word "END" for the final note, this tells the program that there are no more notes, so it exits from the DO...LOOP. Although you enter the word "END" as a note, the program subtracts three characters for the word "END." It also decreases the word count by two, one for the word "END" and one for the end of the sentence.

Then it calls a subprogram (Prnt) to print the notes. The total number of characters and words are printed below the notes, as shown in Figure 2-2.

The word count calculation makes no allowance for double spaces, such as at the end of a sentence. Therefore, the word count

```
This program allows you to enter a number of short notes.
When you have entered all the notes you want, type END to quit.
One FUNCTION counts the number of characters in the notes.
Another FUNCTION counts spaces to calculate the approximate word count.
A SUB prints the notes.

Number of characters in array is:  272
Total number of words is:  49












Press any key to continue
```

Figure 2-2.   Printed notes; character and word count

is not always exact. Since the word count is increased by one for each space, the calculated word count may be a little higher than the actual word count. You could revise the program to take double spaces into consideration in the word count.

A REM Outline of Program 2-1

Program 2-1 is divided into six sections: three in the main program, two functions, and one subprogram. The first lines of the three blocks of the main program, along with the FUNCTION and SUB titles, form a program outline, as shown in the following listing. DECLARE statements are included to show their place at the beginning of the program.

```
DECLARE FUNCTION CountChars (Rec$())
DECLARE FUNCTION CountWords (Rec$())
DECLARE SUB Prnt (Item$())

REM ** NOTE PAD WITH COUNTERS **
REM ** Initialize **
REM ** Input Notes, Count Characters & Words **

FUNCTION CountChars (Rec$())
FUNCTION CountWords (Rec$())
SUB Prnt (Item$())
```

Squeezing and Restoring a String

The next example demonstrates how a program grows from a REM statement outline. The outline is shown in the following listing:

```
DECLARE SUB TakeOut (Squished$)

REM ** PURGE & RESTORE CHARACTERS IN A STRING **
REM ** Initialize & Get Strings **
REM ** Call & Print Squished String **
REM ** Print Restored String **

SUB TakeOut (Squished$)
```

Each block of Program 2-2 performs the functions listed in the REM outline.

The DIM statement in the Initialize & Get Strings block shows several QuickBASIC options. The SHARED attribute in the DIM statement allows the TakeOut subprogram to share the *Final$* array. The upper and lower bounds of the array and the data type (string) are also included in the DIM statement. The upper bound (*num*) is found by using the LEN function to get the length of the string that you enter, as shown in the next listing.

```
        .
        .
        .
PRINT: PRINT "Enter string to be purged: ";
LINE INPUT Original$
num = LEN(Original$)
DIM SHARED Final(1 TO num) AS STRING
```

```
DECLARE SUB TakeOut (Squished$)

REM ** PURGE & RESTORE CHARACTERS IN A STRING **
' Program 2-2   File: PRO0202.BAS

REM ** Initialize & Get Strings **
DEFINT A-Z: CLS
PRINT "Enter characters to be purged: "; : LINE INPUT Purge$
PRINT : PRINT "Enter string to be purged: ";
LINE INPUT Original$
num = LEN(Original$)
DIM SHARED Final(1 TO num) AS STRING

REM ** Call & Print Squished String **
CALL TakeOut(Squished$)
PRINT Squished$
PRINT : PRINT "Press any key to restore original string."
ky$ = INPUT$(1)

REM ** Print Restored String **
yes = 1: no = 1
FOR char = 1 TO num
  CharIn$ = MID$(Squished$, yes, 1)
  CharOrig$ = MID$(Original$, char, 1)
  IF CharIn$ = CharOrig$ THEN
    Restore$ = Restore$ + CharIn$
    yes = yes + 1
  ELSE
    Restore$ = Restore$ + CposOut$(no)
    no = no + 1
  END IF
NEXT char
PRINT : PRINT Restore$
END

SUB TakeOut (Squished$)
  SHARED Purge$, Original$, CposOut$()
  Squished$ = "": no = 1
  FOR cpos1 = 1 TO LEN(Original$)
    char$ = MID$(Original$, cpos1, 1)
    flag = INSTR(Purge$, char$)
    IF flag = 0 THEN
      Squished$ = Squished$ + char$
    ELSE
      CposOut$(no) = char$
      no = no + 1
    END IF
  NEXT cpos1
END SUB
```

Program 2-2.   Purge and Restore Characters in a String

The SHARED statement in the TakeOut subprogram gives the subprogram access to the values of the *Purge$* and *Original$* variables and the *CposOut$* array without including the variables or the array as parameters in the CALL statement of the main program. This is shown in the following listing:

```
SUB TakeOut (Squished$)
   SHARED Purge$, Original$, CposOut$()
      .
      .
      .
END SUB
```

The *Squished$* string value is passed as a parameter in the CALL statement. The following example shows the process:

```
CALL TakeOut(Squished$)
```

Figure 2-3 shows the period (.), comma (,), and space () characters being entered as the characters to be purged from the string

```
Enter characters to be purged: ".,  "

Enter string to be purged: Now, here is a test string.
Nowhereisateststring

Press any key to restore original string.
```

Figure 2-3. Purged string from Program 2-2

"Now, here is a test string." Figure 2-4 shows the string after the purged characters have been restored.

COMPARING
QuickBASIC 4.5
TO OTHER VERSIONS

QuickBASIC 4.5 is easier to use than earlier versions of Quick-BASIC. A separate SETUP program is provided to allow you to configure the QuickBASIC environment to fit your needs. You can choose between two different menu levels to further individualize the environment. You can also change the configuration from the Options menu within the QuickBASIC environment.

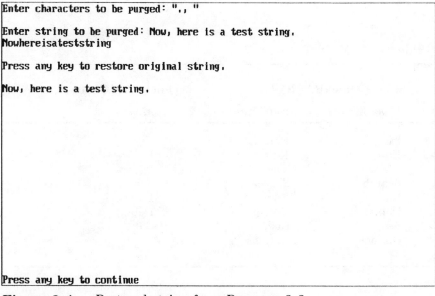

```
Enter characters to be purged: "., "

Enter string to be purged: Now, here is a test string.
Nowhereisateststring

Press any key to restore original string.

Now, here is a test string.




















Press any key to continue
```

Figure 2-4.   Restored string from Program 2-2

SETUP Program

The latest version of QuickBASIC includes an easy-to-use SETUP program, along with documentation on using it. A series of tree-structured menus lets you use arrow keys to make setup choices. The SETUP program allows you to select of all your configuration choices before you begin the actual installation. SETUP has two levels of installation to match the user's level of knowledge and experience. The SETUP program is more completely described in the Microsoft manual *Learning to Use QuickBASIC*.

Edit Screen

If you are familiar with QuickBASIC Version 4.0 screens, you will feel at home with Version 4.5 screens. However, the new screens were changed to make the QuickBASIC user interface conform to the Character Windows interface of Microsoft Works.

Table 2-1.   Menu Titles

| QuickBASIC 4.5 | | QuickBASIC 4.0 |
Easy Menus	*Full Menus*	*Menus*
File	File	File
Edit	Edit	Edit
View	View	View
Search	Search	Search
Run	Run	Run
Debug	Debug	Debug
—	Calls	Calls
Options	Options	—

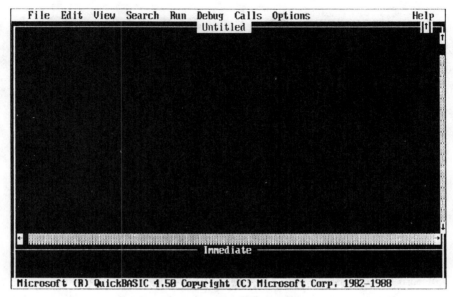

Figure 2-5.   Full Menus option on QuickBASIC 4.5 Edit screen

As in QuickBASIC 4.0, the menu titles of QuickBASIC 4.5 are displayed at the top of the Edit screen in the menu bar. The number of menu titles displayed depends on whether you are using QuickBASIC's Full Menus or the abbreviated Easy Menus.

Table 2-1 lists the menu titles displayed for QuickBASIC 4.5 Easy Menus, Full Menus, and QuickBASIC 4.0 menus. Notice that an Options menu has been added for QuickBASIC 4.5.

Figure 2-5 shows the Full Menus Edit screen of QuickBASIC 4.5. Contrast this figure with Figure 2-6, which shows the Edit screen of QuickBASIC 4.0. The menu bars at the top of the screens reflect the differences between the menus of the two versions. You may also notice differences in the colors of key letters in the menu titles and the background color of the View window and the Immediate window of the Edit screen.

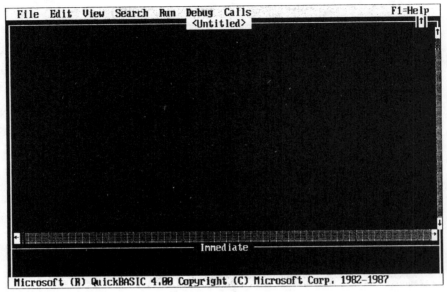

Figure 2-6.   QuickBASIC 4.0 Edit screen

Menus

The Options menu was added to QuickBASIC 4.5 to make it easier to use for both the novice and the experienced programmer. This menu is an expanded version of the options item of the View menu of QuickBASIC 4.0.

Figure 2-7 shows the selection of the Options menu from the Easy Menus mode. Only three items are on the menu: Display, Set Paths, and Full Menus. You can activate Full Menus from Easy Menus by moving the highlight down to Full Menus and pressing the ENTER key. The next time you access the Options menu, the larger Full Menu is displayed.

Figure 2-8 shows the selection of the Options menu from the Full Menus mode. Five items are on this menu: Display, Set Paths, Right Mouse, Syntax Checking, and Full Menus. The marker to the left of Syntax Checking and Full Menus means that these options are active.

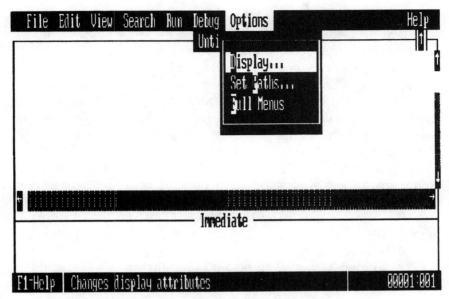

Figure 2-7.   Easy Menus option of the Options menu

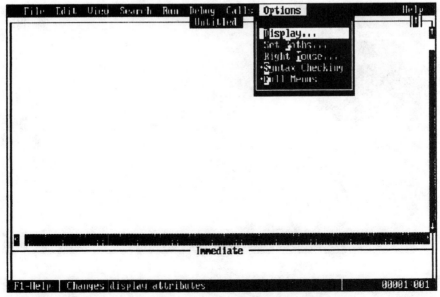

Figure 2-8.   Full Menus option of the Options menu

You can toggle Syntax Checking on and off by moving the highlight down to Syntax Checking and pressing the ENTER key. The marker to the left disappears when Syntax Checking is inactive and reappears when it is active again.

You can change to Easy Menus by moving the highlight down to Full Menus and pressing the ENTER key. This removes the marker to the left of Full Menus and activates Easy Menus. The next time you select the Options menu, the abbreviated Easy Menus is displayed.

You can activate Easy Menus from Full Menus, and Full Menus from Easy Menus. Syntax Checking is always active when you are using Easy Menus. You can toggle Syntax Checking on and off when you are using Full Menus. The number of items on the Options menu depends on whether you are using the Full or Easy Menus mode.

The number of active items on other menus also depends on whether you are using Easy Menus or Full Menus. For example,

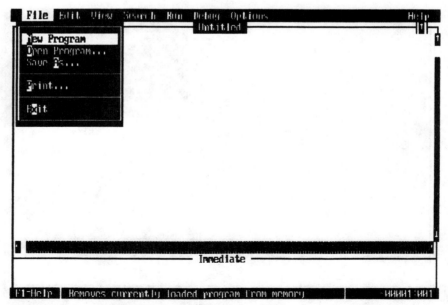

Figure 2-9.   Easy Menus option of the File menu

Figure 2-9 shows how the File menu appears when you are using Easy Menus. Figure 2-10 shows how the File menu looks when you are using Full Menus.

The status line at the bottom of the Edit screen shows the action caused by the highlighted item of the menu. In addition, a Help key reminder appears to the left of the status line.

Dialog Boxes

Some dialog boxes are simplified in the Easy Menus mode. For example, Figure 2-11 shows the selection of the Make EXE dialog box from the Run menu when Easy Menus is active. Figure 2-12 shows the Make EXE dialog box when Full Menus is active. For the simple EXE programs produced in the Easy Menus mode, you do not need to choose between the two types of EXE programs that can be produced in Full Menus mode. You can toggle the

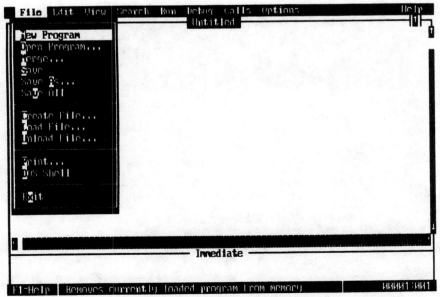

Figure 2-10.   Full Menus option of the File menu

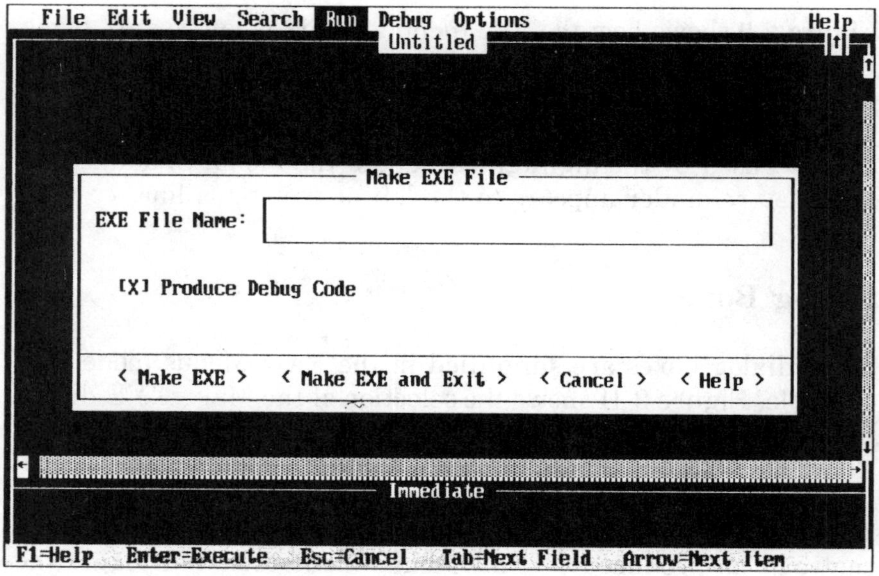

Figure 2-11.   Make EXE on Easy Menus

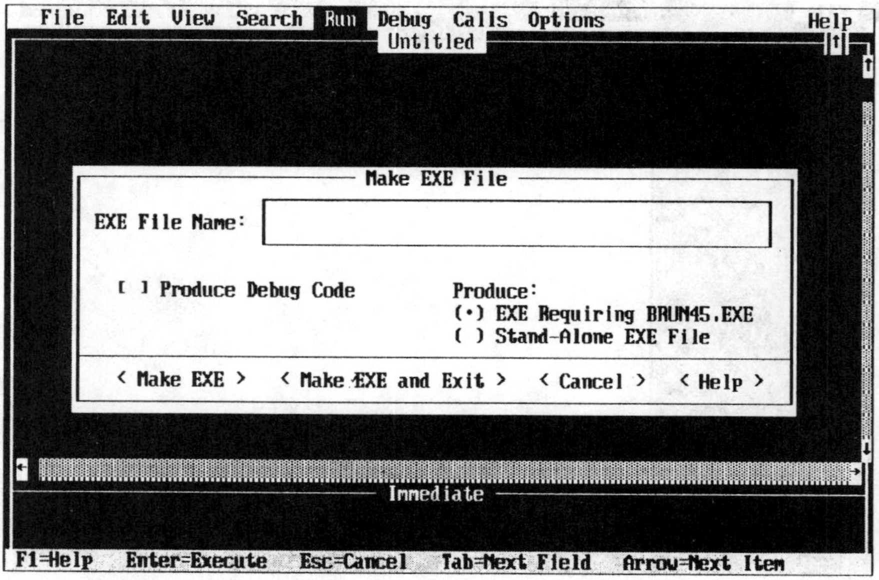

Figure 2-12.   Make EXE on Full Menus

production of Debug code on (as shown in Figure 2-11) or off (as shown in Figure 2-12).

Other dialog boxes have more choices than in earlier Quick-BASIC versions. This simplifies your decision making process by offering you more specific choices. For example, Figure 2-13 shows the dialog box for changing the attributes of the Quick-BASIC Edit screen. This dialog box is accessed from the Display item of the Options menu.

You can quickly display and change foreground and background colors for

1. Normal Text

2. Current Statement

3. Breakpoint Lines

You can delete scroll bars and change tab stops. The status line shows you how to get help and how to execute your selections. It

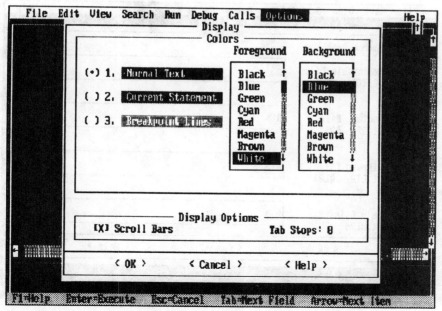

Figure 2-13.   Display dialog box

also shows you how to cancel your selections and how to move between fields and items of a field.

Figure 2-14 shows the Set Paths dialog box that you can also access from the Options menu. You can designate the paths necessary to find each of the fields, Executable Files, Include Files, Library Files and Help File, from this dialog box. Once again, directions for using the dialog box appear in the status line at the bottom of the screen.

All dialog boxes include a button (Help) that provides help on how to use the selections in the box. In general, you will find that you can get help immediately on almost any question you may have from almost any point within QuickBASIC 4.5.

QuickBASIC 4.5 varies in other ways from earlier versions. This book describes such variations as they are encountered. Since this is an advanced book, demonstrations are made using the Full Menus mode.

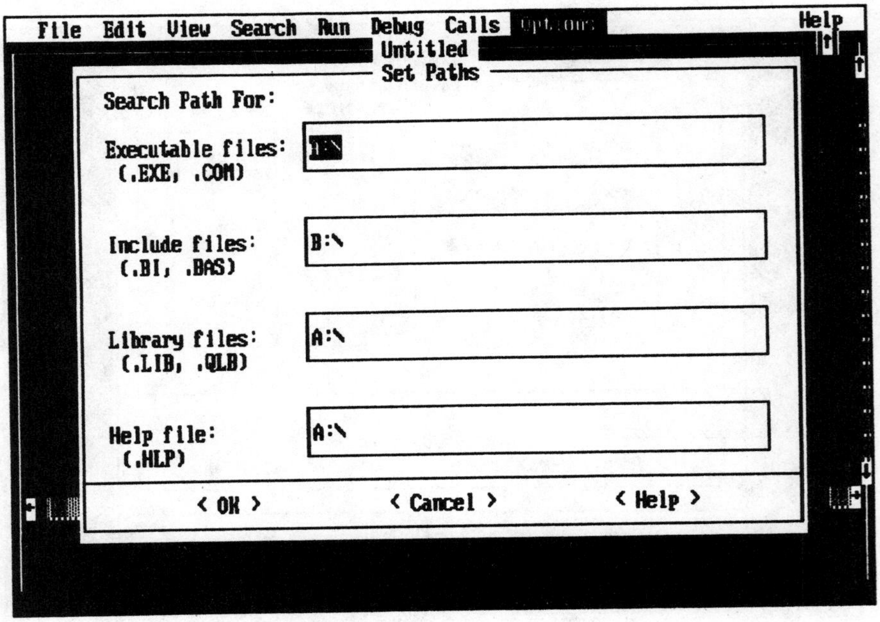

Figure 2-14.   Set Paths dialog box

3

QUICK LIBRARIES

QuickBASIC provides tools for creating two types of libraries. The first type is identified by the file extension .LIB. You create these stand-alone libraries with the Microsoft Library Manager, LIB.EXE.

The second type of library is identified by the file extension .QLB. These special libraries, called Quick libraries, permit you to add frequently used procedures to any of your QuickBASIC programs. A Quick library can contain procedures written in QuickBASIC or other Microsoft languages such as Microsoft C. When QuickBASIC makes a Quick library, it simultaneously creates a stand-alone library (.LIB) containing the same procedures in a somewhat different form. You get two libraries for the price of one.

You can create both types of libraries from within the programming environment or from the command line. Only Quick libraries are discussed in this chapter.

ADVANTAGES OF QUICK LIBRARIES

Think of a Quick library as a set of one or more procedures. This set is "linked" to QuickBASIC when the library is loaded with QuickBASIC.

As you develop a long program, you can add modules that you have completed and run successfully to a Quick library. You can set aside the source files of the completed modules until you want to improve them or bring them up-to-date. Thereafter, you can load the Quick library along with QuickBASIC, and any program you create or load will have instant access to all procedures in the library.

Quick library procedures behave like QuickBASIC statements. For instance, they can be called from your QuickBASIC program or executed from the Immediate window. Therefore, you can test the effects of a Quick library procedure before you use it in other programs.

You can incorporate routines written in other languages into QuickBASIC libraries. All the incorporated routines behave like extensions of the QuickBASIC language when you load the Quick library that contains them at the same time you load Quick-BASIC.

If you develop programs with other programmers, Quick libraries make it easy to combine or update a pool of common procedures. You could offer a library of original procedures for commercial distribution, and all QuickBASIC programmers would be able to use them immediately to enhance their own work. You could leave your Quick library on a bulletin board for others to try before they purchase the library. Because Quick libraries contain no source code and can only be used within the QuickBASIC pro-gramming environment, they protect your proprietary interests while they enhance your marketing opportunities.

BEFORE CREATING A
QUICK LIBRARY

A Quick library automatically contains all the modules present in the QuickBASIC environment when you create the new library. It will also contain any other Quick library that you loaded when you started QuickBASIC.

If you load a program and only want certain modules to be put in the library, you must explicitly unload those you do not want included. You can do this with Unload File from the File menu.

To see which modules are loaded, look at the list from the SUBs command of the View menu. However, this list does not show you which procedures a loaded library contains. You can list the procedures in a library with the QLBDUMP.BAS utility program.

A Quick library must be self-contained; it must not refer to any procedures outside the library. All procedures invoked by a procedure in a Quick library must be in that library.

CREATING A QUICK
LIBRARY

There are two main things to consider when you create a Quick library. The first is the files needed to make the Quick library, and the second is the method to be used to create the library.

Files Needed for a Quick
Library

Make sure you have the necessary files available before you create a Quick library. If you do not have a hard disk, you may need more than one floppy disk.

QuickBASIC prompts you for a path name when it cannot find a file. When this happens, insert the correct disk and respond to the prompt.

Table 3-1 lists and briefly describes the files that should be accessible to QuickBASIC. All these files, which are included on the disks in your QuickBASIC package, easily fit on one 3 1/2-inch disk. Therefore, if you are using 3 1/2-inch disk drives, you should make one or more work disks containing the files in the table.

A Quick Library Created from Within QuickBASIC

When you create a Quick library, you may be creating an entirely new library, or you may be updating an existing library. If you are updating a library, you should start QuickBASIC with the /L command-line option and supply the name of the library to be updated as a command-line argument. This process is discussed later in the chapter.

Table 3-1.   Files for a Quick Library

File Name	Use
QB.EXE	Directs the creation of a Quick library
BC.EXE	Creates the object files from the source code
LINK.EXE	Links object files
LIB.EXE	Manages stand-alone libraries of object modules
BQLB45.LIB	Supplies routines needed by your Quick library

The following discussion outlines the steps necessary to create a new Quick library. You will use these steps later to create and update a Quick library.

1. Access the Run menu and choose the Make Library command as shown in Figure 3-1. When you press ENTER, you will see the dialog box shown in Figure 3-2.

2. Enter the name of the library you wish to create in the Quick-Library File Name text box displayed in Figure 3-2. If you enter only a base name, QuickBASIC automatically appends the extension .QLB when it creates the library. You may enter any base name and any extension, as long as they are consistent with DOS file naming rules. If you do not want an exten-

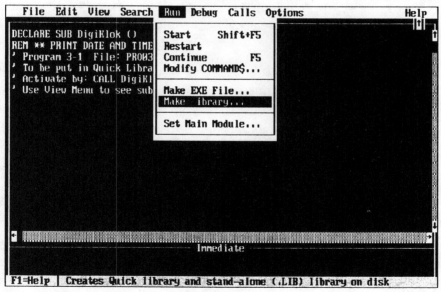

Figure 3-1.   Make Library selected

```
 File  Edit  View  Search  Run  Debug  Calls  Options              Help
                              PRO0301.BAS                            ↨↑
 DECLARE SUB DigiKlok ()                                               ↑
 REM ** PRINT DATE AND TIME SUBPROGRAM **
 ' Program 3-1  File: PRO0301.BAS
 ' To be put in Quick Library
 ' Activate by: CALL DigiKlok
 ' Use View Menu to see subprogram DigiKlok
 ┌──────────────────────── Make Library ────────────────────────┐
 │                                                               │
 │  Quick-Library File Name: ┌─────────────────────────────────┐ │
 │                           └─────────────────────────────────┘ │
 │                                                               │
 │      [ ] Produce Debug Code                                   │
 │ ┌───────────────────────────────────────────────────────────┐│
 │ │ < Make Library >   < Make Library and Exit >  < Cancel >  < Help > ││
 └───────────────────────────────────────────────────────────────┘

 ├─────────────────────────── Immediate ──────────────────────────┤

 F1=Help   Enter=Execute   Esc=Cancel   Tab=Next Field   Arrow=Next Item
```

Figure 3-2.   Request for Quick library file name

sion, add a terminating period to the base name. Here are some typical examples:

a. File name with no extension

Type the file name MAKEFILE in the Quick-Library File Name box with no period and no extension, as shown in the following listing. Do not press ENTER yet. You still have to make other Make Library choices.

```
Quick-Library File Name:    MAKEFILE
```

QuickBASIC will name the file MAKEFILE.QLB.

b. File name with an extension

Type the file name followed by a period and a three-letter extension, as shown in the following listing. Do not press

ENTER yet. You still have to make other Make Library choices.

```
Quick-Library File Name:    MAKEFILE.QLB
```

QuickBASIC will name the file MAKEFILE.QLB. You can use any valid three-letter extension that is consistent with DOS file extensions. If you use an extension different from .QLB, you must remember the extension and use it when you load the Quick library later.

c. File name with a terminating dot, but no extension

Type the file name followed by a period, as shown in the following listing. Do not press ENTER yet. You still have to make other Make Library choices.

```
Quick-Library File Name:    MAKEFILE.
```

The file is created with no extension. If your Quick library file has no extension, you must specify the name in the same way (MAKEFILE.) whenever you load it. If you do not append the dot, QuickBASIC searches in vain for a file with your base name (MAKEFILE) and the .QLB extension.

3. Press the TAB key. The cursor moves to the Produce Debug Code check box, but do not select this option now. If you select the Produce Debug Code option, your library will be larger and your program will execute slower than if you do not select it. This option gives you only a small amount of error control, mostly dealing with checking array bounds.

4. You now have to make one of three final selections. The first two selections ("a" and "b" that follow) complete the preparations for making the Quick library. The third selection ("c") cancels the operation.

You create the Quick library by activating one of two Make Library buttons. These buttons are displayed at the bottom of the dialog box in Figure 3-2.

a. Make Library

Notice that the Make Library button at the bottom left of the dialog box is presently highlighted. This choice allows you to remain in the QuickBASIC environment after the Quick library is created. If this is your choice, press the ENTER key while this button is highlighted.

b. Make Library and Exit

If you want to create your library and automatically exit to DOS, press the TAB key until the Make Library and Exit command button is highlighted. Then press the ENTER key. You will be returned to the DOS command level after the Quick library is created.

c. Cancel

If you change your mind and want to cancel the operation, press the TAB key until the Cancel button is highlighted. Then press the ENTER key.

Demonstrating How to Create a Quick Library

You may have any number of small program fragments, or modules, that you can use in many programs. Rather than enter each of them from the keyboard every time you write a new program, you can enter the fragments once and place them in a common Quick library. Then you can quickly load the library from the command line when you want to include the modules in a new program.

This section uses the steps listed in the previous section to show how to create a Quick library of short utilities. The demonstration begins by loading QuickBASIC and entering Program 3-1.

Notice that this program uses a PRINT #1 statement to send the date and time to whatever I/O device you have previously

```
DECLARE SUB DigiKlok ()
REM ** PRINT DATE AND TIME SUBPROGRAM **
' Program 3-1   File: PRO0301.BAS
' To be put in Quick Library
' Activate by: CALL DigiKlok
' Use View Menu to see subprogram DigiKlok

SUB DigiKlok
  PRINT #1, "Date "; DATE$
  PRINT #1, "Time "; TIME$
END SUB
```

Program 3-1.   Print Date and Time Subprogram

specified in an OPEN statement. Available I/O devices are listed in Table 3-2.

The two most common output devices are a display screen and a printer. The OPEN statements for these devices are shown in the following listing:

```
OPEN "SCRN:" FOR OUTPUT AS #1     'output to screen

OPEN "LPT1:" FOR OUTPUT AS #1     'output to printer
```

This discussion assumes that you are using a two-drive system with QuickBASIC in Drive A and the data file disk in Drive B. If you are using a hard disk system, substitute the appropriate drive designations for your system. Your screen displays will be different, and the data in the tables will appear on your system's directories.

Program 3-1 is very short and is not an executable program by itself. However, when you include it in a library, it can be called by any program that uses that library. After you enter the program, save it to disk. Assuming that QuickBASIC is in Drive A and you are saving programs to Drive B, save it as B:PRO0301.BAS.

Table 3-2.   Devices Supported for I/O

Name	Device	I/O Mode Supported
COM1:	Serial port #1	Input and Output
COM2:	Serial port #2	Input and Output
CONS:	Screen	Output only
KYBD:	Keyboard	Input only
LPT1:	Printer #1	Output only
LPT2:	Printer #2	Output only
LPT3:	Printer #3	Output only
SCRN:	Screen	Output only

You may find it ridiculous to create a library for one small program. If that were the whole library, it would be ridiculous. However, you will add other utilities to the library later in this chapter. This short program just shows you how to begin with a short library and later expand it.

1. Access the Run menu and choose the Make Library command.

2. Type the name of the library to be created, as shown in the following listing, but do not press ENTER yet.

   ```
   Quick-Library File Name:   B:UTIL1.QLB
   ```

3. Press the TAB key to move the cursor to the Produce Debug Code command. Do not select this option. Press the TAB key again.

4. You have now moved the cursor to the Make Library command button. Do not select this option. Press the TAB key once more

to move the cursor to the Make Library and Exit command button. Then press the ENTER key.

QuickBASIC begins to make the library. The program displays a sequence of messages on the screen while it is creating the library. It also displays any errors that it finds. In the example shown in Figure 3-3 no errors were encountered. The Quick library UTIL1.QLB was created and then QuickBASIC returned control to DOS, as you requested by using the Make Library and Exit command.

Now that the computer is back in DOS, check the directories of Drives A and B. This demonstration assumes that the Quick-BASIC .EXE and .LIB files are in Drive A and your source files are in Drive B. Typical directories are shown in Table 3-3.

```
BC B:\PROO301.BAS/T/C:512;
Microsoft (R) QuickBASIC Compiler  Version 4.50
Copyright (C) Microsoft Corp. 1982-1988. All rights reserved.

43740 Bytes Available
43404 Bytes Free

    0 Warning Error(s)
    0 Severe  Error(s)
LINK /QU PROO301,B:\UTIL1.QLB,NUL,A:\BQLB45.LIB;

Microsoft (R) Overlay Linker  Version 3.69
Copyright (C) Microsoft Corp 1983-1988.  All rights reserved.

LIB B:\UTIL1.LIB+PROO301;

Microsoft (R) Library Manager  Version 3.12
Copyright (c) Microsoft Corp 1983-1988.  All rights reserved.

A>_
```

Figure 3-3.   Final Make Library screen

Table 3-3.   Directories After Making UTIL1

Directory of B: \		
PRO0301	BAS	288
UTIL1	QLB	5163
UTIL1	LIB	1551
**Directory of A: **		
QB	EXE	281254
BC	EXE	97449
BQLB45	LIB	23755
LINK	EXE	69091
LIB	EXE	36303
QB	INI	73
PRO0301	OBJ	886

Notice that UTIL1.QLB and UTIL1.LIB have been stored on the disk in Drive B. This path was specified when the Quick library was named (B:UTIL1). Notice also that the object file (PRO0301.OBJ) was saved on the disk in Drive A.

When QuickBASIC makes a Quick library, it directs the work of the BC.EXE, LINK.EXE, and LIB.EXE files. It then combines what they produce into two libraries: a Quick library (.QLB), and a stand-alone library (.LIB). When the process is completed, an object (.OBJ) file exists for each module in your program.

The messages shown in Figure 3-3 outline the steps for creating the library. These steps are described in detail in the next section.

1. The top three lines of Figure 3-3 show you that the QB.EXE file invokes the QuickBASIC BC compiler to process the

QuickBASIC file B:\PRO0301.BAS, which creates an object file (.OBJ). The object file is first used to make the Quick library file (UTIL1.QLB).

When BC.EXE has completed its task, it lists the number of bytes available and number of bytes free. The final message for this part of the process reports 0 warning errors and 0 severe errors.

2. Near the middle of the message list, you will see the word "LINK." This indicates that the LINK.EXE file is working. The linked files PRO0301, B:\UTIL1.QLB, NUL, and A:BQLB45.LIB, are shown on the same line.

   The NUL entry in the linked files list indicates that no map file was created. If you want to output a map file, a device would be named at this place in the list. (See "Creating a Map File" in your Microsoft *Programming in BASIC* manual.)

   The last item on the list, A:BQLB45.LIB, supplies routines needed by your Quick library. When all these files have been linked together properly, the Library Manager takes over.

3. One of the lower lines on the screen starts with the word "LIB." This indicates that the LIB.EXE file has taken control. It creates a stand-alone library (UTIL1.LIB) from the object module.

   The demonstration program had a single module. Therefore, LIB.EXE creates one object file (PRO0301.OBJ). The libraries produced were UTIL1.QLB (the Quick library) and UTIL1.LIB (the stand-alone library).

Files with the .OBJ extension are no longer needed, so you may omit them. For now, leave the object file PRO0301.OBJ so that you can see other object files as you add modules to the library. Files with the .LIB extension are very important, so you should preserve them. These parallel libraries are used to create executable files of your programs.

If you are developing professional software for other Quick-BASIC programmers, you should deliver both the Quick library

and the stand-alone library to customers. Without the .LIB libraries, your customers cannot use your library routines in executable
files produced by QuickBASIC.

USING QUICK LIBRARY UTIL1

To make sure the UTIL1 Quick library works, load QuickBASIC
and the library from the command line with the following
command:

```
A>QB /L B:UTIL1
```

where

> /L tells the computer to load a library
> B: is the path where the library is found
> UTIL1 is the library name

A nearly blank Untitled Edit screen appears. If you use the
View menu to check for SUBs, you will find nothing. Although
the library is loaded, you will not see any list of procedures in the
library.

You could write a short program to test the library UTIL1.
However, you can easily use QuickBASIC's Immediate window to
enter a Call command to the subprogram DigiKlok in UTIL1.

Press the F6 key to move the cursor to the Immediate window.
Open the necessary I/O device. If you want to use the screen as
output, perform the following steps:

1. Type **CLS** and press ENTER.
2. When the "Press any key to continue" message appears, press
   ENTER again to get back to the Immediate window.
3. Type **OPEN "SCRN:" FOR OUTPUT AS #1** and press ENTER.
4. Type **CALL DigiKlok** and press ENTER.

The date and time are obtained from DigiKlok and sent to the screen.

If you want to send the date and time to your printer, be sure your printer is on line. Then if you opened device #1 as the screen, perform these steps:

1. Type **CLOSE** #1 and press ENTER.
2. Open the printer as I/O device #1.
3. Type **OPEN** ″**LPT1:**″ **FOR OUTPUT AS** #1 and press ENTER.
4. Type **CALL DigiKlok** and press ENTER.

The date and time information is output to your printer.

ADDING TO A QUICK LIBRARY

If you want to write professional-looking programs, you often need to use the cursor and function keys. These keys return a two-character ASCII code when pressed, instead of a one-character ASCII code. The first character is always the null code, CHR$(0). The second character is in the range of one-character ASCII codes. For example, the RIGHT ARROW key produces a null code followed by code 59.

A procedure that identifies which key has been pressed would be useful here. Program 3-2 consists of a few remarks and a subprogram (ScanKey) that performs this function.

When you press a key, the ScanKey subprogram reads it with the INKEY$ function and assigns what it reads to the variable *ky$*. The INKEY$ function returns a one-character string for

```
DECLARE SUB ScanKey (ky$)
REM ** SCAN THE KEYBOARD SUB **
' Program 3-2  File: PRO0302.BAS
' To be put in Quick Library
' Activate by: CALL ScanKey(ky$)
' Use View Menu to see subprogram ScanKey(ky$)

SUB ScanKey (ky$)
  ky$ = ""
  DO WHILE ky$ = ""
    ky$ = INKEY$
  LOOP
  IF LEN(ky$) = 2 THEN
    ky$ = "0 +" + STR$(ASC(RIGHT$(ky$, 1)))
  ELSE
    ky$ = STR$(ASC(ky$))
  END IF
END SUB
```

Program 3-2.   Scan the Keyboard SUB

ASCII coded keys (such as A, a, 1, 2, and so on). It returns a
two-character string for extended ASCII codes (such as F1, F2,
and the cursor movement keys). The first character of a two-
character string is always zero (null). The second character is an
ASCII code (used for other keys in the ASCII set). A complete list
of these extended codes is given in Microsoft's *Programming in
BASIC* manual.

When you press a key, Program 3-2 first assigns the value of
the key to the variable *ky$*. It then determines the length of *ky$*.
If the length is two, *ky$* is modified by the following statement:

```
ky$ = "0 +" + STR$(ASC(RIGHT$(ky$,1)))
```

This statement concatenates the null portion of the code (″0 +″) to the string equivalent of the ASCII code of the second character of the extended code.

If the length of *ky$* is 1, the variable is modified to be the string equivalent of the ASCII code returned. This allows the program to recognize nonprintable characters (such as the ENTER key).

When you add to a Quick library, you must give the resulting library a different name. The name UTIL2 is used in the following demonstration to distinguish it from UTIL1, which was used for the first Quick library.

To begin creating a new Quick library, load QuickBASIC and UTIL1 from the DOS command line, as shown in the following listing. These commands assume that Drive B contains your programs and libraries.

```
A>QB /L B:UTIL1
```

After you press ENTER and the QuickBASIC Edit screen appears, do one of the following steps:

1. Load Program 3-2 if you have already entered and saved it, or
2. Enter Program 3-2 now.

When Program 3-2 is displayed in the Edit window, access the Make Library command from the Run menu and press ENTER. In the File Name text box, enter **B:UTIL2** as the new library's file name. Then press TAB to move the cursor to the Make Library and Exit command button. The screen should now look like Figure 3-4. Press ENTER to make the new library.

Once again, you can watch the library being created on the display screen. The final result is shown in Figure 3-5.

You successfully made a Quick library (UTIL2) and then returned to DOS. You can verify this by looking at the directories

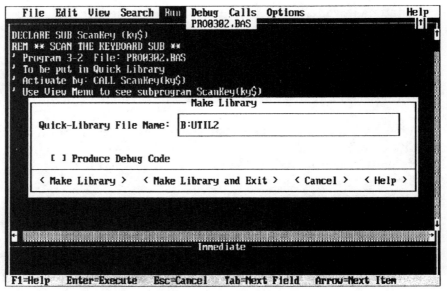

```
 File  Edit  View  Search  Run  Debug  Calls  Options              Help
                         PRO0302.BAS                                    ↑↓
DECLARE SUB ScanKey (ky$)
REM ** SCAN THE KEYBOARD SUB **
' Program 3-2  File: PRO0302.BAS
' To be put in Quick Library
' Activate by: CALL ScanKey(ky$)
' Use View Menu to see subprogram ScanKey(ky$)
          ┌──────────────────── Make Library ────────────────────┐
          │                                                       │
          │  Quick-Library File Name: ┌─────────────────────────┐ │
          │                           │B:UTIL2                   │ │
          │                           └─────────────────────────┘ │
          │                                                       │
          │      [ ] Produce Debug Code                           │
          │                                                       │
          │  < Make Library >   < Make Library and Exit >   < Cancel >   < Help > │
          └───────────────────────────────────────────────────────┘


                              Immediate
F1=Help   Enter=Execute   Esc=Cancel   Tab=Next Field   Arrow=Next Item
```

Figure 3-4.   Quick library name entered

```
BC B:\PRO0302.BAS/T/C:512;
Microsoft (R) QuickBASIC Compiler  Version 4.50
Copyright (C) Microsoft Corp. 1982-1988. All rights reserved.

43740 Bytes Available
43200 Bytes Free

    0 Warning Error(s)
    0 Severe  Error(s)
LINK /QU /NOE /NOD:BCOM45.LIB PRO0302+B:UTIL1.LIB,B:\UTIL2.QLB,NUL,A:\BQLB45.LIB
;

Microsoft (R) Overlay Linker  Version 3.69
Copyright (C) Microsoft Corp 1983-1988.  All rights reserved.

LIB B:\UTIL2.LIB+PRO0302+B:UTIL1.LIB;

Microsoft (R) Library Manager  Version 3.12
Copyright (c) Microsoft Corp 1983-1988.  All rights reserved.

A>_
```

Figure 3-5.   Make Quick library UTIL2

Table 3-4. Directories After UTIL2 Is Made

Directory of B:

PRO0301	BAS	288
UTIL1	QLB	5163
UTIL1	LIB	1551
PRO0302	BAS	410
UTIL2	QLB	5778
UTIL2	LIB	2581

Directory of A:

QB	EXE	281254
BC	EXE	97449
BQLB45	LIB	23755
LINK	EXE	69091
LIB	EXE	36303
PRO0301	OBJ	886
PRO0302	OBJ	1064

of Drive A and Drive B. This demonstration added files to both drives, as shown in Table 3-4.

Notice that there are two .OBJ files in the Drive A directory, one for each module. You can delete these object files now if you wish, since you will have no further use for them. Remember to keep the .LIB and .QLB files on Drive B.

Testing Quick Library UTIL2

Load QuickBASIC and the Quick library UTIL2 from the DOS prompt with the following command:

```
A>QB /L B:UTIL2
```

Before you test UTIL2, go to the View menu and select SUBs to see if you can find any subprograms. Remember, the subprograms are now in the UTIL2 Quick library. Because a Quick library is essentially a binary file, you cannot view its contents from QuickBASIC or any other text editor. However, one of your QuickBASIC distribution disks contains a file called QLBDUMP. BAS. This utility allows you to list all the procedures in a given library.

Follow these steps to use this utility to view the contents of a Quick library:

1. Load QuickBASIC.
2. Load and run QLBDUMP.BAS.
3. Enter the name of the Quick library you wish to examine. In this case, enter the following name:

```
B:UTIL2.QLB
```

If the specified file exists, and it is a Quick library, the QLBDUMP program displays a list of symbol names included in the library. Procedures in the library are included in this list of symbol names.

For example, QLBDUMP.BAS produced the list shown in Table 3-5 for the demonstration library UTIL2. Observe the last few items listed under Code Symbols. You will see the names ScanKey and DigiKlok. These are the names of the included procedures.

Now, test UTIL2. This Quick Library has two subprograms, DigiKlok and ScanKey(*ky$*). You tested DigiKlok in UTIL1, but make sure it is in UTIL2 by moving the cursor to the Immediate window (by pressing F6). Also make sure your printer is on line if you plan to use it as the output device. Then perform the following steps:

1. Type **CLS** and press ENTER.

Table 3-5.   Output of QLBDUMP.BAS

Code Symbols	Data Symbols
_brtctl	b_ULVars
_execve	_end
_exit	b_erradr
_main	b_errlin
_spawnve	b_errmod
_TEXT_END	b_errnum
ScanKey	b_ULSymSeg
SetUEvent	STKHQQ
DigiKlok	_environ
	_edata
	_edata
	_errno
	FIDRQQ

2. Press ENTER again to return to the Immediate window.

3. Enter the appropriate OPEN statement for your output device ("SCRN:" or "LPT1:").

4. Type **CALL DigiKlok** and press ENTER.

The date and time are sent to your output device (screen or printer). The subprogram in the demonstration Quick library printed the following lines:

```
Date 09-27-1988
Time 18:14:13
```

To test the ScanKey subprogram, follow these steps:

1. Type **CALL ScanKey(*ky$*)** and press ENTER.

2. Press the UP ARROW key. Then press ENTER to return to the Immediate window

3. Type **PRINT** *ky$* and press ENTER.

Your printer (or display) should print 0 + 72, the extended character code for the UP ARROW key. Then the message "Press any key to continue" is displayed at the bottom of the screen.

Now, try another test by performing these steps:

1. Press any key to return to the Immediate window.

2. Move the cursor back up to the line with the CALL Scan-Key(*ky$*) command in the Immediate window, and press ENTER again.

3. Press the F4 key. Then press ENTER to return to the Immediate window.

4. Type **PRINT** *ky$* in the Immediate window and press ENTER.

Your printer (or display) should print 0 + 62, the extended character code for the F4 key, just below the previous code for the UP ARROW key. This proves that UTIL2, the demonstration Quick library, passed the test.

Adding More to a Quick Library

Program 3-3 is the last feature to add to the demonstration Quick library. It produces a time delay of a specified number of seconds. The length of the delay is set in a main program, and then the time delay routine is called. QuickBASIC's TIMER function terminates the delay when the specified number of seconds have elapsed.

Enter Program 3-3 and save it as PRO0303.BAS. Then exit QuickBASIC and return to DOS. Load QuickBASIC, Program

```
DECLARE SUB Delay (sec!)
REM ** TIME DELAY SUB **
' Program 3-3  File: PRO0303.BAS
' To be put in Quick Library
' Main program must set number of seconds (sec!)
' Activate by: CALL Delay(sec!)
' Use View Menu to see subprogram Delay(sec!)

SUB Delay (sec!)
  TurnOn! = TIMER
  DO UNTIL TIMER >= TurnOn! + sec!
  LOOP
END SUB
```

Program 3-3.   Time Delay SUB

3-3, and the Quick library UTIL2 from the command line with the following command:

```
A>QB B:PRO0303 /L B:UTIL2
```

When you have loaded all of these files, Program 3-3 appears in the Edit window. Use the same steps as before to make a new Quick library: access the Run menu; Select the Make Library command; enter the Quick library file name, **B:UTIL3;** press TAB to move to the Make Library and Exit command button; and press the ENTER key.

Watch the screen as the new Quick library is created. By now you will recognize when Microsoft's compiler, linker, and Library Manager begin to build Quick library UTIL3.

When the process is finished, notice how full the directory of the disk in Drive B is getting. The directory of the demonstration disk is shown in Table 3-6.

Since UTIL3.QLB contains all the subprograms in UTIL1.QLB and UTIL2.QLB, keep UTIL3.QLB and erase the other two. Do the same for the .LIB files: keep UTIL3.LIB; erase UTIL1. LIB

Table 3-6.   Directory of Demonstration Disk

Directory of B:

PRO0301	BAS	288
UTIL1	QLB	5163
UTIL1	LIB	1551
PRO0302	BAS	410
UTIL2	QLB	5778
UTIL2	LIB	2581
PRO0303	BAS	340
UTIL3	QLB	5957
UTIL3	LIB	3611

Table 3-7.   Directories After Erasures

Directory of A:

QB	EXE	281254
BC	EXE	97449
BQLB45	LIB	23755
LINK	EXE	69091
LIB	EXE	36303
QB	INI	73

Directory of B:

UTIL3	QLB	5957
UTIL3	LIB	3611

and UTIL2.LIB. You can also erase the QuickBASIC programs
PRO0301.BAS, PRO0302.BAS, and PRO0303.BAS from the disk
in Drive B, as they are all incorporated in UTIL3.QLB and
UTIL3.LIB. This leaves the disk with only two files: UTIL3.QLB

```
REM ** TEST UTIL3 **
'Program 3-4   File: PRO0304.BAS
' Used to test Quick Library UTIL3

CLS
DO
  INPUT "Output to screen or printer (S or P)"; ky$
LOOP WHILE INSTR("SsPp", ky$) = 0
SELECT CASE ky$
  CASE "S", "s"
    OPEN "SCRN:" FOR OUTPUT AS #1
  CASE "P", "p"
    OPEN "LPT1:" FOR OUTPUT AS #1
END SELECT
CALL DigiKlok
sec! = 5
LOCATE 12, 25: PRINT "Please wait, I'm thinking."
CALL Delay(sec!)
LOCATE 12, 25: PRINT SPACE$(27)
PRINT "Press a key to print character values."
PRINT : PRINT "Press the ENTER key to quit."

REM ** Wait for Keypress **
DO
  CALL ScanKey(ky$)
  PRINT #1, : PRINT #1, ky$
LOOP UNTIL ky$ = " 13"
CLOSE #1
END
```

Program 3-4.   Test UTIL3

and UTIL3.LIB. In addition, you can erase all .OBJ files created with the Quick libraries from the disk in Drive A. Table 3-7 shows the files on this disk after the .OBJ files are erased.

Testing Quick Library UTIL3

You used immediate commands to test the first two Quick libraries. This time you can use Program 3-4 to test all three subprograms in the UTIL3 Quick library. Do not enter Program 3-4 yet. First load QuickBASIC and UTIL3 with the following command.

```
A>QB /L B:UTIL3
```

When these files are loaded, a nearly blank screen appears with the cursor in the Edit window. Now enter Program 3-4.

Save Program 3-4 as B:PRO0304.BAS. Make sure your printer is on line if you plan to use it. Then run the program.

First the prompt "Output to screen or printer (S or P)?" appears at the top of the display screen. Enter **S** or **P**. If you enter "P," the date and time are sent to the printer. Then the following message is printed at the center of the display screen:

```
Please wait, I'm thinking.
```

The computer waits for five seconds (because a time delay was set for that length) before calling the subprogram Delay. After the delay, you are prompted, as follows, to press a key.

```
Press a key to print character values.
Press the ENTER key to quit.
```

When you press a key, your printer prints the key's character code. Figure 3-6 shows the date and time that was printed plus the character codes for the keys that were pressed: UP ARROW, DOWN ARROW, LEFT ARROW, RIGHT ARROW, F1, F2, F3, F4, and ENTER.

This Quick library demonstration just begins to describe the utilities that you might put in a Quick library. You can use UTIL3 as a base and add a more complete set of utilities, or you can discard it and build your own Quick library. In fact, you will probably want to create many Quick libraries for different purposes. With a little planning, your Quick libraries can save you much time when you write, load, and run programs.

```
Date 03-10-1988
Time 17:39:03
0 + 72
0 + 80
0 + 75
0 + 77
0 + 59
0 + 60
0 + 61
0 + 62
 13




Press any key to continue
```

Figure 3-6.   Output of Program 3-4

4

INTRODUCTORY GRAPHICS

You can create a wide variety of patterns, colors, and shapes with QuickBASIC graphics statements and functions. Graphics add a new dimension to text-oriented programs, whether they are games, educational tools, math and science applications, or business applications.

To run the graphics programs in this book, your computer must have a graphics adapter such as a Color Graphics Adapter (CGA), Extended Graphics Adapter (EGA), or Video Graphics Adapter (VGA). To make this book useful to the largest possible number of readers, the demonstrations are limited to display screen modes 0, 1, and 2, which are common to all of these graphics adapters. You can alter the programs used here for other screen modes if your adapter can handle them. The discussions and demonstrations of this chapter and the following two chapters assume that you are using a CGA.

TEXT MODE GRAPHICS

The SCREEN 0 text mode is limited to block graphics. Each of these blocks occupies an area the same size as a text character. The block shapes are printed by the extended ASCII character codes 128 to 255, which are available on most CGAs (see Appendix B). These blocks are useful for creating colorful menus and rectangular patterns.

Program 4-1 shows all foreground, background, and border colors available in the SCREEN 0 text mode. Block graphics are used to form a boundary around the displayed text. The text describes the colors as they are displayed. Before entering and running the program, you should read the description of the SCREEN and COLOR statements in this section.

The SCREEN 0 statement provides a screen display of either 40 or 80 columns specified by a WIDTH 40 or WIDTH 80 statement. Eight pages are available in the 40-column mode, and four

```
DECLARE SUB RightSide ()
DECLARE SUB Delay (sec!)
REM ** TEXT COLOR DEMONSTRATION **
' Program 4-1  PR00401.BAS

REM ** Set Screen and Display Foreground Colors **
SCREEN 0: WIDTH 80: CLS
DEFINT A-Z: DIM SHARED bord AS INTEGER
COLOR 0, 7: LOCATE 2, 3: PRINT " Foreground Colors  "
LOCATE 3, 2: PRINT STRING$(22, 223)
LOCATE 20, 2: PRINT STRING$(22, 220)
FOR bord = 0 TO 15
  col = 3: row = 4
  FOR fore = 0 TO 15
    LOCATE row, 2: COLOR 7, 0: PRINT CHR$(219)
    COLOR fore, 1, bord
    LOCATE row, col: PRINT STRING$(20, 219);
    LOCATE row, 24: COLOR 7, 0: PRINT fore;
    LOCATE row, 23: COLOR 7, 0: PRINT CHR$(219)
    row = row + 1
```

Program 4-1.   Text Color Demonstration

```
   NEXT fore
   CALL RightSide
   sec! = 1: CALL Delay(sec!)
NEXT bord
COLOR 7, 0, 0
END

SUB Delay (sec!)
   TurnOn! = TIMER
   DO UNTIL TIMER >= TurnOn! + sec!
   LOOP
END SUB

SUB RightSide
   DEFINT A-Z
   COLOR bord, 0, bord
   LOCATE 2, 40: PRINT STRING$(22, 220)
   FOR row = 3 TO 9
      COLOR bord: LOCATE row, 40: PRINT CHR$(219); : COLOR 7
      PRINT SPACES$(20); : COLOR bord: PRINT CHR$(219): COLOR 7
   NEXT row
   COLOR bord: LOCATE 3, 40: PRINT CHR$(219); : COLOR 7
   PRINT " Background     "; SPACES$(5); : COLOR bord:
   PRINT CHR$(219): LOCATE 4, 40: PRINT CHR$(219);
   COLOR 7: PRINT " Border        "; SPACES$(5);
   COLOR bord: PRINT CHR$(219)
   FOR row = 5 TO 17
      COLOR bord: LOCATE row, 40: PRINT CHR$(219); : COLOR 7
      PRINT SPACES$(20); : COLOR bord: PRINT CHR$(219)
   NEXT row
   LOCATE 18, 40: PRINT STRING$(22, 223)
   FOR back = 0 TO 7
      IF back = 0 THEN
         txt = 7
      ELSE txt = 0
      END IF
      COLOR txt, back, bord
      LOCATE 3, 41: PRINT " Border     "; STR$(bord);
      IF bord < 10 THEN
         PRINT SPACES$(5);
      ELSE PRINT SPACES$(4);
      END IF
      LOCATE 4, 41: PRINT " Background   "; STR$(back);
         PRINT SPACES$(5);
      FOR row = 5 TO 17
         LOCATE row, 41: PRINT SPACES$(20);
      NEXT row
      sec! = 1: CALL Delay(sec!)
   NEXT back
END SUB
```

Program 4-1.   Text Color Demonstration (*continued*)

pages are available in the 80-column mode. You can specify an active page to write to (the page where CLS, PRINT, LOCATE, and so on are performed) and a visual page to be displayed with the following statement:

```
SCREEN 0, colorswitch, apage, vpage
```

where

> *colorswitch, apage,* and *vpage* are all optional
> *colorswitch* values: 0 = color on, 1 = color off
> *apage* = a number (1 to 8 or 1 to 4) of the actual page
> *vpage* = a number (1 to 8 or 1 to 4) of the visual page

Another statement used for text mode graphics is the COLOR statement. As shown in the following listing, COLOR can set foreground colors (0-31), background colors (0-7), and border colors (0-15) in the text mode. It is used differently in graphics modes.

```
COLOR foregrndnumber, Backgrndnumber, Bordernumber
```

Table 4-1 shows colors available in the text mode with a color adapter.

Program 4-1 displays the text mode foreground colors as a block of color bands within a white border on the left side of the screen. The color number is displayed to the right of each color band. On the right side of the screen, a rectangle is displayed as the program cycles through the background and border colors. The rectangle displays the current border color as its border and

Table 4-1.   Color Numbers

Number	Color	Number	Color
0	Black	8	Gray
1	Blue	9	Light blue
2	Green	10	Light green
3	Cyan	11	Light cyan
4	Red	12	Light red
5	Magenta	13	Light magenta
6	Brown	14	Yellow
7	White	15	Bright white

Foreground numbers 16-31 produce blinking characters in colors 0-15.

the current background color as its background. A text description of the changing colors is displayed in the rectangle.

Note: Most EGAs cannot display a border, even in the CGA mode.

Figure 4-1 shows a typical screen in the cycle. The program needs a subprogram containing a time delay; it passes the length of the delay (in seconds) to this subprogram. The demonstration program was loaded from the command line with the Quick library UTIL3 of Chapter 3, as shown in the following listing:

```
A>QB B:PRO0401.BAS /L B:UTIL3.QLB
```

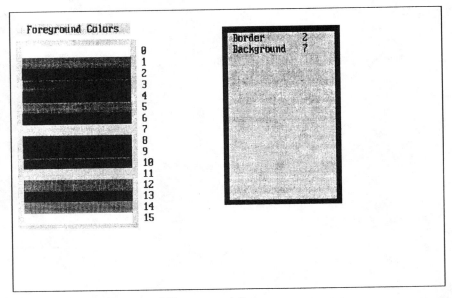

Figure 4-1.   Output of Program 4-1

You can do the same or add your own time delay subprogram such as the one shown in the next listing:

```
SUB Delay (sec!)
  TurnOn! = TIMER
  DO UNTIL TIMER >= TurnOn! + sec!
  LOOP
END SUB
```

A time delay of one second is used in Program 4-1. You can modify this to suit your needs.

Most computers use a particular key combination to hold a given color combination on the screen, and another key combination to resume the action. The CTRL-NUMLOCK combination is used on many computers to halt action, and any other key is used to resume action. Some computers have a HOLD key to halt action. Since this key is a toggle, pressing HOLD again resumes the action.

You may want to record the color combinations you find pleasing. Then you can refer to that record when you plan future programs.

In Program 4-1, the main program and subprograms share information in two ways. A DIM SHARED statement is used in the main program so that any, or all, subprogram(s) share the variable *bord*. The CALL DELAY(*sec!*) statement uses the parameter *sec!* to pass a value to be shared only between the main program and the Delay subprogram.

LOOKING AT WINDOWS

Program 4-2 shows how you can use block text mode characters to form the border and background for pull-down windows. The window area is 10 rows deep by 32 characters wide. The upper left corner of the window is displayed at column 26 in row 1. The lower right corner of the window is at column 57 in row 10. This area of the screen is saved in an array and replaced after you make a selection from the menu displayed in the window.

```
DECLARE SUB Menu ()
DECLARE SUB List1 ()
DECLARE SUB List2 ()
REM ** WINDOW DEMONSTRATION **
' Program 4-2  File: PRO0402.BAS

REM ** Dimension Array, Define Screen and Print Text **
DIM Block%(1 TO 10, 1 TO 32): DEFINT A-Z
SCREEN 0: WIDTH 80: CLS
PRINT "This program has a pull-down menu."
PRINT "Press a key and the menu drops down."
PRINT "Select menu item, and the menu will go away."
PRINT "The original information will be replaced.";

REM ** Copy Window Area and Wait for Key Press **
FOR row = 1 TO 10
```

Program 4-2. Window Demonstration

```
    FOR col = 1 TO 32
      Block%(row, col) = SCREEN(row, col + 25)
    NEXT col
NEXT row
LOCATE 6, 1: PRINT "Press a key to see menu.";
ky$ = INPUT$(1)

REM ** Print Menu 1 and Choose an Item **
CALL Menu
CALL List1
DO
   ky$ = INPUT$(1)
   IF INSTR("CcSsPp", ky$) = 0 THEN BEEP
LOOP WHILE INSTR("CcSsPp", ky$) = 0
SELECT CASE ky$
   CASE "C", "c"
      Choice$ = "Create Note Pad"
   CASE "S", "s"
      Choice$ = "Scan Note Pad"
   CASE "P", "p"
      Choice$ = "Print Note Pad"
END SELECT

REM ** Show Original Screen with Menu Choice **
COLOR 7, 0
FOR row = 1 TO 10
   FOR col = 1 TO 32
      LOCATE row, col + 25
      PRINT CHR$(Block%(row, col));
   NEXT col
NEXT row
LOCATE 7, 1: PRINT "You chose "; Choice$
PRINT "Press a key to choose disk drive."
ky$ = INPUT$(1)
LOCATE 7, 1: PRINT SPACE$(35): PRINT SPACE$(35)

REM ** Print Menu 2 and Choose Item **
CALL Menu
CALL List2
DO
   ky$ = INPUT$(1)
   IF INSTR("AaBbCc", ky$) = 0 THEN BEEP
LOOP WHILE INSTR("AaBbCc", ky$) = 0
SELECT CASE ky$
   CASE "A", "a"
      Choice$ = "Drive A"
   CASE "B", "b"
      Choice$ = "Drive B"
   CASE "C", "c"
      Choice$ = "Drive C"
END SELECT

REM ** Return to Original Screen and End **
COLOR 7, 0
```

Program 4-2.   Window Demonstration (*continued*)

```
FOR row = 1 TO 10
  FOR col = 1 TO 32
    LOCATE row, col + 25
    PRINT CHR$(Block%(row, col));
  NEXT col
NEXT row
LOCATE 7, 1: PRINT "You chose "; Choice$
PRINT "Press any key to end program."
ky$ = INPUT$(1)
COLOR 7, 0: CLS : END
SUB List1
  LOCATE 3, 35: COLOR 11, 1: PRINT "Function List";
  LOCATE 5, 32: COLOR 7: PRINT " ( )reate Note Pad "
  LOCATE 6, 32: PRINT " ( )can Note Pad   "
  LOCATE 7, 32: PRINT " ( )rint Note Pad "
  COLOR 12: LOCATE 5, 34: PRINT "C";
  LOCATE 6, 34: PRINT "S";
  LOCATE 7, 34: PRINT "P";
  COLOR 12
  LOCATE 9, 28: PRINT "Press First Letter of Choice";
  LOCATE 9, 27: COLOR 27: PRINT "*"; : LOCATE 9, 56, 0
  PRINT "*"; : BEEP
END SUB

SUB List2
  LOCATE 3, 35: COLOR 11, 1: PRINT "Select Drive ";
  LOCATE 5, 33: COLOR 7: PRINT "( ) Drive for file "
  LOCATE 6, 33: PRINT "( ) Drive for file"
  LOCATE 7, 33: PRINT "( ) Drive for file"
  COLOR 12: LOCATE 5, 34: PRINT "A";
  LOCATE 6, 34: PRINT "B";
  LOCATE 7, 34: PRINT "C";
  COLOR 12
  LOCATE 9, 28: PRINT "    Press Letter of Drive   ";
  LOCATE 9, 27: COLOR 27: PRINT "   *"; : LOCATE 9, 54, 0
  PRINT "*  "; : BEEP
END SUB

SUB Menu
  LOCATE 6, 1: PRINT SPACE$(24)
  COLOR 1, 0: DEFINT A-Z
  FOR row = 2 TO 9
    LOCATE row, 27: PRINT STRING$(30, 219);
  NEXT row
  COLOR 11, 0: LOCATE 1, 26: PRINT STRING$(32, 220)
  LOCATE 10, 26: PRINT STRING$(32, 223)
  COLOR 11, 1
  FOR row = 2 TO 9
    LOCATE row, 26: PRINT CHR$(221);
    LOCATE row, 57: PRINT CHR$(222);
  NEXT row
END SUB
```

Program 4-2.   Window Demonstration (*continued*)

The following four lines of text are originally displayed at the top of the screen:

```
This program has a pull-down menu.
Press a key and the menu drops down.
Select menu item, and the menu will go away.
The original information will be replaced.
```

Each character in the area to be replaced by the window is saved as an element of a two-dimensional array named *Block%*. These characters would be saved by the following statement:

```
Block%(row, col) = SCREEN(row, col + 25)
```

The SCREEN statement, in this format, returns the ASCII code of the character in the specified screen position (*row, col* + 25). This code is assigned to the specified element of the array (*row, col*). Since the two values following the SCREEN keyword are enclosed in parentheses, QuickBASIC recognizes that you are not specifying a screen mode.

Then the message "Press a key to see menu." appears below the four lines of text. When you press a key, the Menu subprogram is called. This subprogram draws the border and background for the first menu. The List1 subprogram is then called to print the menu items. Figure 4-2 shows the first menu.

To make a selection from the menu, press the first letter (upper or lower case) of one of the following three items:

1. (C)reate Note Pad

2. (S)can Note Pad

3. (P)rint Note Pad

If you press a key other than C, S, or P, the computer beeps once and then waits for you to enter one of the specified letters. When you press one of the specified keys, the SELECT CASE *ky$* structure assigns the appropriate choice to the variable *Choice$*.

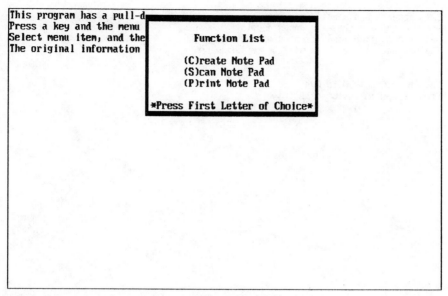

Figure 4-2.   First menu of Program 4-2

The characters replaced by the window are recalled from the *Block%* array and displayed at their original screen positions. When this process is finished, the window is gone and the original four lines of text are again displayed.

A message displays your menu choice, and another requests that you press a key to choose a disk drive. Figure 4-3 shows the restored screen with four text lines and two message lines.

When you press a key, the Menu subprogram is called again to draw new borders and background for the second menu. Since this menu outline is the same size as the previous menu, the same subprogram is used to draw the border and background. The List2 subprogram is then called to print the text of the second menu.

A second menu appears, as shown in Figure 4-4. The following three items are listed on the Disk Drive menu:

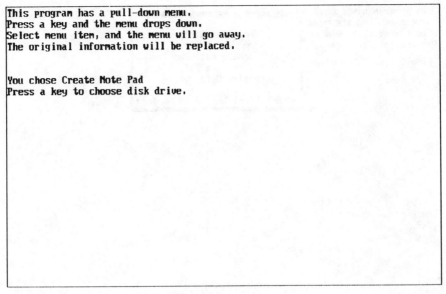

Figure 4-3.   Restored screen with messages

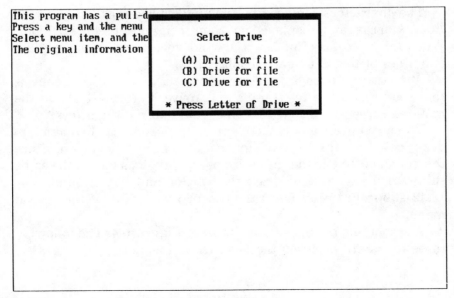

Figure 4-4.   Second menu of Program 4-2

1. (A) Drive for file
2. (B) Drive for file
3. (C) Drive for file

You select the letter of the disk drive where the Note Pad file has been or is to be saved. When you select a drive the menu is replaced by the original screen (screen page 1). A message echoing your second selection is added, and then another message requests that you press any key to end the program.

If this were a working program rather than a demonstration, then your selected action would be executed on the appropriate disk drive. Since this is a demonstration, the program ends at this point.

OTHER CHARACTER SHAPES

You can draw more delicate borders using character codes that form thin lines and double lines. Codes are also provided that draw pieces of borders, such as those shown with their character codes in Figure 4-5.

By combining the corner shapes and the vertical and horizontal thin and double lines, you can form a variety of rectangles. Figure 4-6 shows rectangles formed by character codes that display corners and straight lines. The character codes are shown within the rectangles.

Codes that form the corners are in the corresponding corner of the rectangles. Codes that form top and bottom lines are shown at the center top and bottom positions in the rectangles. Codes that form the sides are shown at the center left and right positions in the rectangles.

In addition to the solid block shape formed by character code 219, character codes 176, 177, and 178 provide three similar shapes of different gray levels. Vertical bars formed by these codes are shown with additional rectangle variations in Figure 4-7. You can display additional shapes by using character codes in the range of 1 to 31.

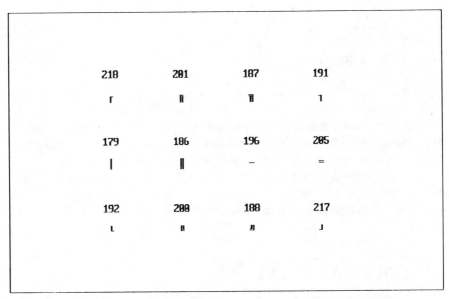

Figure 4-5. Character code line shapes

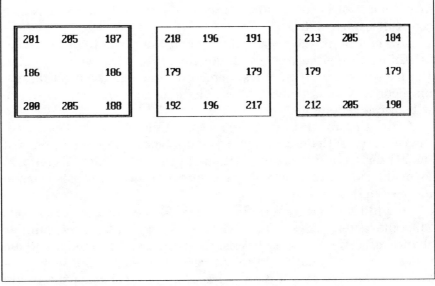

Figure 4-6. Character code rectangles

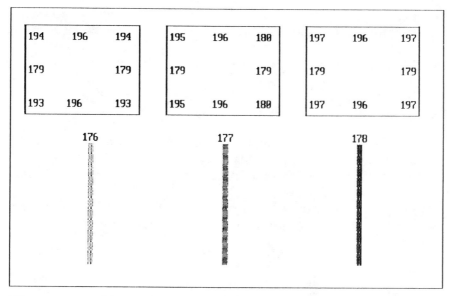

Figure 4-7.   Using character codes

PASSING DATA

When you write computer programs, you invariably use some blocks of code over and over. To avoid repeatedly entering these blocks, you can make them readily available in subprograms or in Quick libraries. The block of code, whether large or small, could then be called by a single instruction. A single instruction that causes a whole sequence of operations to be performed is a CALL statement that invokes a subprogram.

To be effective, a subprogram should perform operations that are general enough to satisfy a wide variety of uses. Then to use the subprogram in a given situation, you can provide information specific to that application. This information, when passed to the subprogram, serves as a template (or a pattern) that makes the general subprogram fit a specific situation.

Consider the windows displayed in Program 4-2. Suppose you wish to create a subprogram to display the background and border for a window. You would need to provide the following information in a template:

1. Location of the window by row and column
2. Height and width of the window
3. Border and background colors

The subprogram would then use the template's background color and location information to draw the interior of the window. It would also use the template's border color and location information to draw the border.

For example, the following subprogram provides the operations necessary to draw a colorful background and border for a pull-down window:

```
SUB PullDown (Backcol%, Bordcol%, column%, row%, hgt%, wdth%)
   DEFINT A-Z
   REM ** Draw Background **
   COLOR Backcol: wide = wdth - 2
   FOR lyne = row + 1 TO row + hgt - 2
     LOCATE lyne, column + 1: PRINT STRING$(wide, 219)
   NEXT lyne

   REM ** Draw Border **
   COLOR Bordcol
   LOCATE row, column: PRINT STRING$(wdth, 219)
   LOCATE row + hgt - 1, column: PRINT STRING$(wdth, 219)
   FOR lyne = row + 1 TO row + hgt - 2
     LOCATE lyne, column: PRINT CHR$(219)
     LOCATE lyne, column + wide + 1: PRINT CHR$(219)
   NEXT lyne
END SUB
```

The template for the PullDown subprogram supplies values for the following variables:

row	Top row of window
column	Left column of window
hgt	Height of window (including border)

wdth	Width of window (including border)
Backcol	Background color
Bordcol	Border color

Each value is passed as a parameter in a CALL statement to the subprogram. This is shown in the following listing:

```
CALL PullDown(Backcol%, Bordcol%, column%, row%, hgt%, wdth%)
   .
   .
   .
SUB PullDown (Backcol%, Bordcol%, column%, row%, hgt%, wdth%)
   .
   .
   .
```

Program 4-3 shows how the PullDown subprogram uses its template.

```
DECLARE SUB PullDown (Backcol%, Bordcol%, column%, row%, hgt%, wdth%)
REM ** TINY TEMPLATE DEMO **
' Program 4-3  File: PRO0403.BAS

REM ** Initialize **
SCREEN 0: CLS
DEFINT A-Z

REM ** Template for Window **
INPUT "Row for top of window"; row
INPUT "Column for left side of window"; column
INPUT "Height of window"; hgt
INPUT "Width of window"; wdth
INPUT "Background color number for window (0 - 15)"; Backcol
INPUT "Border color number for window (0 - 15)"; Bordcol

REM ** CALL SUB and Pass Data **
CALL PullDown(Backcol%, Bordcol%, column%, row%, hgt%, wdth%)
END
```

Program 4-3.   Tiny Template Demo

```
SUB PullDown (Backcol%, Bordcol%, column%, row%, hgt%, wdth%)
  DEFINT A-Z
  REM ** Draw Background **
  COLOR Backcol: wide = wdth - 2
  FOR lyne = row + 1 TO row + hgt - 2
    LOCATE lyne, column + 1: PRINT STRING$(wide, 219)
  NEXT lyne

  REM ** Draw Border **
  COLOR Bordcol
  LOCATE row, column: PRINT STRING$(wdth, 219)
  LOCATE row + hgt - 1, column: PRINT STRING$(wdth, 219)
  FOR lyne = row + 1 TO row + hgt - 2
    LOCATE lyne, column: PRINT CHR$(219)
    LOCATE lyne, column + wide + 1: PRINT CHR$(219)
  NEXT lyne
END SUB
```

Program 4-3.   Tiny Template Demo (*continued*)

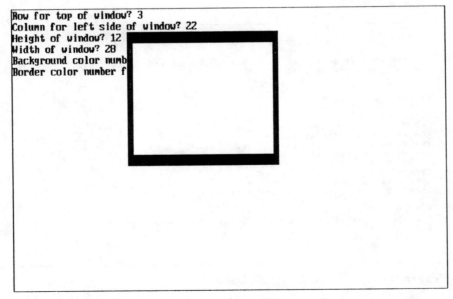

Figure 4-8.   Window displayed by PullDown subprogram

Figure 4-8 shows a window produced by this template. The template is created by passing the following variable values to the subprogram:

row = 3
column = 22
hgt = 12
wdth = 28
Backcol = 3 (cyan)
Bordcol = 1 (blue)

CORRELATING TEXT AND PIXEL POSITIONS

Quite often graphics screens that you create need to include some textual information. For instance, if you create a bar graph, you will need labels to indicate what the bars represent and a scale to indicate what the relative sizes of the bars represent. You will probably also want to add a title for the graph. To coordinate the placement of text characters on a pixel-oriented graphics screen, you need a quick way to relate text positions to graphic pixel positions.

SCREEN 1 Text Character/Pixel Positions

Each text character occupies an eight-by-eight pixel area, as shown in Figure 4-9. Thus, corresponding positions of adjacent text characters are eight pixels apart.

Unfortunately, the numbering conventions for text character and pixel positions are different. You can see this in the following formats for the LOCATE statement (used for text) and the PSET statement (used for graphics):

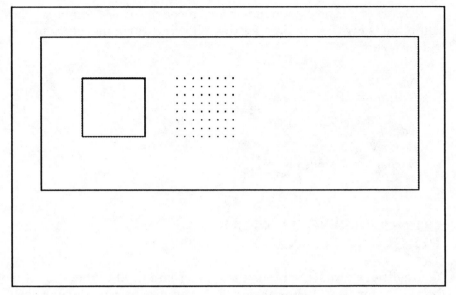

Figure 4-9.   Comparing character and pixel size

```
LOCATE row, column        'row first, then column

PSET(column, row)         'column first, then row
```

For the upper left corner of the screen, the numbering conventions for text characters and pixels are

   (*row, column*) = (1,1) for text characters
   (*column, row*) = (0,0) for graphic pixels

Compare how the first row of text character positions and the corresponding pixel positions of the upper left corner of each character position are numbered in Figure 4-10.

   Using *tcol* to represent text column values and *pcol* to represent the column value of the text character's upper left corner pixel, you can set up the following algebraic equation:

```
tcol = pcol / 8 + 1
```

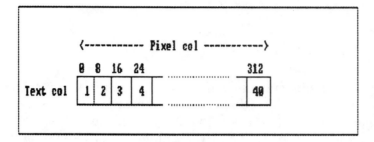

Figure 4-10.   Pixel and text column numbering

For example, for *pcol* = 32, *tcol* = 32 / 8 + 1 = 4 + 1 or 5. Correspondingly, *pcol* = 8 * (*tcol* − 1). In words, to calculate the text column of a corresponding pixel, divide the pixel column value by 8 and add 1. To calculate the pixel column of the upper left corner of a corresponding text character position, subtract 1 from the character's column value and multiply the result by 8.

Next, compare how the rows of the first column of text character positions and the corresponding pixel row of the upper left corner of the character are numbered in Figure 4-11. Using *trow* to represent text row values and *prow* to represent the row value of the corresponding upper left corner pixel, you can set up the following algebraic equation:

```
trow = prow / 8 + 1
prow = 8 * (trow -1)
```

You can now relate text positions in a LOCATE statement to the graphics position of a pixel occupying the upper left corner of the text position. You can also relate pixel positions to the upper left corner of a text position. Both relationships are shown in the following listing:

```
LOCATE trow, tcol is equivalent to:

LOCATE prow / 8 + 1, pcol / 8 + 1

PSET (pcol, prow) is equivalent to:

PSET (8 * (tcol - 1), 8 *(trow - 1)
```

For example, suppose you wish to place a text character on a SCREEN 1 graphics display with the upper left corner of the character at the pixel position that would be set by PSET (32, 112). Remember, 32 in the PSET statement represents the column position (*pcol*) and 112 represents the row position (*prow*). You

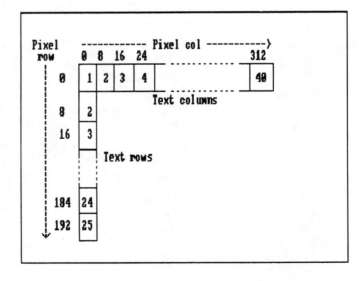

Figure 4-11.   Pixel and text row numbering

could calculate the LOCATE statement to place this character in the following manner:

```
LOCATE prow / 8 + 1, pcol / 8 + 1 =

LOCATE 112 / 8 + 1, 32 / 8 + 1 = LOCATE 15,5
```

Notice that the variables *prow* and *pcol* used in the example are multiples of 8. Since text character positions are 8 pixels apart, they cannot be placed at exact pixel positions. If you use a *prow* or *pcol* value that is not a multiple of 8, the value is rounded to the next lower integer. An example for *prow* = 30 and *pcol* = 110 is shown in the following listing:

```
LOCATE 110 /8 + 1, 30 /8 + 1 = LOCATE 14.75, 4.75
```

The character here would be located at row 14, column 4.

Putting Text/Pixel Relationships to Work

Since pixels are placed more precisely on the screen than text, first place the text on the screen and then calculate the corresponding pixel positions. Program 4-4 places a line of text near the center of the screen. The first letter of the text is placed at row 8, column 8. The text, "WRAP A RECTANGLE AROUND ME", is 26 characters long. Therefore, the last character occupies the position at row 8, column 33.

Suppose you want to place a rectangle around this text. The top of this rectangle should be one character position above the text, the bottom one character position below the text, and the sides one character position to the right and left of the text string.

First calculate the ending positions for the top of the rectangle. Using the previously defined relationships for *prow* (pixel row)

```
REM ** RECTANGLE 'ROUND THE TEXT **
' Program 4-4   File: PRO0404.BAS

REM ** Initialize **
SCREEN 1: CLS

REM ** Print Text & Enclose **
LOCATE 13, 8: PRINT "WRAP A RECTANGLE AROUND ME"
LINE (48, 88)-(272, 88)
LINE (48, 112)-(272, 112)
LINE (48, 88)-(48, 112)
LINE (272, 88)-(272, 112)

REM ** Wait for Keypress & End **
ky$ = INPUT$(1): CLS : END
```

Program 4-4.   Rectangle Around the Text

and *trow* (text row), calculate *prow* and *pcol* for the left-most character in the text with the following equations:

```
trow = 13, tcol = 8
prow = 8 * (trow - 1) = 8 * 12 = 96
pcol = 8 * (tcol - 1) = 8 * 7 = 56
```

The top of the rectangle starts eight pixels to the left of and eight pixels above the PSET point (56, 96). Remember that graphics point positions are specified in the reverse order of text point positions. The correct starting point for the line is the point (48, 88).

The last character in the text string lies at text row 13 and text column 33. However, the pixel associated with this character is at the upper left corner of the character. Add an extra character to move the rectangle side beyond the last character in the string. This addition makes *tcol* equal 34. Now calculate the pixel point using this adjusted text position with the following equations:

```
trow = 13, tcol = 34
prow = 8 * (trow - 1) = 8 * 12 = 96
pcol = 8 * (tcol - 1) = 8 * 33 = 264
```

The line above the text ends eight pixels to the right of and eight pixels above the pixel point (264, 96), which is the point

(272, 88). The next listing shows the appropriate LINE statement to draw the top line of the rectangle.

```
LINE (48,88)-(272,88)
```

From the end points of the top line, you know that the pixel end points of the bottom line start at *pcol* = 48 and end at *pcol* = 272. You only need to calculate the row coordinates of these end points.

Since text characters occupy eight pixel positions, calculate the bottom line of the rectangle by adding three text positions (24 pixels)—one for the space between the top of the rectangle and the text, one for the text, and one for the space between the text and the bottom of the rectangle. This relationship is shown in Figure 4-12. This calculation results in the following end points for the bottom of the rectangle:

    Left point = (48, 88 + 24)
    Right point = (272, 88 + 24)

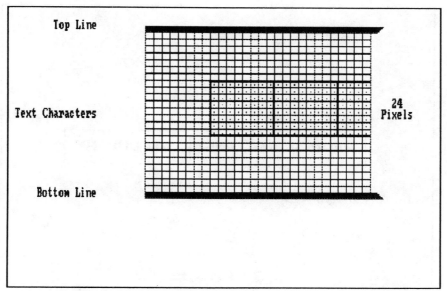

Figure 4-12.   Top and bottom of the rectangle

The next listing shows the appropriate LINE statement for the bottom line of the rectangle:

```
LINE (48, 112)-(272,112)
```

To draw the sides, you merely connect the end points of the top and bottom lines with the LINE statements shown in this listing:

```
LINE (48, 88)-(48, 112)
LINE (272, 88)-(272, 112)
```

Figure 4-13 shows the rectangle wrapped around the text.

The LINE statement efficiently replaces a series of PSET statements. Therefore, PSET is usually used to turn on single or irregularly placed points.

Program 4-4 uses the LINE statement to draw individual sides of the rectangle to illustrate the text character and pixel position relationship. You can use the box option (B) of the LINE

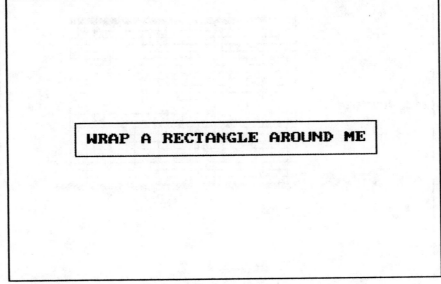

Figure 4-13. Rectangle wrapped around text

statement to replace the four individual LINE statements in the program as shown in the following listing:

```
LINE (48,88) - (272, 112), , B     can replace:

LINE (48, 88) - (272, 88)
LINE (48, 112) - (272, 112)
LINE (48, 88) - (48, 112)
LINE (272, 88) - (272, 112)
```

If you use the B option shown in this listing, you only need to calculate the upper left pixel (48, 88) and the lower right pixel (272, 112) of the rectangle.

You could also write the executable statements of Program 4-4 and only reference the position of the first text character (13, 8), as shown in the next listing:

```
SCREEN 1: CLS
LOCATE 13, 8: PRINT "WRAP A RECTANGLE AROUND ME"
LeftCol = 8 * (8 - 2):   TopRow = 8 * (13 - 2)
RiteCol = 8 * (8 + 26): BotRow = 8 * (13 + 1)
LINE(LeftCol, TopRow) - (RiteCol, BotRow), , B
```

Program 4-5 provides a more general way to enclose text within a rectangle.

Enter the number of text rows and the column and row location of the first text line. The program stores each text line in an array and finds the length of the longest line as shown in the next listing:

```
   .
   .
   .
Lng = 0
   .
   .
   .
  LINE INPUT Array$(num)
  temp = LEN(Array$(num))
  IF temp > Lng THEN
    Lng = temp
  END IF
```

Typical entries are shown in Figure 4-14.

The program uses the location you entered for the left-most character of the first line to calculate the location of the upper left

```
REM ** GENERAL RECTANGLE/TEXT DEMONSTRATION **
' Program 4-5   File:  PRO0405.BAS

REM ** Initialize & Get Data **
SCREEN 1: CLS : DEFINT A-Z
INPUT "How many lines of text "; LineNum
INPUT "Row number for first line "; trow
INPUT "Column number for first line "; tcol
REDIM Array(1 TO LineNum)  AS STRING
Lng = 0
FOR num = 1 TO UBOUND(Array$)
   PRINT "Enter line number"; num
   LINE INPUT Array$(num)
   temp = LEN(Array$(num))
   IF temp > Lng THEN
     Lng = temp
   END IF
NEXT num
CLS

REM ** Print Array & Box **
FOR lyne = 1 TO UBOUND(Array$)
   LOCATE trow + lyne - 1, tcol: PRINT Array$(lyne)
NEXT lyne
pco1 = (tcol - 2) * 8: prw1 = (trow - 2) * 8
pco2 = (tcol + Lng) * 8: prw2 = (trow + LineNum) * 8
LINE (pco1, prw1)-(pco2, prw2), , B

REM ** Wait for Keypress & End **
a$ = INPUT$(1): CLS : END
```

Program 4-5.   General Rectangle/Text Demonstration

corner of the rectangle. Next it uses the length of the longest line (*Lng*) and the number of lines (*LineNum*) to calculate the lower right corner of the rectangle. Then it draws the rectangle. This section of the program is shown in the following listing:

```
   .
   .
   .
pco1 = (tcol - 2) * 8: prw1 = (trow - 2) * 8
pco2 = (tcol + Lng) * 8: prw2 = (trow + LineNum) * 8
LINE (pco1, prw1)-(pco2, prw2) , , B
```

The output of the entries shown in Figure 4-14 is illustrated in Figure 4-15.

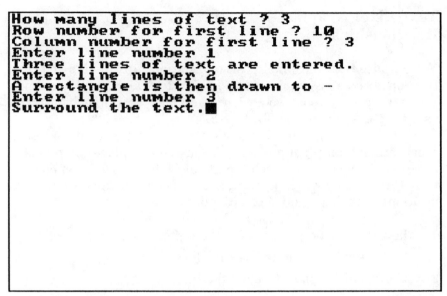

Figure 4-14. Input for Program 4-5

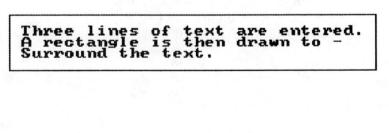

Figure 4-15. Output of Program 4-5

Text/Pixel Graph Relationships

You can use text and pixel position relationships to help you plan the appearance of graphs that combine text and graphic shapes. For example, suppose you wish to display a simple bar graph using the data shown in Table 4-2.

You should begin to plan such a graph in terms of text positions rather than pixel positions. Then you can place the pixels of the graphic portion to match the more crudely placed text characters. First decide which general areas of the screen to use for text positions. You might do this as follows:

1. The title will be placed near the top of the screen.
2. The bars will be plotted vertically.
3. Labels will be placed below the bars.

Table 4-2.   Mean Temperatures for Six Months

Month	Mean Temperature (in degrees Fahrenheit)
January	12
February	15
March	43
April	68
May	75
June	80

For a graph displayed on SCREEN 1, you have 25 rows of 40 characters each. You might plan the areas in more detail as shown in Figure 4-16 and described here:

1. The title will be placed on line 3.
2. Bars will be placed at least two rows below the title; columns will be centered, leaving room at the bottom for labels.
3. Bar labels will be placed near the bottom of the screen.

Program 4-6 uses this plan to display a bar graph of the data in Table 4-2. This program was written generically so that a tem-

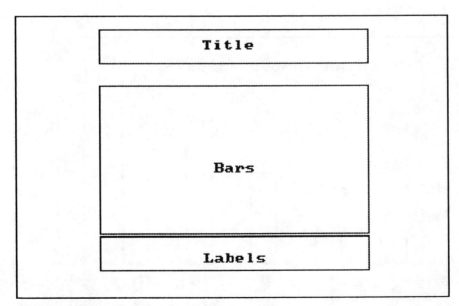

Figure 4-16.   Screen plan for bar graph

plate and a subprogram could readily be designed. The title and bar labels are automatically centered. The bars are then placed by the text and pixel relationships discussed earlier.

You only need to enter information at the beginning of the program. The program requests that you enter the graph's title, the number of bars to be drawn, the number of rows needed for the labels, and the values that the bars are to represent. You might want to add a section to provide a scale at either side of the graph.

The output of Program 4-6, after entering the data in Table 4-2, is shown in Figure 4-17.

Text and pixel position relationships are also used in the next two chapters.

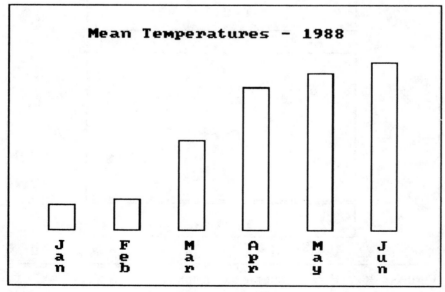

Figure 4-17.   Output of Program 4-6

```
REM ** BAR GRAPH TITLE/LABEL DEMONSTRATION **
' Program 4-6   File:   PRO0406.BAS

REM ** Initialize and Get Data **
SCREEN 1: CLS : DEFINT A-Z
INPUT "Title of graph "; Title$
INPUT "Number of bars "; BarNum
INPUT "Number of rows for label "; NumRows
REDIM Amount!(1 TO BarNum)

REM ** Get Data & Calculate Scale for Bars **
biggest! = 0
FOR num = 1 TO BarNum
  PRINT "ENTER amount number"; num; ": ";
  INPUT Amount!(num)
  IF Amount!(num) > biggest! THEN biggest! = Amount!(num)
NEXT num
Scale! = 120 / biggest!

REM ** Calculate Positions; Print Title & Labels **
HalfTitle = INT(LEN(Title$) / 2)
CLS
LOCATE 3, 20 - HalfTitle: PRINT Title$
Interv = INT(30 / BarNum) + 1
UpLim = Interv * BarNum
FOR row = 22 TO 22 + NumRows - 1
  FOR column = 5 TO UpLim STEP Interv
    READ Month$
    LOCATE row, column: PRINT Month$;
  NEXT column
NEXT row
DATA J, F, M, A, M, J
DATA a, e, a, p, a, u
DATA n, b, r, r, y, n

REM ** Calculate positions and Draw Bars **
prw1 = 160
FOR num = 1 TO BarNum
  tco1 = 5 + (Interv * (num - 1))
  pco1 = 8 * (tco1) - 2 * Interv
  pco2 = (pco1 + 7) + 2 * Interv
  prw2 = prw1 - Scale! * Amount!(num)
  LINE (pco1, prw1)-(pco2, prw2), , B
NEXT num

REM ** Wait for Keypress & End **
a$ = INPUT$(1): END
```

Program 4-6.   Bar Graph Demonstration

5

GRAPHICS: PAINT
AND TILE

Chapter 4 concluded with Program 4-6, which drew a rather drab bar graph with a title and labels. Using that graph as a base, this chapter shows you how to liven up uncolorful graphic images. You can do this by painting or tiling the interior of geometric figures.

ADDING COLOR

You can create a wide variety of patterns, colors, and shapes with QuickBASIC graphics statements and functions. The graphics introduced in Chapter 4 started with SCREEN 0 (the text mode) and went on to SCREEN 1 (the medium resolution graphics mode). This chapter discusses more about SCREEN 1 graphics.

The COLOR statement for graphics modes differs from that used in the text mode. If you are using a CGA, you can set the colors in SCREEN 0 as follows:

```
COLOR [foreground][,[background][,border]]
```

Table 5-1.   Background Colors for SCREEN 1

Number	Color	Number	Color
0	Black	8	Gray
1	Blue	9	Light blue
2	Green	10	Light green
3	Cyan	11	Light cyan
4	Red	12	Light red
5	Magenta	13	Light magenta
6	Brown	14	Yellow
7	White	15	Bright white

Table 5-2.   Foreground Colors from Two Palettes

Palette 0		**Palette 1**	
Number	*Color*	*Number*	*Color*
0	Background	0	Background
1	Green	1	Cyan
2	Red	2	Magenta
3	Brown	3	White

where

> *foreground* = 0 to 31
> *background* = 0 to 15
> *border* = 0 to 15

The COLOR statement in SCREEN 1 mode has a different format. In this graphics mode, you may specify a background color and one of two palettes as shown in the next listing:

```
COLOR [background][,[palette]]
```

where

> *background* = 0 to 15
> *palette* = 0 or 1

This gives you four colors to work with. You may use any one of the sixteen background colors shown in Table 5-1.

You can use foreground colors to draw images on the background you have chosen. Since the background color may also be used as a foreground color, you can use one of two four-color palettes for drawing and painting. Foreground colors for the two palettes are shown in Table 5-2.

Notice that the colors used in palettes 0 and 1 are also included in the table of background colors. If you want to use four colors with SCREEN 1, do not select a background that corresponds to one of the palette colors you are using.

Drawing with Color

The PSET and LINE graphics statements were introduced in Chapter 4. You specify the color to be used to set a point or to draw a line with these statements in the following way:

```
PSET(column, row), color
LINE(col1, row1)-(col2, row2), color
```

When you use the box option (B) as follows, a box is drawn using the specified color:

```
LINE(col1, row1)-(col2, row2), color, B
```

You can add more color to the box with one other LINE option. The fill (F) option colors the interior of the box with the color you specify, or defaults to color 3 of the palettes in use if you do not specify a color. The use of this option is shown in the following listing:

```
LINE(col1, row1)-(col2, row2), color, BF
```

You could modify Program 4-6 in Chapter 4 by adding the fill option to the LINE statement that draws the bars in the Calculate Positions and Draw Bars block. The computer would then draw solid colored bars. The next section shows you how to use the PAINT statement, which provides another way to color the inside of closed shapes.

Using COLOR and PAINT Statements

Program 5-1 is a variation of Program 4-6, the bar graph program in Chapter 4. This program places the bars horizontally and adds a scale. The box (B) option is used to draw empty bars. The PAINT statement is used to fill the bars with color.

Figure 5-1 shows a sample input set for the mean temperature data used in Program 4-6. Figure 5-2 shows the output for that data. The COLOR statement is used to set a blue background and to select palette 1.

```
SCREEN 1: CLS
COLOR 1, 1
```

```
REM ** BAR GRAPH WITH PAINT **
' Program 5-1   File: PRO0501.BAS

REM ** Enter Data and Dimension Arrays **
CLS : DEFINT A-Z
INPUT "Title of graph "; Title$
INPUT "Number of bars "; BarNum
REDIM Amount!(1 TO BarNum)
REDIM Label$(1 TO BarNum)
REDIM Text$(1 TO BarNum)
biggest! = 0
FOR num = 1 TO BarNum
  PRINT "Enter bar label"; num; "(up to 5 letters)";
  INPUT Text$(num)
  PRINT "Enter amount"; num; : INPUT Amount!(num)
  IF Amount!(num) > biggest! THEN biggest! = Amount!(num)
NEXT num

REM ** Scale Bars, Set Graphics Screen, & Calculate **
Scale! = 2.2
SCREEN 1: CLS
COLOR 1, 1                              'blue background, palette 1
HalfTitle = INT(LEN(Title$) / 2)
LOCATE 2, 20 - HalfTitle: PRINT Title$
TextInterv = 6 - INT(BarNum / 2)
PixInterv = TextInterv * 8
trows = 5: pcol = 60: kolr = 0
LOCATE 2, 20 - HalfTitle: PRINT Title$

REM ** Draw and Label Graph **
FOR num = 1 TO BarNum
  trow = trows + (num - 1) * TextInterv
  LOCATE trow, 2: PRINT Text$(num)
  prow = (trow - 1) * 8
  pcol2 = (Scale! * Amount!(num)) + 60
  prow2 = prow + PixInterv / 2
  LINE (pcol, prow)-(pcol2, prow2), 3, B
  kolr = kolr + 1: IF kolr = 4 THEN kolr = 1
  PAINT ((pcol + pcol2) / 2, (prow + prow2) / 2), kolr, 3
NEXT num
prow = prow + 28
LINE (pcol, prow + 2)-(280, prow + 2)
LOCATE trow + 4, 8: PRINT "0    20    40    60    80    100";
FOR pcol = 60 TO 280 STEP 22
  LINE (pcol, prow - 2)-(pcol, prow + 1)
NEXT pcol

REM ** Wait for Keypress, Restore Graphics Screen, End **
ky$ = INPUT$(1)
SCREEN 0: CLS : END
```

Program 5-1.   Bar Graph with Paint

```
Title of graph ? Mean Temperatures - 1988
Number of bars ? 6
Enter bar label 1 (up to 5 letters)? Jan
Enter amount 1 ? 12
Enter bar label 2 (up to 5 letters)? Feb
Enter amount 2 ? 15
Enter bar label 3 (up to 5 letters)? Mar
Enter amount 3 ? 43
Enter bar label 4 (up to 5 letters)? Apr
Enter amount 4 ? 68
Enter bar label 5 (up to 5 letters)? May
Enter amount 5 ? 75
Enter bar label 6 (up to 5 letters)? Jun
Enter amount 6 ? 80
```

Figure 5-1.   Program 5-1 entries

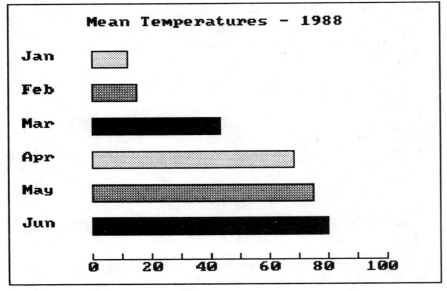

Figure 5-2.   Output of Program 5-1

The bars are drawn using color 3. The interior of each bar is painted in one of the three foreground colors of palette 1. Color 1 is used to paint the first bar, color 2 is used for the second bar, and color 3 for the third bar. When it reaches color 4, an IF...THEN statement cycles the color number back to 1. The colors then recycle through numbers 1, 2, and 3. Therefore, no two adjacent bars are the same color. This process is shown in the next listing:

```
trows = 5: pcol = 60: kolr = 0
   .
   .
   .
LINE(pcol, prow)-(pcol2, prow2), 3, B
kolr = kolr + 1: IF kolr = 4 THEN kolr = 1
PAINT((pcol + pcol2) / 2, (prow + prow2) / 2), kolr, 3
```

The following PAINT statement specifies the point (pixel position) at which to start painting, the paint color, and the boundary color. The program does not paint beyond the boundary color of a closed figure.

```
PAINT(col1, row1), colornumber, boundcolornum
```

When you are painting, you must satisfy these two conditions:

1. The figure to be painted must be closed so that paint does not spill out beyond the figure.

2. The starting point for painting must be within the boundary of the figure being painted.

Try running Program 5-1 to draw bar graphs with your own data. Be sure to keep labels within the five-letter limit.

LAYING TILES

You can PAINT an enclosed figure with multi-color patterns as well as solid colors. This process is called *tiling*. In SCREEN 1 mode tiling is done by using different colors to form a pattern

within a four-by-four block of pixels. This block is called a *tile*.
You then lay those tiles next to each other with a PAINT statement to fill an enclosed figure.

Two tiles are shown in Figure 5-3. The left tile has a pattern of
cyan pixels running diagonally from the upper left corner to the
lower right corner. All the other pixels of the tile are black, the
background color.

Defining Tiles

Binary and hexadecimal numbers are usually used to define the
pixel arrangement within a tile. The color numbers for palette 1
in SCREEN 1 mode are background 0, cyan 1, magenta 2, and
white 3. Table 5-3 shows the binary equivalents for these decimal

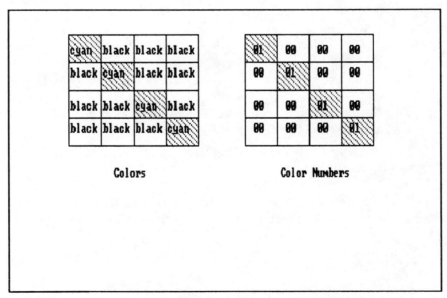

Figure 5-3.   Pixel colors and color numbers

Table 5-3.   Binary and Decimal Color Numbers

Color	Decimal	Binary
Background	0	00
Cyan	1	01
Magenta	2	10
White	3	11

color values of palette 1. The right tile in Figure 5-3 shows the binary color numbers for the pixels making up the tile.

When you are tiling, you replace the color argument in the PAINT statement with a string expression, as shown here:

```
PAINT(col1, row1)-(col2, row2), Tile$, boundcolornum
```

The variable *Tile$* here and in Figure 5-3 is defined by concatenating CHR$ expressions for individual rows of the tile. To do this, first consider the following binary expressions for the rows of the tile:

Row 1	01 00	00 00	cyan, black,	black, black
Row 2	00 01	00 00	black, cyan,	black, black
Row 3	00 00	01 00	black, black,	cyan, black
Row 4	00 00	00 01	black, black,	black, cyan

Next convert each four-bit block of the binary number to a hexadecimal digit. Use Table 5-4 if you are not familiar with

Table 5-4.   Binary and Hexadecimal Equivalents

Binary	Hexadecimal	Binary	Hexadecimal
0000	0	1000	8
0001	1	1001	9
0010	2	1010	A
0011	3	1011	B
0100	4	1100	C
0101	5	1101	D
0110	6	1110	E
0111	7	1111	F

binary to hexadecimal conversions. These conversions result in the following hexadecimal values for the tile:

Row 1	40	cyan, black	black, black
Row 2	10	black, cyan	black, black
Row 3	04	black, black	cyan, black
Row 4	01	black, black	black, cyan

Use these hexadecimal row values to define the variable *Tile$*. Then draw a figure and use *Tile$* in a PAINT statement like the following listing:

```
Tile$ = CHR$(&H40) + CHR$(&H10) + CHR$(&H4) + CHR$(&H1)
```

You could also convert the hexadecimal numbers to decimal and write the expression as follows:

```
Tile$ = CHR$(64) + CHR$(16) + CHR$(4) + CHR$(1)
```

However, changing to decimal numbers requires more work. The computer can convert the hexadecimal values to decimal for you. The &H symbols tell QuickBASIC that the numbers following the symbols are hexadecimal values.

The left side of Figure 5-4 shows the pattern for the defined tile. Four adjacent tiles of the same pattern are shown on the right side of the figure.

You can produce many color patterns by combining the four colors of the palette in this way. You can achieve many patterns with just two colors, but you can even create the illusion of more than four colors by combining the available colors in different patterns.

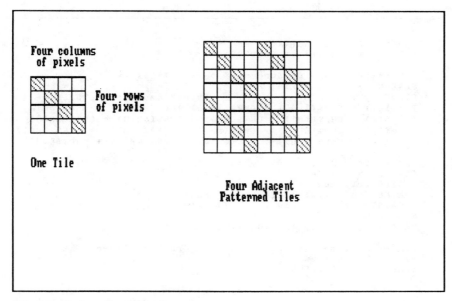

Figure 5-4.   Laying tiles

Program 5-2 draws four boxes on the screen and fills each box with a different tile pattern. Figure 5-5 shows the result.

Instead of using color to fill bars in bar graphs, you can use patterns such as those shown in Figure 5-5. In this way you can create a unique pattern for each bar instead of having to repeat colors that are limited. Try substituting tiles for color numbers in the PAINT statement of Program 5-1.

Deciding on Tile Patterns

Visualizing a tile pattern from a pattern of binary or hexadecimal numbers is difficult. It is also tedious to draw tile patterns by hand when planning their use in a program.

Luckily the computer is good at performing tedious tasks. It can display a tile pattern quickly on the screen when it is

```
REM ** TILE DEMONSTRATOR **
' Program 5-2  File: PRO0502.BAS

REM ** Set Graphics Screen, & Define Tiles **
SCREEN 1: CLS : DEFINT A-Z
COLOR 0, 1                    'black background, palette 1
Tile$(1) = CHR$(&H40) + CHR$(&H10) + CHR$(&H4) + CHR$(&H1)
Tile$(2) = CHR$(&H1) + CHR$(&H4) + CHR$(&H10) + CHR$(&H40)
Tile$(3) = CHR$(&H41) + CHR$(&H14) + CHR$(&H14) + CHR$(&H41)
Tile$(4) = CHR$(&H0) + CHR$(&H14) + CHR$(&H14) + CHR$(&H0)

REM ** Draw Boxes and Lay Tiles **
FOR num = 1 TO 4
   READ col, row
   LINE (col, row)-(col + 100, row + 80), 3, B
   PAINT (col + 5, row + 5), Tile$(num)
NEXT num
DATA 10, 10, 160, 10, 10, 110, 160, 110

REM ** Wait for Keypress, Restore Graphics Screen, End **
ky$ = INPUT$(1)
SCREEN 0: CLS : END
```

Program 5-2.   Tile Demonstrator

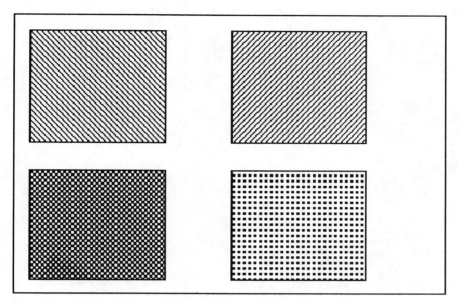

Figure 5-5. Tile patterns

informed of the desired pattern. Therefore, a computer program to allow you to preview tile patterns should prove useful.

Program 5-3 lets you select from the tile patterns you enter, which it displays on the screen. It not only lets you preview these tile patterns, but it also gives you the PAINT statement CHR$ codes necessary to produce the pattern you select.

The Initialize block of Program 5-3 dimensions and types several variables that are shared between the main program and its subprograms. Color names are assigned as elements of a two-dimensional array (*Forgrnd$(palet, kolor)*) and a one-dimensional array (*Backgrnd$(bgcolor)*). Only 8 of the possible 16 background colors are used in this program.

The Get Data block first requests you to enter a number to choose a palette for the tile, as shown in the following listing:

```
Which palette, please (0 or 1)?

   0   green, red, and brown
   1   cyan, magenta, and white
```

```
DECLARE SUB Choose ()
DECLARE SUB Custom (Back%, Pal%)
DECLARE SUB SetTile ()

REM ** TILE SELECTOR **
' Program 5-3  File: PRO0503.BAS

REM ** Initialize **
DIM SHARED size(0 TO 12) AS INTEGER, cschm(0 TO 80) AS INTEGER
DIM SHARED Forgrnd$(0 TO 1, 0 TO 3), pics%
DEFINT A-Z

begin: SCREEN 0: WIDTH 80: CLS : RESTORE
FOR palet = 0 TO 1
  FOR kolor = 1 TO 3
    READ Forgrnd$(palet, kolor)
  NEXT kolor
NEXT palet
DATA green, red, brown, cyan, magenta, white
FOR bgcolor = 0 TO 7
  READ Backgrnd$(bgcolor)
NEXT bgcolor
DATA black, blue, green, cyan, red, magenta, brown, white

REM ** Get Data **
LOCATE 5, 1: PRINT "Which palette, please (0 or 1)?"
LOCATE 7, 3: PRINT "0  green, red, and brown"
LOCATE 8, 3: PRINT "1  cyan, magenta, and white"
DO
  ky$ = INPUT$(1)
LOOP WHILE INSTR("01", ky$) = 0
Pal = VAL(ky$)
CLS : PRINT "Palette is "; Forgrnd$(Pal, 1); ", ";
PRINT Forgrnd$(Pal, 2); ", and "; Forgrnd$(Pal, 3); "."
LOCATE 3, 1: PRINT "Which background color?"
PRINT TAB(3); "(0-7,  but not in the palette)": PRINT
FOR bgcolor = 0 TO 7
  PRINT TAB(2); bgcolor; " "; Backgrnd$(bgcolor)
NEXT bgcolor
DO
  DO
    ky$ = INPUT$(1)
  LOOP WHILE INSTR("01234567", ky$) = 0
  Back = VAL(ky$): Forgrnd$(Pal, 0) = Backgrnd$(Back)
  FOR num = 1 TO 3
    IF Backgrnd$(Back) = Forgrnd$(Pal, num) THEN
      flag = 0
      LOCATE 24, 1: PRINT "Same color as in palette!";
      PRINT " - Try again";
      EXIT FOR
    ELSE flag = 1
    END IF
```

Program 5-3. Tile Selector

```
   NEXT num
LOOP WHILE flag = 0
CLS : PRINT "Which color boundary do you want?": PRINT
FOR num = 1 TO 3
   PRINT TAB(2); num; " "; Forgrnd$(Pal, num)
NEXT num
DO
   ky$ = INPUT$(1)
LOOP WHILE INSTR("123", ky$) = 0
PRINT ky$: bordcol = VAL(ky$)

REM ** Pick and Choose **
CALL Custom(Back%, Pal%)
CALL Choose

REM ** Display Result and PAINT Statement **
SCREEN 1: COLOR Back, Pal: CLS
LINE (1, 1)-(80, 40), bordcol, B
PAINT (40, 20), Tile$, bordcol
LOCATE 3, 14: PRINT "This is the pattern"
LOCATE 4, 14: PRINT "you generated."
LOCATE 10, 1: PRINT "The commands for this pattern are:"
PRINT : PRINT "Tile$ = "; TileHex$
PRINT : PRINT "PAINT (X,Y), Tile$, " + MID$(STR$(bordcol), 2)

REM ** Go Again? **
LOCATE 20, 1: PRINT "Try another pattern (Y or N)"
DO
   ky$ = UCASE$(INPUT$(1))
LOOP WHILE INSTR("YN", ky$) = 0
IF ky$ = "Y" THEN
   GOTO begin
ELSE
   CLS : SCREEN 0: COLOR 7, 0, 0: WIDTH 80
   END
END IF

SUB Choose
   DEFINT A-Z
   SHARED Tile$, TileHex$
   column = 0: row = 0
   lyne = row * 8: col = column * 10 + 200
   PUT (col + 1, lyne + 1), size, XOR
   DO
getkey:
   ky$ = INKEY$
   IF ky$ = "" THEN GOTO getkey
   IF ky$ = CHR$(0) + "M" AND column < 3 THEN
     PUT (col + 1, lyne + 1), size, XOR
     column = column + 1: col = column * 10 + 200
     PUT (col + 1, lyne + 1), size, XOR
```

Program 5-3.   Tile Selector (*continued*)

```
      ELSEIF ky$ = CHR$(0) + "K" AND column > 0 THEN
        PUT (col + 1, lyne + 1), size, XOR
        column = column - 1: col = column * 10 + 200
        PUT (col + 1, lyne + 1), size, XOR
      ELSEIF ky$ = CHR$(0) + "P" AND row < pics THEN
        PUT (col + 1, lyne + 1), size, XOR
        row = row + 1: lyne = row * 8
        PUT (col + 1, lyne + 1), size, XOR
      ELSEIF ky$ = CHR$(0) + "H" AND row > 0 THEN
        PUT (col + 1, lyne + 1), size, XOR
        row = row - 1: lyne = row * 8
        PUT (col + 1, lyne + 1), size, XOR
      ELSEIF ky$ >= "0" AND ky$ <= "3" THEN
        PUT (col + 1, lyne + 1), size, XOR
        ppt = VAL(ky$)
        LINE (col, lyne)-(col + 10, lyne + 8), 0, BF
        LINE (col, lyne)-(col + 10, lyne + 8), 3, B
        PAINT (col + 5, lyne + 4), ppt, 3
        cschm(column + row * 4) = ppt
        PUT (col + 1, lyne + 1), size, XOR
        CALL SetTile
      END IF
    LOOP WHILE ky$ <> CHR$(13)
    Tile$ = "": TileHex$ = ""
    FOR row = 0 TO pics
      des1 = cschm(3 + 4 * row) + 4 * cschm(2 + 4 * row)
      des2 = 16 * cschm(1 + 4 * row) + 64 * cschm(4 * row)
      Descrip = des1 + des2
      Tile$ = Tile$ + CHR$(Descrip)
      TileHex$ = TileHex$ + "CHR$(&H" + HEX$(Descrip) + ") + "
    NEXT row
    TileHex$ = LEFT$(TileHex$, LEN(TileHex$) - 3)
  END SUB

  SUB Custom (Back%, Pal%)
    CLS : DEFINT A-Z
    DO
      INPUT "Number of pixel rows (1-20)"; pics
      IF pics < 1 OR pics > 20 THEN
        PRINT "Number not in range, try again."
      END IF
    LOOP UNTIL pics < 21 AND pics > 0
    pics = pics - 1: SCREEN 1: COLOR Back, Pal: CLS
    CIRCLE (5, 4), 2, 3: GET (1, 1)-(9, 7), size: CLS
    PRINT "Possible colors:"
    FOR kolor = 0 TO 3
```

Program 5-3.   Tile Selector (*continued*)

```
      PRINT kolor; "   "; Forgrnd$(Pal, kolor)
    NEXT kolor
    PRINT
    FOR trw = 0 TO pics
    FOR column = 0 TO 3
      col = column * 10 + 200: row = trw * 8
      LINE (col, row)-(col + 10, row + 8), 3, B
      PAINT (col + 5, row + 4), 1, 3
      cschm(column + trw * 4) = 1
    NEXT column
  NEXT trw
  CALL SetTile
END SUB

SUB SetTile
  DEFINT A-Z
  Tile$ = ""
  FOR trw = 0 TO pics
    csc1 = cschm(3 + 4 * trw) + 4 * cschm(2 + 4 * trw)
    csc2 = 16 * cschm(1 + 4 * trw) + 64 * cschm(4 * trw)
    Tile$ = Tile$ + CHR$(csc1 + csc2)
  NEXT trw
  LINE (260, 0)-(300, 40), 0, BF
  LINE (260, 0)-(300, 40), 3, B
  PAINT (280, 20), Tile$, 3
END SUB
```

Program 5-3.   Tile Selector (*continued*)

If you select palette 0, you can use the colors green, red, brown, and the background color for pixel colors in the tile pattern. If you select palette 1, the colors available to you are cyan, magenta, white, and the background color. The palette number you select is assigned to the variable *Pal*.

When you have selected a palette, the computer displays the names of the colors in the palette. Then it displays a list of background colors and asks you to select one. If you chose palette 0, the following listing shows the request for the background color you would see:

```
Palette is green, red, and brown.

Which background color?
  (0-7, but not in the palette)

  0   black
  1   blue
  2   green
  3   cyan
  4   red
  5   magenta
  6   brown
  7   white
```

If you selected palette 1, the first statement would be "Palette is cyan, magenta, and white." Notice that the program reminds you not to choose a background color that is in your palette. If you ignore this reminder, you will be able to use only three colors.

The computer uses your palette and background selections, as well as two more selections, to draw a "working" tile. Later you may reset pixels in this tile to the desired color. But before it can draw the working tile, the program must know what color to use to draw around it (the boundary color). The following listing shows this request:

```
Which color boundary do you want?

  1   green
  2   red
  3   brown
```

Previous discussions have used only four rows of pixels to define a tile. A tile grid can have up to 64 rows of pixels; however, that many are seldom necessary. Program 5-3 allows you to use up to 20 rows of pixels for your tile, but you will usually find even that many are unnecessary.

After you select the color boundary, the computer goes to a subprogram (Custom) and makes one last request. This time it asks you to enter the number of rows for your working tile. This request is shown in the next listing:

```
Number of pixel rows (1-20)?
```

When you have made this selection, the computer clears the screen, prints a list of colors you can use, and draws the pixels for the working tile. It then goes to the SetTile subprogram to draw the "preview" rectangle. When you change a pixel's color in the working tile, the new pattern is shown in the preview rectangle. This rectangle is large enough to show several adjacent tiles, so you can see what the current arrangement will look like. After the preview rectangle is drawn, the computer calls the Choose subprogram, which places a small circle in the upper left corner of the working tile. The computer is now ready for you to start manipulating pixels. The current display is shown in Figure 5-6.

Selecting Pixels for a Tile

The circle drawn by the Choose subprogram indicates the active pixel in the working tile. You can color the active pixel by pressing the 0, 1, 2, or 3 key. To move the circle to a different pixel, press the LEFT, RIGHT, UP, or DOWN ARROW key. You many set any

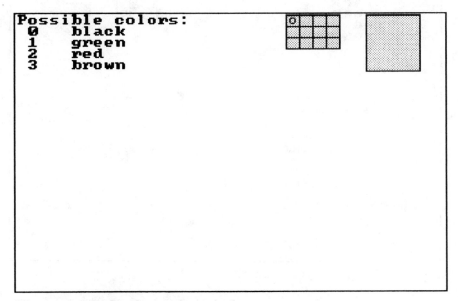

Figure 5-6.   Ready to select pixels

pixel in the tile to any one of the four colors by making it the active pixel and then pressing the desired color number. If you change your mind, you may recolor the pixel by returning the circle to the pixel and pressing a new color number. Figure 5-7 shows a typical screen with final pixel colors.

The Final Result

When the pixels are colored the way you want, press the ENTER key. The program clears the screen and draws a large rectangle filled with the selected tile pattern. Beneath the rectangle, it displays the PAINT statement that would produce the tile pattern displayed. The color selections shown in Figure 5-7 are displayed

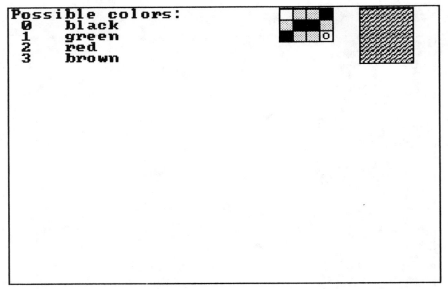

Figure 5-7.   Final pixel pattern

in Figure 5-8 with the following *Tile\$* definition and PAINT statement:

```
Tile$ =
CHR$(&H16) + CHR$(&H69) + CHR$(&H94)

PAINT (X,Y), Tile$, 3
```

ANALYSIS OF KEY PROGRAM FEATURES

Since QuickBASIC works easily with decimal numbers, nearly all the calculations in Program 5-3 are performed using decimal values.

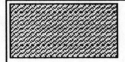

Figure 5-8.   Final result of Program 5-3

The Choose subprogram manipulates the pixel. The bulk of this subprogram is a single IF...THEN...ELSEIF...END IF block that draws the circle and moves it around the working tile with PUT statements. You probably did not see it, but the program draws a circle before this. It draws, saves, and quickly erases a circle in the Custom subprogram with the following multi-statement line:

```
CIRCLE (5, 4), 2, 3: GET (1, 1)-(9, 7), size: CLS
```

The CIRCLE statement first draws the circle. Then the graphics GET statement saves a rectangle with opposite corners at the pixel coordinates (1, 1) and (9, 7). The rectangle is saved in an array named *size*. As soon as the area containing the circle has been saved, the screen is cleared. It happens so fast you probably will not see it.

When the Choose subprogram is called, the circle is PUT in the upper left corner of the working tile, as shown in the following listing:

```
SUB Choose
  DEFINT A-Z
  SHARED Tile$, TileHex$
  column = 0: row = 0
  lyne = row * 8: col = column * 10 + 200
  PUT (col + 1, lyne + 1), size, XOR
```

Moving the Circle and Selecting Pixel Colors

The PUT statement places the *size* array on the screen with the upper left corner at (*col* + 1, *lyne* + 1). The XOR option to the PUT statement is called an *actionverb*. XOR is used in animation such as the circle movement because of its unique effect on the pixel colors under an array image. The XOR actionverb inverts the colors of the pixels that coincide with the image. When a second PUT statement places the image in the same place, the colors of the coinciding pixels are again inverted. This restores the background to its original color. This double PUT action effectively draws the circle and then erases it, leaving the background as it was originally.

So far, the circle has been PUT in the upper left corner of the working tile. You can now select a color for that pixel or you can move the circle with one of the arrow keys.

First, consider moving the circle. You cannot move it up or to the left, as it is already in the upper left corner of the working tile. The program will reject any attempt to move the circle out of the tile area.

If you press the RIGHT ARROW, the circle disappears from the upper left corner and reappears one square to the right. The circle is moved by the first part of the long IF...THEN...END IF block of the Choose subprogram, as shown in this listing:

```
ky$ = INKEY$
    .
    .
    .
IF ky$ = CHR$(0) + "M" AND column < 3 THEN
  PUT(col + 1, lyne + 1), size, XOR
  column = column + 1: col = column * 10 + 200
  PUT(col + 1, lyne + 1), size, XOR
    .
    .
    .
```

The IF clause detects the RIGHT ARROW key and restricts any movement past column 3, the right-most column of the working tile. The first PUT statement erases the circle from its original position. The column value is then increased by one. The second PUT statement places the circle in the new position. The first three ELSEIF clauses perform similar operations for the LEFT, DOWN, and UP ARROW keys.

The last ELSEIF clause in the IF...THEN...END IF block colors the square that contains the circle. The number keys 0, 1, 2, and 3 activate this clause. A PUT statement erases the circle, the first LINE statement fills the box representing the pixel with the background color, and the second LINE statement outlines the box. Finally, a PAINT statement recolors the interior of the box. The new color is assigned to the variable *ppt*, and the circle is replaced by another PUT statement. Finally, the SetTile subprogram is called to reformat the preview rectangle with the latest change.

```
ELSEIF ky$ >= "0" AND ky$ <= "3" THEN
   PUT (col + 1, lyne + 1), size, XOR
   ppt = VAL(ky$)
   LINE (col, lyne)-(col + 10, lyne + 8), 0, BF
   LINE (col, lyne)-(col + 10, lyne + 8), 3, B
   PAINT (col + 5, lyne + 4), ppt, 3
   cschm(column + row * 4) = ppt
   PUT (col + 1, lyne + 1), size, XOR
   CALL SetTile
```

The computer stays in the DO...LOOP containing the IF... THEN...END IF block until you press the ENTER key. This action selects your final tile pattern. The computer then calculates the string necessary to draw your pattern.

Calculating the Tile$ String

While the Choose subprogram is performing its functions, the computer stores color numbers in the color scheme array (cschm( )) as you manipulate the circle. The *Tile$* string is calculated from these numbers by several steps in the FOR...NEXT loop shown in the next listing:

```
FOR row = 0 TO pics
   des1 = cschm(3 + 4 * row) + 4 * cschm(2 + row)
   des2 = 16 * cschm(1 + 4 * row) + 64 * cschm(4 * row)
   Descrp = des1 + des2
       .
       .
       .
```

Table 5-5.   Color Numbers for a Tile Pattern

cschm% (Index)	Color Number	Tile Pattern Stored in Array			
0	0	0	1	1	2
1	1	1	2	2	1
2	1	2	1	1	0
3	2				
4	1				
5	2				
6	2				
7	1				
8	2				
9	1				
10	1				
11	0				

Table 5-5 shows the color values stored in the array *cschm* for the calculations used in this discussion. The following decimal values are calculated as the computer executes the FOR... NEXT loop for the three pixel rows numbered 0, 1, and 2:

row = 0

des1 = 6   *cschm*(3) + 4 * *cschm*(2)

des2 = 16   16 * *cschm*(1) + 64 * *cschm*(0)

Descrp = 22   6 + 16

$$row = 1$$

$$des1 = 9 \qquad cschm(7) + 4 * cschm(6)$$

$$des2 = 96 \qquad 16 * cschm(5) + 64 * cschm(4)$$

$$Descrp = 105 \qquad 9 + 96$$

$$row = 2$$

$$des1 = 4 \qquad cschm(11) + 4 * cschm(10)$$

$$des2 = 144 \qquad 16 * cschm(9) + 64 * cschm(8)$$

$$Descrp = 148 \qquad 4 + 144$$

Converting Decimal CHR$ to Hexadecimal

Each time the decimal value of a CHR$ code (*Descrp%*) is calculated in the FOR...NEXT loop, the result is concatenated to the decimal *Tile$* string. This string is then converted to hexadecimal form as shown in the next listing:

```
Tile$ = Tile$ + CHR$(Descrip)
TileHex$ = TileHex$ + "CHR$(&H" + HEX$(Descrip) + ") + "
```

When the string, called *TileHex$*, is completely constructed, the last three characters (space, +, space) are stripped from the string by the following line:

```
TileHex$ = LEFT$(TileHex$, LEN(TileHex$) -3)
```

The resulting *TileHex$* string is

```
CHR$(&H16) + CHR$(&H69) + CHR$(&H94)
```

You can use Program 5-3 to decide what tile patterns you want to use in the PAINT statements of any program. You may want to add it or a similar program to your library of utilities.

USING TILES

Program 5-4 uses tiling to provide backgrounds for ellipses. As shown in Figure 5-9, you can overlay printed characters on the patterned background.

The CIRCLE statement is used to draw the rounded forms. Some of the shapes are circles, but most of them are ellipses. The eccentricity (*ecc!*) option in the CIRCLE statement allows you to

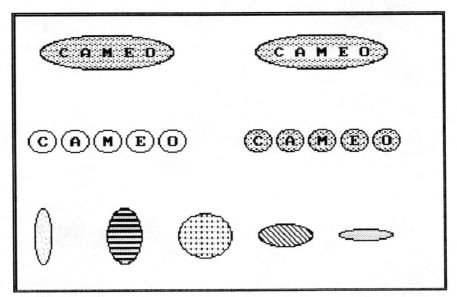

Figure 5-9.   Tiling rounded shapes

```
REM ** TILING ROUNDED SHAPES **
' Program 5-4   File: PRO0504.BAS

REM ** Initialize **
SCREEN 1: CLS : COLOR 0, 1: DEFINT A-Z
Tile$(1) = CHR$(&H14) + CHR$(&H42) + CHR$(&H24) + CHR$(&H41)
Tile$(2) = CHR$(&H41) + CHR$(&H10) + CHR$(&H4) + CHR$(&HO)
Tile$(3) = CHR$(&HFF) + CHR$(&HAA) + CHR$(&H55) + CHR$(&HO)
Tile$(4) = CHR$(&HO) + CHR$(&H21) + CHR$(&H21) + CHR$(&HO)
Tile$(5) = CHR$(&HCO) + CHR$(&H30) + CHR$(&HC) + CHR$(&H3)
Tile$(6) = CHR$(&H55) + CHR$(&H55) + CHR$(&H55) + CHR$(&H55)

REM ** Two Tiled Ellipses **
LOCATE 4, 5: PRINT "C A M E O"
CIRCLE (9 * 8 - 4, 27), 49, , , , , .25
PAINT (68, 20), Tile$(1)
CIRCLE (29 * 8 - 4, 27), 49, , , , , .25
PAINT (228, 20), Tile$(1)
LOCATE 4, 25: PRINT "C A M E O"

REM ** Cameo Letters **
FOR col = 3 TO 15 STEP 3
  READ Ltr$
  LOCATE 12, col: PRINT Ltr$
  CIRCLE ((col) * 8 - 4, 91), 10
  CIRCLE ((col + 20) * 8 - 4, 91), 10
  PAINT ((col + 20) * 8 - 13, 91), Tile$(1)
  LOCATE 12, col + 20: PRINT Ltr$
NEXT col
DATA C, A, M, E, O

REM ** Tiled Ellipses with Changing Eccentricities **
ecc! = 3.2
FOR col = 20 TO 280 STEP 60
  num = (col - 20) / 60 + 2
  CIRCLE (col, 160), 20, , , , ecc!
  PAINT (col, 160), Tile$(num%)
  ecc! = ecc! / 2
NEXT col
LINE (0, 0)-(319, 199), , B


REM ** Wait for Keypress and Restore Screen **
ky$ = INPUT$(1)
SCREEN 1: CLS
END
```

Program 5-4.   Tiling Rounded Shapes

stretch a circle vertically or horizontally to form ellipses of different shapes. The format of the eccentricity option is

```
CIRCLE (column, row), radius, color, , , ecc!
```

where

> *column, row* is the center of the circle
> *radius* is the ellipse's major axis
> *color* is the drawing color
> *ecc* is the circle's eccentricity

The top shapes in Figure 5-9 are tiled ellipses overlayed with printing. The order in which printing and tiling are done causes a slight difference in the appearance of the ellipses. The word in the left ellipse is printed before the tiles are laid. The word in the right ellipse is printed after the tiles are laid.

The center shapes show letters enclosed in untiled circles on the left, and the same letters in tiled circles on the right. The bottom row of shapes are ellipses with various eccentricities (3.2, 1.6, .8, .4, and .2) and tile patterns (*Tile$*(2), *Tile$*(3), *Tile$*(4), *Tile$*(5), and *Tile$*(6)). These shapes were calculated as follows:

```
ecc! = 3.2
FOR col = 20 TO 280 STEP 60
   num = (col - 20) / 60 + 2
   CIRCLE (col, 160), 20, , , , ecc!
   PAINT (col, 160), Tile$(num%)
   ecc! = ecc! / 2
NEXT col
```

Mixing Colors

Program 5-5 draws a series of eight rectangles in each of two rows. Each rectangle has a uniquely tiled interior. Figure 5-10 shows the result of one run of the program.

```
REM ** TILING RECTANGLES **
' Program 5-5   File: PRO0505.BAS

REM ** Initialize **
SCREEN 1: CLS : COLOR 0, 1: DEFINT A-Z
DIM Tile$(1 TO 12)

Tile$(1)  = CHR$(&H11) + CHR$(&H11) + CHR$(&H11) + CHR$(&H11)
Tile$(2)  = CHR$(&H22) + CHR$(&H22) + CHR$(&H22) + CHR$(&H22)
Tile$(3)  = CHR$(&H33) + CHR$(&H33) + CHR$(&H33) + CHR$(&H33)
Tile$(4)  = CHR$(&H18) + CHR$(&H18) + CHR$(&H18) + CHR$(&H18)
Tile$(5)  = CHR$(&H1C) + CHR$(&H1C) + CHR$(&H1C) + CHR$(&H1C)
Tile$(6)  = CHR$(&H2C) + CHR$(&H2C) + CHR$(&H2C) + CHR$(&H2C)
Tile$(7)  = CHR$(&H36) + CHR$(&H36) + CHR$(&H36) + CHR$(&H36)
Tile$(8)  = CHR$(&H66) + CHR$(&H66) + CHR$(&H66) + CHR$(&H66)
Tile$(9)  = CHR$(&H77) + CHR$(&H77) + CHR$(&H77) + CHR$(&H77)
Tile$(10) = CHR$(&H1) + CHR$(&H10) + CHR$(&H4) + CHR$(&H40)
Tile$(11) = CHR$(&HBB) + CHR$(&HBB) + CHR$(&HBB) + CHR$(&HBB)
Tile$(12) = CHR$(&HDB) + CHR$(&HB7) + CHR$(&HDE) + CHR$(&HE7)

REM ** Draw Rectangles and Tile Them **
FOR box = 1 TO 4
  col = box * 30
  LINE (col, 10)-(col + 25, 90), , B
  PAINT (col + 5, 20), box - 1, 3
NEXT box
FOR box = 5 TO 8
  col = box * 30
  LINE (col, 10)-(col + 25, 90), , B
  PAINT (col + 5, 20), Tile$(box - 4)
NEXT box
FOR box = 1 TO 8
  col = box * 30
  LINE (col, 110)-(col + 25, 190), , B
  PAINT (col + 5, 120), Tile$(box + 4)
NEXT box
LINE (0, 0)-(319, 199), , B


REM ** Wait for Keypress and Restore Screen **
ky$ = INPUT$(1)
SCREEN 1: CLS
END
```

Program 5-5.   Tiling Rectangles

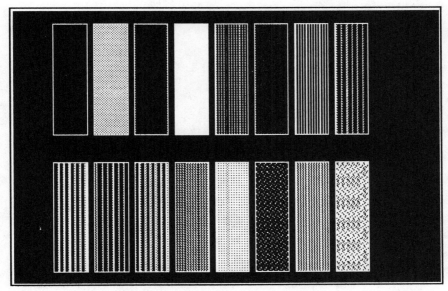

Figure 5-10.   Tiling rectangles

In the top row of Figure 5-10, the four left rectangles are filled with solid colors (black, cyan, magenta, and white). The rest of the rectangles (including the bottom row) are formed by mixing the four colors in various ways through tiles (*Tile$*(1) through *Tile$*(12)) designed with Program 5-4.

Color Shading

You can mix colors to make it appear that you are using a palette with more than four colors. Program 5-6 draws the eleven rectangles shown in Figure 5-11. Only cyan and white pixels are used to form the tile patterns. Magenta is used to form the boundaries of the rectangles.

```
REM ** CYAN TO WHITE **
' Program 5-6  File: PRO0506.BAS

REM ** Initialize **
SCREEN 1: CLS : COLOR 0, 1: DEFINT A-Z
DIM Tile$(1 TO 11)

Tile$(1) = CHR$(&H55) + CHR$(&H55) + CHR$(&H55) + CHR$(&H55)
Tile$(2) = CHR$(&HD5) + CHR$(&H55) + CHR$(&H5D) + CHR$(&H55)
Tile$(3) = CHR$(&HD5) + CHR$(&H57) + CHR$(&H55) + CHR$(&H5D)
Tile$(4) = CHR$(&HD5) + CHR$(&H57) + CHR$(&HDD) + CHR$(&H77)
Tile$(5) = CHR$(&HDD) + CHR$(&H57) + CHR$(&HDD) + CHR$(&H77)
Tile$(6) = CHR$(&HDD) + CHR$(&H77) + CHR$(&HDD) + CHR$(&H77)
Tile$(7) = CHR$(&H7F) + CHR$(&HFD) + CHR$(&H77) + CHR$(&HDD)
Tile$(8) = CHR$(&H7F) + CHR$(&HFD) + CHR$(&HFF) + CHR$(&HF7)
Tile$(9) = CHR$(&H7F) + CHR$(&HFF) + CHR$(&HF7) + CHR$(&HFF)
Tile$(10) = CHR$(&H7F) + CHR$(&HFF) + CHR$(&HFF) + CHR$(&HFF)
Tile$(11) = CHR$(&HFF) + CHR$(&HFF) + CHR$(&HFF) + CHR$(&HFF)

REM ** Draw Rectangles and Tile Them **
FOR box = 1 TO 11
  col = box * 25
  LINE (col, 10)-(col + 20, 60), 2, B
  PAINT (col + 5, 20), Tile$(box), 2
NEXT box
LINE (0, 0)-(319, 70), , B

REM ** Wait for Keypress and Restore Screen **
ky$ = INPUT$(1)
SCREEN 1: CLS
END
```

Program 5-6.   Cyan to White

At the extreme left of Figure 5-11 is a rectangle filled with only cyan tiles. As each rectangle to the right is drawn, it is filled with a mixture of cyan and white pixels (the percentage of white pixels increases from left to right). The final rectangle on the right is filled with only white tiles.

Your monitor screen will display much better shading than the screen print shown in Figure 5-11. Run Program 5-6 to see the

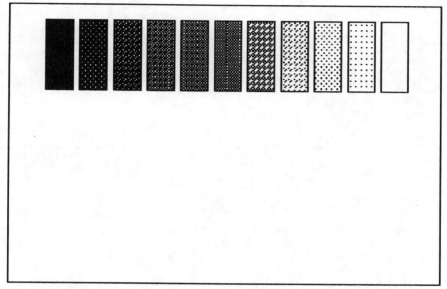

Figure 5-11.   Shading from cyan to white

screen results. You can display a greater variety of colors by mixing in the other colors (black and magenta) in various percentages.

Pie Graphs

You can use tiling to create pie graphs that are interesting and easy to read. You can produce a variety of tiles to shade the interior of circle sectors that represent unique quantities. You do not have to repeat patterns, since you are not limited to a given number as you are with a four-color palette.

Program 5-7 is a versatile program that creates pie graphs using six separate tile patterns. If you wish to cut the pie into more than six pieces, you can add more tiles.

```
DECLARE SUB FinalDraw ()
DECLARE SUB Drawing ()
DECLARE SUB Info ()
DECLARE SUB Menu (KeyChoice$)
DECLARE SUB Label ()

REM ** PIE GRAPH **
' Program 5-7  File: PRO0507.BAS

REM ** Initialize **
COMMON SHARED sec AS INTEGER, col AS INTEGER, row AS INTEGER
COMMON SHARED radius AS SINGLE, ecc AS SINGLE, x() AS INTEGER
COMMON SHARED y() AS INTEGER, A() AS STRING, col() AS INTEGER
COMMON SHARED angle() AS SINGLE, row() AS INTEGER
DIM percent!(0 TO 12), amount!(0 TO 12)

REM ** Print Menu and Make Choices **
DO
  CALL Menu(KeyChoice$)
  SELECT CASE KeyChoice$
    CASE "I"
       CALL Info
    CASE "P"
       CALL Drawing
    CASE "F"
       CALL FinalDraw
    CASE "Q"
       EXIT DO
  END SELECT
LOOP
REM ** Reset Graphics Screen and End **
SCREEN 1: CLS : COLOR 0, 1
END

SUB Drawing STATIC
  SCREEN 1, 0: CLS : DEFINT A-Z
  CIRCLE (col, row), radius!, 3, , , ecc!
  FOR sector = 1 TO sec
    LINE (col, row)-(col(sector), row(sector))
  NEXT sector
  CALL Label
  SCREEN 0: WIDTH 80
END SUB

SUB FinalDraw STATIC
  SCREEN 1, 0: CLS : DEFINT A-Z
  CIRCLE (col, row), radius!, 3, , , ecc!
  FOR sector = 1 TO sec
```

Program 5-7.   Pie Graph

```
      LINE (col, row)-(col(sector), row(sector))
   NEXT sector
   TileNum = 1: angle!(sec + 1) = 6.283
   Tile$(1) = CHR$(&H80) + CHR$(&H20) + CHR$(&H8) + CHR$(&H2)
   Tile$(2) = CHR$(&HBB) + CHR$(&HBB) + CHR$(&HBB) + CHR$(&HBB)
   Tile$(3) = CHR$(&H82) + CHR$(&H28) + CHR$(&H28) + CHR$(&H82)
   Tile$(4) = CHR$(&HDB) + CHR$(&HB7) + CHR$(&HDE) + CHR$(&HE7)
   Tile$(5) = CHR$(&H80) + CHR$(&H80) + CHR$(&HAA) + CHR$(&H80)
   Tile$(6) = CHR$(&H1) + CHR$(&H10) + CHR$(&H4) + CHR$(&H40)
   FOR sector = 1 TO sec
      plotangle! = (angle!(sector + 1) + angle!(sector)) / 2
      colpaint = col + (radius! * COS(plotangle!) / 2)
      rowpaint = row - (radius! * SIN(plotangle!) / 2)
      PAINT (colpaint, rowpaint), Tile$(TileNum)
      TileNum = TileNum + 1
      IF TileNum > 6 THEN TileNum = 1
   NEXT sector
   FOR sector = 1 TO sec + 1
      LOCATE y(sector), x(sector): PRINT A$(sector);
   NEXT sector
   BEEP
   waitkey$ = INPUT$(1)
   SCREEN 0: WIDTH 80
END SUB

SUB Info
   REDIM amount(0 TO 12) AS SINGLE
   REDIM percent(0 TO 12) AS SINGLE
   REDIM angle(0 TO 12) AS SINGLE
   REDIM col(0 TO 12) AS INTEGER
   REDIM row(0 TO 12) AS INTEGER
   CLS : DEFINT A-Z
   INPUT "Number of sections"; sec
   INPUT "Center of circle (col,row)"; col, row
   INPUT "Radius of circle"; radius!
   INPUT "Ratio height/width"; ecc!
   CLS : pi! = 3.14159
   FOR sector = 1 TO sec
      PRINT "Amount for item "; sector;
      INPUT amount!(sector)
      amount!(0) = amount!(0) + amount!(sector)
   NEXT sector
   FOR sect = 1 TO sec
      angle!(sect) = percent!(0) * pi! / 50
      percent!(sect) = amount!(sect) * 100 / amount!(0)
      percent!(0) = percent!(0) + percent!(sect)
      col(sect) = col + radius! * COS(angle!(sect))
```

Program 5-7.   Pie Graph (*continued*)

```
      row(sect) = row - radius! * SIN(angle!(sect)) * ecc!
  NEXT sect
END SUB

SUB Label
  REDIM x(0 TO 12) AS INTEGER
  REDIM y(0 TO 12) AS INTEGER
  REDIM A(0 TO 12) AS STRING
  DEFINT A-Z
  FOR sector = 1 TO sec + 1
    LOCATE 1, 1
    IF sector <= sec THEN
    PRINT "Start of lable"; sector; "(row, column)";
  ELSE
    PRINT "Start of title"; sector; "(row, column";
  END IF
  INPUT y(sector), x(sector)
  LOCATE 2, 1: INPUT "String to print "; A$(sector)
  LOCATE 1, 30: PRINT SPACE$(10);
  LOCATE 2, 1: PRINT SPACE$(38);
NEXT sector
FOR sector = 1 TO sec + 1
  LOCATE y(sector), x(sector): PRINT A$(sector);
NEXT sector
DO
  flag = 0
  FOR sector = 1 TO sec + 1
    LOCATE 1, 1: PRINT SPACE$(30);
    LOCATE 2, 1: PRINT SPACE$(30);
    LOCATE 1, 1: PRINT "Change"; sector; "?"
    LOCATE y(sector), x(sector): PRINT "";
    answer$ = UCASE$(INPUT$(1))
    IF answer$ = "Y" THEN
      flag = 1
      LOCATE 1, 1: PRINT "Start of label is ";
      PRINT y(sector); ","; x(sector);
      LOCATE 2, 1: INPUT "New start point "; ytemp, xtemp
      LOCATE y(sector), x(sector)
      PRINT SPACE$(LEN(A$(sector)));
      y(sector) = ytemp: x(sector) = xtemp
      LOCATE y(sector), x(sector): PRINT A$(sector);
    END IF
  NEXT sector
LOOP WHILE flag = 1
END SUB

SUB Menu (KeyChoice$) STATIC
```

Program 5-7.   Pie Graph (*continued*)

```
    COLOR 4, 0, 12: CLS
    COLOR 9: LOCATE 5, 33: PRINT "PIE GRAPH MENU"
    LOCATE 10, 27: PRINT "("; : COLOR 4: PRINT "I";
    COLOR 9: PRINT ")nput Information"
    LOCATE 12, 27: PRINT "("; : COLOR 4: PRINT "P";
    COLOR 9: PRINT ")reliminary Draw and Label"
    LOCATE 14, 27: PRINT "("; : COLOR 4: PRINT "F";
    COLOR 9: PRINT ")inal Drawing"
    LOCATE 16, 27: PRINT "("; : COLOR 4: PRINT "Q";
    COLOR 9: PRINT ")uit"
    COLOR 27, 1
    LOCATE 22, 24: PRINT CHR$(219);
    COLOR 10: PRINT " PRESS A LETTER (I, P, F, or Q) ";
    COLOR 27: PRINT CHR$(219);
    COLOR 7, 0
    DO
       BEEP: KeyChoice$ = UCASE$(INPUT$(1))
    LOOP WHILE INSTR("IPFQ", KeyChoice$) = 0
END SUB
```

Program 5-7.   Pie Graph (*continued*)

The opening Initialize block of the program declares and types variables that are shared between the main program and its subprograms. It also dimensions and types arrays.

Then the Print Menu and Make Choices block calls a menu subprogram. The menu lists the four functions shown in Figure 5-12. The items are listed in the usual order of selection: Input Information, Preliminary Draw and Label, Final Drawing, and Quit.

To emphasize the keys used to select the options, the first letter of each is enclosed in parentheses. The first letter is also printed in red to add more emphasis. Valid entries are limited to the keys I, P, F, or Q by the following DO...LOOP.

```
DO
   BEEP: KeyChoice$ = UCASE$(INPUT$(1))
LOOP WHILE INSTR("IPFQ", KeyChoice$) = 0
```

This loop assigns the upper case form of the key you pressed to the variable *KeyChoice$*. The INSTR function returns the posi-

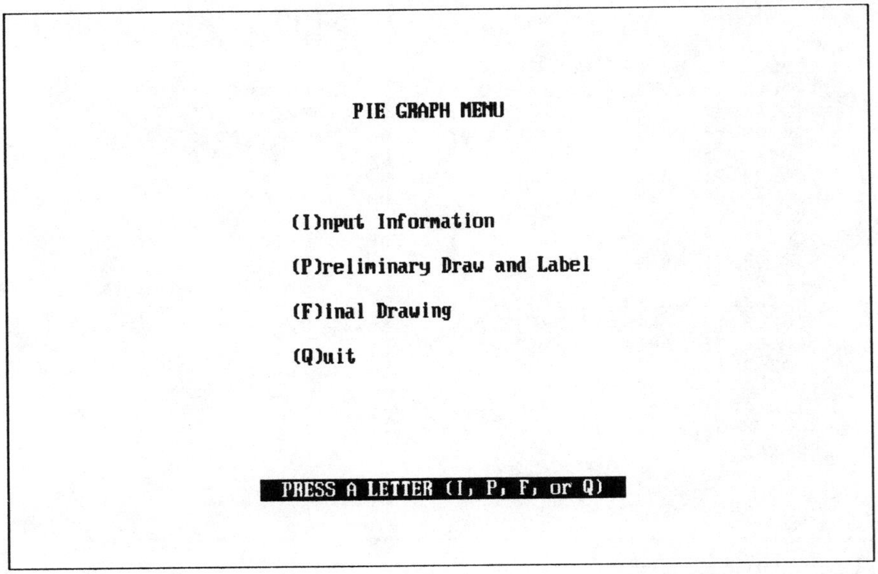

```
                    PIE GRAPH MENU


              (I)nput Information

              (P)reliminary Draw and Label

              (F)inal Drawing

              (Q)uit




              PRESS A LETTER (I, P, F, or Q)
```

Figure 5-12.   Pie Graph menu

tion of *KeyChoice$* in the string "IPFQ". The following values are returned by INSTR when you press the given key:

Key	= I	Value of 1 returned (1st in the string)
Key	= P	Value of 2 returned (2nd in the string)
Key	= F	Value of 3 returned (3rd in the string)
Key	= Q	Value of 4 returned (4th in the string)
Any other key		Value of 0 returned (not in the string)

When you press the I, P, F, or Q key, the computer returns from the Menu subprogram to the main program. You must input some data for the graph to be drawn, so your first selection is naturally I, Input Information.

When you select this option, the Info subprogram is called from the main program. This subprogram requests you to enter the following information:

1. **Number of sections**   The number of slices in the pie graph to be drawn.

2. **Center of circle (*col,row*)**   The pixel location of the center of the pie graph.

3. **Radius of circle**   The distance from the perimeter to the center of the circle. The radius determines how large the pie graph will be. Remember, the diameter (or width) of the circle is twice the radius.

4. **Ratio of height/width**   The height of the circle divided by the width; the eccentricity of the circle to make the center appear more or less round.

When you have entered this information about the circle, the computer executes a FOR...NEXT loop that requests you to enter the numeric value of each item to be represented in the graph. As you make entries, the program keeps a running total so that the circle can be sectioned off by percentages. This loop is shown in the following listing:

```
FOR sector = 1 to sec
  PRINT "Amount for item "; sector;
  INPUT amount!(sector)
  amount!(0) = amount!(0) + amount!(sector)
NEXT sector
```

All arrays in this program are dynamically dimensioned with subscripts of 0 to 12. The element indexed zero in the *amount* array is used to hold the running total.

Another FOR...NEXT loop is used to calculate the beginning and ending coordinates of each sector. The percentage for each sector is calculated and assigned to the *percent* array. Once again the element indexed zero is used to keep a running total of the percentages used to calculate the column and row coordinates that limit each sector. This loop is shown in the following listing:

```
FOR sect = 1 to sec
  angle!(sect) = percent!(0) * pi! / 50
  .
  .
  .
  col(sect) = col + radius! * COS(angle!(sect))
  row(sect) = row - radius! * SIN(angle!(sect))* ecc!
NEXT sect
```

When all positions have been calculated, the computer redisplays the menu.

The next step is to display the information in circle graph form. You do this by selecting the letter "P" (Preliminary Draw and Label). This selects CASE "P" in the SELECT CASE structure that calls the Drawing subprogram.

The Drawing subprogram draws the circle graph. Then it calls the Label subprogram, where you choose the placement of the graph's labels and title. You may enter approximate positions, as the program cycles through the selections and allows you to view and correct the positions of the text. The cycles continue until you have gone through a complete cycle without changing any positions. Figure 5-13 shows this process in progress. When you have chosen the final positions, you are returned to the menu.

The final graph is shown when you select the letter "F" (Final Drawing) from the menu. CASE "F" of SELECT CASE calls the FinalDraw subprogram. This subprogram draws the graph, tiles the sectors, and places the labels and title. Then the computer stops so that you can look at the final product or print the pie graph. Figure 5-14 shows a screen print of a typical graph. Press any key to return to the Pie Graph menu.

Select the letter "Q" to end the program. CASE "Q" of SELECT CASE exits the DO...LOOP, restores the graphics screen to its original condition, and ends the program. Try using Program 5-7 a few times with your own data before going on to the next chapter.

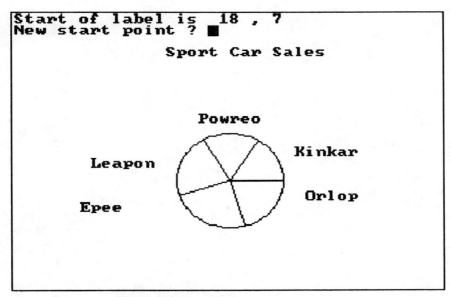

Figure 5-13.   Placing labels and title

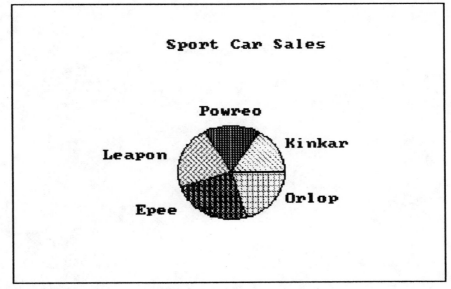

Figure 5-14.   Final pie graph

6

SPRITES AND ANIMATION

A sprite is an elfish thing: a soul, a ghost, a pixie, a spirit that moves with the wind, appearing and disappearing as if by magic. In this chapter, you will learn to create sprite graphics and to move them on, about, and off the display screen. Sprites are small so they can flit quickly about; the smaller they are, the quicker they can move.

A SPRITE IS BORN

You can create sprites in color if you use a color graphics mode like SCREEN 1, which is used in the discussions and programs of this chapter. A higher resolution graphics mode with many colors is even more desirable.

You create a sprite pixel by pixel. You should be able to easily change its shape and colors while it is being created. Once it is created, you should be able to "hide" it (save its shape on disk) and make it reappear when you want it. Therefore, each of your sprites should have a separate name. Then you can "call" a specific sprite when you want it.

The following listing is a REM outline of a program that does all of those necessary spritely things:

```
REM ** SPRITE CREATOR **
REM ** Initialize Screens, etc. **
REM ** Get Color Data **
REM ** Pick and Choose Sprite Attributes **
REM ** Display Final Results **
REM ** Save Sprite Data ? **
REM ** Do Another ? **
```

Program 6-1 uses this outline to let you create sprites and save the sprite data. You can then use QuickBASIC's PUT statement to place the sprite anywhere you wish on the screen. By using PUT statements repeatedly, you can move the sprite about the screen.

```
DECLARE SUB Saver (dimen%)
DECLARE SUB Choose (dimen%)
DECLARE SUB Custom (Back%, Pal%)
DECLARE SUB SetPixel (ppt%, column%, row%)

REM ** SPRITE CREATOR **
' Program 6-1   File: PRO0601.BAS

REM ** Initialize **
DIM SHARED size(0 TO 12) AS INTEGER, sprite%(0 TO 170)
DIM SHARED Forgrnd$(0 TO 1, 0 TO 3), picol%, pirow%
DEFINT A-Z
begin: SCREEN 0: WIDTH 80: CLS : RESTORE
FOR palet = 0 TO 1
  FOR kolor = 1 TO 3
    READ Forgrnd$(palet, kolor)
  NEXT kolor
NEXT palet
DATA green, red, brown, cyan, magenta, white
FOR bgcolor = 0 TO 7
  READ Backgrnd$(bgcolor)
NEXT bgcolor
DATA black, blue, green, cyan, red, magenta, brown, white
```

Program 6-1.   Sprite Creator

```
REM ** Get Color Data **
LOCATE 5, 1: PRINT "Which palette, please (0 or 1)?"
LOCATE 7, 3: PRINT "0  green, red, and brown"
LOCATE 8, 3: PRINT "1  cyan, magenta, and white"
DO
  ky$ = INPUT$(1)
LOOP WHILE INSTR("01", ky$) = 0
Pal = VAL(ky$)
CLS : PRINT "Palette is "; Forgrnd$(Pal, 1); ", ";
PRINT Forgrnd$(Pal, 2); ", and "; Forgrnd$(Pal, 3); "."
LOCATE 3, 1: PRINT "Which background color?"
PRINT TAB(3); "(0-7,  but not in the palette)": PRINT
FOR bgcolor = 0 TO 7
  PRINT TAB(2); bgcolor; " "; Backgrnd$(bgcolor)
NEXT bgcolor
DO
  DO
    ky$ = INPUT$(1)
  LOOP WHILE INSTR("01234567", ky$) = 0
  Back = VAL(ky$): Forgrnd$(Pal, 0) = Backgrnd$(Back)
  FOR num = 1 TO 3
    IF Backgrnd$(Back) = Forgrnd$(Pal, num) THEN
      flag = 0
      LOCATE 24, 1: PRINT "Same color as in palette!";
      PRINT " - Pick a different color";
      EXIT FOR
    ELSE flag = 1
    END IF
  NEXT num
LOOP WHILE flag = 0
CLS : PRINT "Which color boundary do you want?": PRINT
FOR num = 1 TO 3
  PRINT TAB(2); num; " "; Forgrnd$(Pal, num)
NEXT num
DO
  ky$ = INPUT$(1)
LOOP WHILE INSTR("123", ky$) = 0
PRINT ky$: bordcol% = VAL(ky$)

REM ** Pick and Choose **
CALL Custom(Back%, Pal%)
CALL Choose(dimen%)

REM ** Display Result and DIM Statement **
SCREEN 1: COLOR Back, Pal: CLS
LOCATE 3, 14: PRINT "This is the sprite"
LOCATE 4, 14: PRINT "you generated."
PUT (40, 20), sprite, PSET
LOCATE 10, 1: PRINT "Here is the data for the array"
LOCATE 11, 1: PRINT "to create the sprite."
LOCATE 13, 1
```

Program 6-1.   Sprite Creator (*continued*)

```
FOR elem = 0 TO dimen
  PRINT sprite(elem);
NEXT elem
PRINT : PRINT : PRINT "Dimension sprite array:"
PRINT "DIM sprite(0 TO"; RTRIM$(STR$(dimen)); ") AS INTEGER"

REM ** Save Sprite Data ? **
LOCATE 20, 1: PRINT "Save sprite data (Y or N)? ";
DO
  ky$ = UCASE$(INPUT$(1))
LOOP WHILE INSTR("YN", ky$) = 0
IF ky$ = "Y" THEN
  CALL Saver(dimen)
END IF

REM ** Go Again? **
LOCATE 20, 1: PRINT "Try another pattern (Y or N) ? "
DO
  ky$ = UCASE$(INPUT$(1))
LOOP WHILE INSTR("YN", ky$) = 0
IF ky$ = "Y" THEN
  GOTO begin
ELSE
  SCREEN 1: CLS
  SCREEN 0: COLOR 7, 0, 0: CLS : WIDTH 80
  END
END IF

SUB Choose (dimen%)
  DEFINT A-Z
  column = 0: row = 0
  lyne = row * 8 + 10: col = column * 10 + 140
  PUT (col + 1, lyne + 1), size, XOR
  DO
getkey:
    ky$ = INKEY$
    IF ky$ = "" THEN GOTO getkey
    IF ky$ = CHR$(0) + "M" AND column% < picol THEN
      PUT (col + 1, lyne + 1), size, XOR
      column = column + 1: col = column * 10 + 140
      PUT (col + 1, lyne + 1), size, XOR
    ELSEIF ky$ = CHR$(0) + "K" AND column > 0 THEN
      PUT (col + 1, lyne + 1), size, XOR
      column = column - 1: col = column * 10 + 140
      PUT (col + 1, lyne + 1), size, XOR
    ELSEIF ky$ = CHR$(0) + "P" AND row% < pirow THEN
      PUT (col + 1, lyne + 1), size, XOR
      row = row + 1: lyne = row * 8 + 10
      PUT (col + 1, lyne + 1), size, XOR
    ELSEIF ky$ = CHR$(0) + "H" AND row > 0 THEN
      PUT (col + 1, lyne + 1), size, XOR
```

Program 6-1.   Sprite Creator (*continued*)

```
        row = row - 1: lyne = row * 8 + 10
        PUT (col + 1, lyne + 1), size, XOR
      ELSEIF ky$ >= "0" AND ky$ <= "3" THEN
        PUT (col + 1, lyne + 1), size, XOR
        ppt = VAL(ky$)
        LINE (col, lyne)-(col + 10, lyne + 8), 0, BF
        LINE (col, lyne)-(col + 10, lyne + 8), 3, B
        PAINT (col + 5, lyne + 4), ppt, 3
        PUT (col + 1, lyne + 1), size, XOR
        CALL SetPixel(ppt%, column%, row%)
      END IF
    LOOP WHILE ky$ <> CHR$(13)
    part = INT((2 * (picol + 1) + 7) / 8)
    dimen = INT((4 + part * (pirow + 1)) / 2) + 1
    GET (80, 60)-(80 + picol, 60 + pirow), sprite
END SUB

SUB Custom (Back%, Pal%)
  CLS : DEFINT A-Z
  DO
    LOCATE 2, 2: INPUT "Number of columns (1-16)"; picol
    IF picol < 1 OR picol > 16 THEN
      LOCATE 3, 2: PRINT "Not in range, try again."
    END IF
  LOOP UNTIL picol <= 16 AND picol >= 1
  CLS
  DO
    LOCATE 2, 2: INPUT "Number of rows (1-16)"; pirow
    IF pirow < 1 OR pirow > 16 THEN
      LOCATE 3, 2: PRINT "Not in range, try again."
    END IF
  LOOP UNTIL pirow <= 16 AND pirow >= 1
  CLS : picol = picol - 1: pirow = pirow - 1
  SCREEN 1: COLOR Back, Pal: CLS
  CIRCLE (5, 4), 2, 3: GET (1, 1)-(9, 7), size: CLS
  LOCATE 2, 2: PRINT "Possible colors:"
  FOR kolor = 0 TO 3
    PRINT kolor; "  "; Forgrnd$(Pal, kolor)
  NEXT kolor
  PRINT
  LOCATE 24, 1
  PRINT "Press ENTER when sprite is complete";
  FOR trw = 0 TO pirow
    FOR column = 0 TO picol
      col = column * 10 + 140: row = trw * 8 + 10
      LINE (col, row)-(col + 10, row + 8), 3, B
    NEXT column
  NEXT trw
END SUB
```

Program 6-1.   Sprite Creator (*continued*)

```
SUB Saver (dimen%)
  DEFINT A-Z: SCREEN 0: CLS : WIDTH 80
  INPUT "Array file name with extension"; nayme$
  INPUT "Save to drive: (A, B, C, etc.)"; drive$
  nayme$ = LEFT$(drive$, 1) + ":" + nayme$
  DEF SEG = VARSEG(sprite(1))
  BSAVE nayme$, VARPTR(sprite(0)), 2 * dimen
  DEF SEG
END SUB

SUB SetPixel (ppt%, column%, row%)
  DEFINT A-Z
  pcol = column + 80
  prow = row + 60
  PSET (pcol, prow), ppt
END SUB
```

Program 6-1.   Sprite Creator (*continued*)

Initializing Program 6-1

The Initialize block of Program 6-1 uses the SHARED option of a
DIM statement to declare several variables that are used in more
than one part of the program (main program and subprograms).
Some variables are passed between parts of the program, and
some are passed when a subprogram is called.

   The Initialize block also sets the screen to the text mode and
reads foreground and background color data into separate arrays.
This data is used to display the actual names of the colors so you
can make color choices later in the program.

Choosing Colors for
Your Sprite

The Get Color Data block of the program first displays data for
the color palette and then asks you to choose a palette for your

sprite, as shown in Figure 6-1. Palette 1 was chosen in this example.

Then this block shows your sprite palette color choice, lists the palette colors, and asks you to choose a background color on which to create the sprite. This process is shown in Figure 6-2. Eight background colors are provided, and you can add more if you wish. The program will not let you use a background color that is included in the palette you chose. Otherwise, you would end up with only three colors available for the sprite. If you pick a background color that is in the palette, the following message is displayed at the bottom of the screen:

```
Same color as in palette! - Pick a different color
```

After you select a background color (black (0) was chosen in this example), QuickBASIC asks you to choose a boundary color.

```
Which palette, please (0 or 1)?

  0  green, red, and brown
  1  cyan, magenta, and white
```

Figure 6-1.   Palette choice

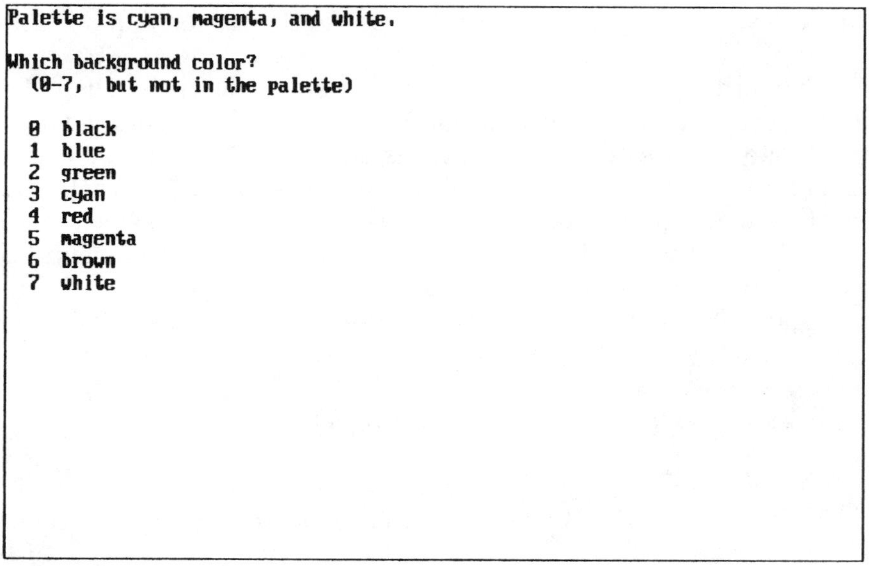

```
Palette is cyan, magenta, and white.

Which background color?
  (0-7, but not in the palette)

  0  black
  1  blue
  2  green
  3  cyan
  4  red
  5  magenta
  6  brown
  7  white
```

Figure 6-2.   Background colors

This color will be used to draw the grid on which you create your sprite. The boundary color prompt is shown in Figure 6-3. White (3) was chosen in this example.

Creating the Sprite

The Pick and Choose block calls two subprograms, Custom and Choose. The Custom subprogram requests the information shown in the following listing:

```
Number of columns (1-16)?

Number of rows (1-16)?
```

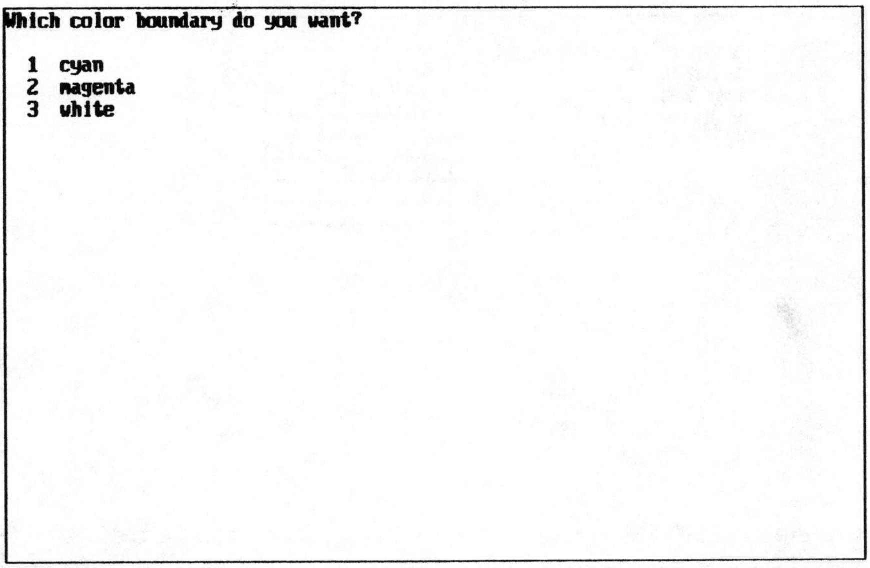

```
Which color boundary do you want?

   1  cyan
   2  magenta
   3  white
```

Figure 6-3.   Boundary colors for palette 1

Eight columns and eight rows were chosen for a particular program run. When you have entered these two values, the program changes the screen to the SCREEN 1 graphics mode. Then it draws a grid at the top right corner of the screen using the selected number of columns and rows. You create the sprite within this grid.

The Pick and Choose block next calls the Choose subprogram to allow you to create the sprite pixel by pixel. A small circular cursor appears in the upper left pixel position on the grid. This cursor marks the active pixel, whose color you can immediately change. The top left corner of the screen lists the colors that you can use to fill in this active pixel. The opening screen of the Choose subprogram is shown in Figure 6-4.

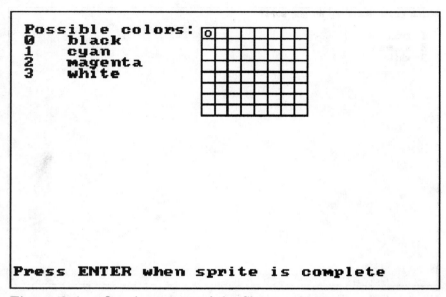

Figure 6-4.   Opening screen of the Choose subprogram

You create a sprite by moving the cursor within the grid to the desired pixel and pressing the desired color number key. You can change the color of a pixel again by returning the cursor to the pixel and pressing a new color number.

Press one of the arrow keys to move the cursor and activate a different pixel within the grid. The arrow keys move the cursor as follows:

- RIGHT ARROW moves the cursor one pixel to the right.
- LEFT ARROW moves the cursor one pixel to the left.
- UP ARROW moves the cursor one pixel upward.
- DOWN ARROW moves the cursor one pixel downward.

The program is written so that you cannot move the cursor off

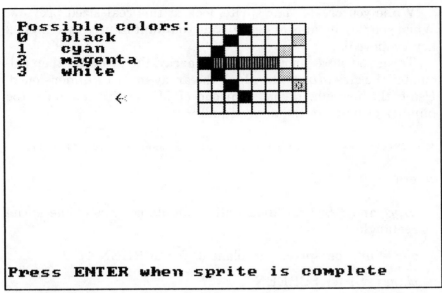

Figure 6-5.   Final stages of sprite creation

the grid. If you reach a boundary and try to move beyond it, the cursor remains motionless at the boundary.

To change the color of the pixel under the cursor, press the number key corresponding to the desired color. This action causes the program to paint the simulated pixel in the grid and to call the SetPixel subprogram. This subprogram sets the corresponding pixel in the real-sized sprite to the selected color. Then it returns you to the Choose subprogram for more pixel changes. The real-sized sprite is shown beneath the list of colors. It grows and changes colors like a chameleon as you make additional choices.

Figure 6-5 shows a sprite in the final stages of creation. Notice the sprite shown in actual size below the list of colors. This gives you a preview of what the completed sprite will look like.

While you create your sprite, look at this real-sized preview. When your sprite appears exactly as you want it, press the ENTER key to move on.

To let you store your sprite on an array, the program then calculates the size (*dimen*) to which the array must be dimensioned. Using the formula taken from one of Microsoft's manuals, the number of bytes in the array equals

```
4 + INT(((x2-x1) * (bits) + 7) / 8) * planes * ((y2-y1) + 1)
```

where

x1,y1 and *x2,y2* are diagonally opposite corners of the sprite rectangle

bits = bits-per-pixel-per-plane (2 for SCREEN 1)

planes = 1 for SCREEN 1

If you store the sprite in an integer array, each element of the array consists of two bytes. Divide the number of bytes by two to get the number of elements for which the array must be dimensioned.

The Choose subprogram calculates the value needed for dimensioning the array with the following two formulas:

```
part = INT((2 * picol + 1) + 7) / 8)
dimen = 4 + INT((part * (pirow + 1)) / 2) + 1
```

where

bits = 2: *picol* = $x2 - x1$

pirow = $y2 - y1$

After the dimension value is calculated, the sprite is stored by the following GET statement:

```
GET(80, 60)-(80 + picol, 60 + pirow), sprite
```

where

(80, 60) and (80 + *picol*, 60 + *pirow*) are opposite corners of the real-sized sprite

You are then returned to the main program in the Display Result and DIM statement block. This block displays the final sprite at the top left corner of the screen, as shown in Figure 6-6. It lists the elements of the sprite array, and then shows you the DIM statement needed to access the sprite.

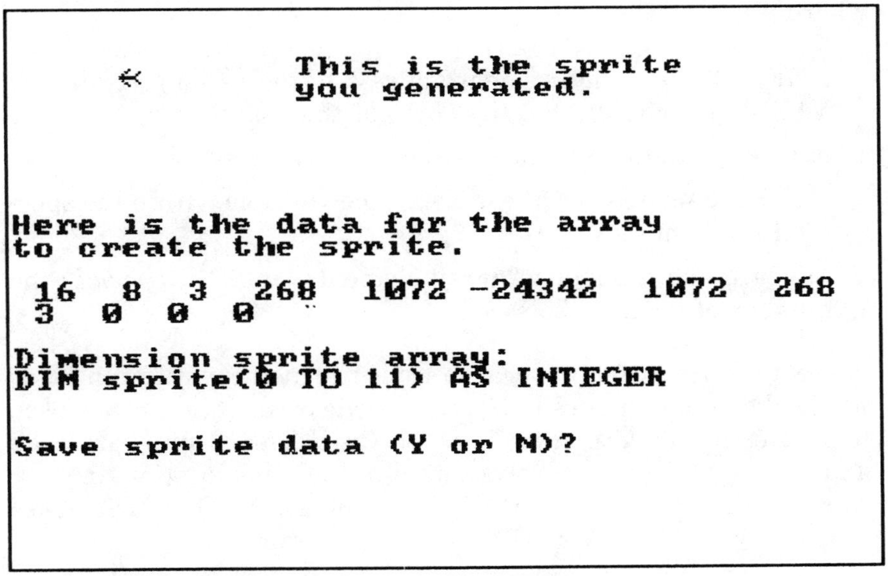

Figure 6-6.   Sprite data and save prompt

Control passes to the Save Sprite Data? block, which prints a prompt just below the DIM statement, asking if you want to save the array. If you respond to the prompt with a Y for yes, the Saver subprogram is called. This subprogram saves the array as a memory-image file with a BSAVE statement. You may then load it into another program with a BLOAD statement and use it in that program.

BSAVE and BLOAD are much faster than other methods of saving and loading numeric arrays. The memory-image file saved is a byte-for-byte copy of the data in memory. It also includes control information used by the BLOAD command when the file is reloaded.

The entire array is saved with only the following two statements:

```
DEF SEG = VARSEG(sprite(0))
BSAVE nayme$, VARPTR(sprite(0)), 2 * dimen
```

where

DEF SEG sets the segment address to the value returned by VARSEG(sprite(0)), the first byte of the sprite array

nayme$ is the name under which the file is saved

VARPTR(sprite(0)) is the offset of the variable within the specified segment

dimen is the number of array elements, and 2 * *dimen* is the number of bytes to be saved

Note: Because different screen modes use memory differently, do not load graphic images in a screen mode other than the one used to create the images. Also, because QuickBASIC program code and data items are not always stored in the same locations as they were in BASICA or GW-BASIC, do not use BLOAD with files created by a BASICA or GW-BASIC program.

After the file has been saved, the BASIC segment is restored with the following statement:

```
DEF SEG
```

Figure 6-7 shows the screen after a yes response to the "Save Sprite Data?" prompt. The demonstration sprite data was saved in a file named PLANE.DAT to a disk in drive B.

Remember to save your sprites under unique names. Keep a record of the sprite shapes and names for future use.

The Go Again? block of the main program allows you to create more than one sprite at a sitting. The following prompt appears after you save a sprite or after you enter N for no to the "Save Sprite Data?" prompt:

```
Try another pattern (Y or N) ? _
```

This prompt appears near the bottom of the screen shown in Figure 6-7. If you enter Y for yes, the Go Again? block returns you to

```
Array file name with extension? plane.dat
Save to drive: (A, B, C, etc.)? b:




















Try another pattern (Y or N) ?
```

Figure 6-7.   Sprite saved

the beginning of the main program (begin:). If you enter N for no, both SCREEN 0 and SCREEN 1 are cleared and the program ends.

Save Program 6-1, as you will use it to create some sprites for future programs.

USING SPRITES

Once you have saved a sprite to disk, you can use it in any program. Program 6-1 was used to create the arrow shown previously in Figure 6-6. Program 6-2 used a subprogram (Sprite-Load) to load the arrow and then "shoot" it across the screen.

The SpriteLoad subprogram requests the file name under which the sprite array was saved, and then the name of the drive it can retrieve the array from. The following listing shows these prompts with the responses used in this demonstration:

```
Array file name with extension? plane.dat
Disk drive (A, B, C, etc.)? B
```

The subprogram uses the entered data as the file name (fyle$) in the BLOAD statement. The name of the array used in the subprogram is *sprite*, which is so general that it lets you use the subprogram with any sprite array. You can merge the SpriteLoad subprogram with any program or put it in a library and load the library when you wish to use the subprogram.

The elements read into the general array can be assigned to elements of a specific array after the file containing the array elements has been loaded. When the array has been loaded, the value needed to dimension the array is calculated, and the file is closed.

Back in the main program of Program 6-1, the elements of the sprite array are duplicated in an array named *arrow*, using the statements shown in this listing:

```
FOR num = 0 to dimen
   arrow(num) = sprite(num)
NEXT num
```

The animation of the arrow is achieved by two PUT statements separated by a time delay. The XOR mode is often used with PUT statements to create animation. When an image is PUT on the screen twice in the XOR mode, the background is restored. This

```
DECLARE SUB SpriteLoad ()
REM ** SPRITE TEST **
' Program 6-2   File: PRO0602.BAS

REM ** Initialize **
DIM SHARED dimen AS INTEGER, sprite%(0 TO 34)
DEFINT A-Z
CALL SpriteLoad
REDIM SHARED arrow(0 TO dimen) AS INTEGER
FOR num = 0 TO dimen
  arrow(num) = sprite(num)
NEXT num

REM ** Shoot Arrow; then Repeat? **
SCREEN 1: CLS : LOCATE 24, 1
PRINT "Press Q to quit; another key to repeat";
begin:
FOR col = 300 TO 10 STEP -8
  PUT (col, 100), sprite, XOR
  begin! = TIMER
  DO
  LOOP UNTIL TIMER >= begin! + .1
  PUT (col, 100), arrow, XOR
NEXT col
a$ = INPUT$(1)
IF UCASE$(a$) = "Q" THEN END ELSE GOTO begin

SUB SpriteLoad
  DEFINT A-Z: SCREEN 0: CLS : WIDTH 80
  INPUT "Array file name with extension"; fyle$
  INPUT "Disk drive (A, B, C, etc.)"; drive$
  fyle$ = LEFT$(drive$, 1) + ":" + fyle$
  DEF SEG = VARSEG(sprite(0))
  BLOAD fyle$, VARPTR(sprite(0))
  DEF SEG
  some = INT((sprite(0) + 7) / 8)
  dimen = INT(4 + some * sprite(1)) / 2 + 1
END SUB
```

Program 6-2.   Sprite Test

allows an image to move across a complex background without "destroying" the background. Table 6-1 shows how the XOR option affects a pixel color on the screen.

The 8-by-8 arrow sprite has the color pattern shown in Figure 6-8. Originally the screen is colored with the background color (0).

The first PUT statement, with XOR, changes the colors of the pixels that make up the sprite position according to the first row of the XOR table.

1. Array color 0 put on background color 0 gives 0.

2. Array color 1 put on background color 0 gives 1.

3. Array color 2 put on background color 0 gives 2.

4. Array color 3 put on background color 0 gives 3.

Therefore, the sprite is displayed as desired. A time delay allows you to see the sprite.

The second PUT statement, with XOR, changes the colors as follows according to Table 6-1.

Table 6-1.   Pixel Colors Produced by XOR

Original Pixel	Array	Pixel	Color	
	0	1	2	3
0	0	1	2	3
1	1	0	3	2
2	2	3	0	1
3	3	2	1	0

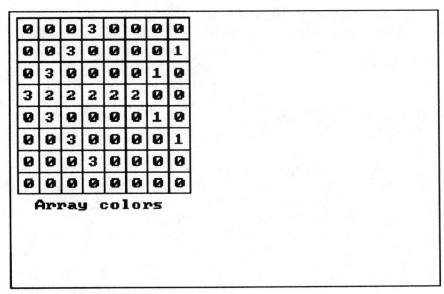

Figure 6-8.   Sprite color pattern

1. Array color 0 put on itself gives 0.

2. Array color 1 put on itself gives 0.

3. Array color 2 put on itself gives 0.

4. Array color 3 put on itself gives 0.

Therefore, the sprite area is all returned to color 0, which restores the background. The sprite is erased.

The following program statements animate the sprite:

```
FOR col = 300 to 10 step -8
  PUT (col, 100), plane, XOR
  begin! = TIMER
  DO
  LOOP UNTIL TIMER >= begin! + .1
  PUT (col, 100), plane, XOR
NEXT col
```

These statements make the arrow move across the screen from right to left, disappearing off the left side of the screen. Press any key except the letter "Q" to shoot the arrow again. Press Q to end the program.

USING MULTIPLE SPRITES

You can handle multiple sprites at the same time as long as you define each sprite in a separate array. Program 6-3 uses the SpriteLoad subprogram to load two sprites created by Program 6-1. The arrow sprite produced by Program 6-2 is one of the sprites. The other sprite is an arrow rotated 45 degrees counter-clockwise from the first sprite. Figure 6-9 shows the second sprite with the array elements and dimension data. It was saved as an array named *plane2*.

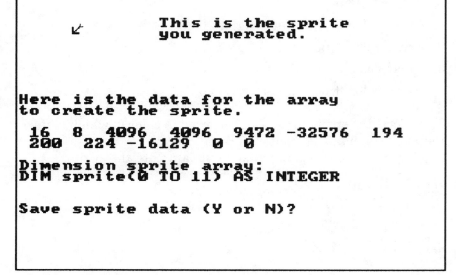

Figure 6-9.   Plane2 sprite data

```
DECLARE SUB SpriteLoad ()
REM ** TWO SPRITE TEST **
' Program 6-3   File: PRO0603.BAS

REM ** Initialize **
DIM SHARED dimen AS INTEGER, sprite%(0 TO 34)
DEFINT A-Z

REM ** Load Sprites **
CALL SpriteLoad
REDIM SHARED plane(0 TO dimen) AS INTEGER
FOR num = 0 TO dimen
   plane(num) = sprite(num)
NEXT num
CALL SpriteLoad
REDIM SHARED plane2(0 TO dimen) AS INTEGER
FOR num = 0 TO dimen
   plane2(num) = sprite(num)
NEXT num

REM ** Move Sprites **
SCREEN 1: CLS : COLOR 1, 1: LOCATE 24, 1
PRINT "Press Q to quit; another key to repeat";
begin:
row = 50
FOR col = 300 TO 10 STEP -5
   PUT (col, 100), plane, XOR
   PUT (col, row), plane2, XOR
   begin! = TIMER
   DO
   LOOP UNTIL TIMER >= begin! + .1
   PUT (col, 100), plane, XOR
   PUT (col, row), plane2, XOR
   row = row + 2
NEXT col
a$ = INPUT$(1)
IF UCASE$(a$) = "Q" THEN END ELSE GOTO begin
COLOR 0, 1

SUB SpriteLoad
   DEFINT A-Z: SCREEN 0: CLS : WIDTH 80
   INPUT "Array file name with extension"; fyle$
   INPUT "Disk drive (A, B, C, etc.)"; drive$
   fyle$ = LEFT$(drive$, 1) + ":" + fyle$
   DEF SEG = VARSEG(sprite(0))
   BLOAD fyle$, VARPTR(sprite(0))
   DEF SEG
   some = INT((sprite(0) + 7) / 8)
   dimen = INT(4 + some * sprite(1)) / 2 + 1
END SUB
```

Program 6-3.   Two Sprite Test

The arrow sprite used in Program 6-2 is loaded first. This program copies it into an array named *plane* with the following FOR...NEXT loop:

```
FOR num = 0 to dimen
  plane(num) = sprite(num)
NEXT num
```

It then loads the sprite named *plane2* and copies it into an array of the same name.

The sprites are placed in different locations and travel different paths. The *plane* sprite moves from east to west, and *plane2* moves from northeast to southwest. Their paths cross but neither sprite is destroyed because the XOR option is used in the PUT statements, as shown in the next listing:

```
row = 50
FOR col = 300 TO 10 STEP -5
  PUT (col, 100), plane, XOR        'First sprite
  PUT (col, row), plane2, XOR       'Second sprite
  begin! = TIMER
  DO
  LOOP UNTIL TIMER >= begin! + .1
  PUT (col, 100), plane, XOR        'Restore
  PUT (col, row), plane2, XOR       'background
  row = row + 2                     'Change row for plane2
NEXT col
```

After flying across the screen, the two planes disappear. Press Q to end the program; press any other key to begin a new flight.

CHANGING TEXT COLORS

When you are working in the SCREEN 1 graphics mode, text is printed in the default color 3 of the palette selected in the last COLOR statement. If no COLOR statement has been executed, the default palette of 1 is used with a black background. Therefore, text is printed as white (color 3 in palette 1) on black.

To highlight a character, a word, or a group of words in a block of text, you may want to change the colors of the characters in that block. You can use PUT and GET statements to move a pointer through the text. Then you can use PSET to change the color of a character by setting the color of each pixel that differs from the background.

Using this method you could create a sprite shape with Program 6-1, as before, but a simple, rectangular cursor is more appropriate now. You can quickly create a cursor with a LINE statement (BOX option) and save it as an array with a GET statement. Then clear the screen, as shown in the following listing:

```
LINE(1, 1) - (8, 8), 1, B
GET(1, 1) - (8, 8), kursor: CLS
```

Program 6-4 uses this cursor to mark the location within a block of text.

```
DECLARE SUB Adjust2 (col%, lyne%)
DECLARE SUB Adjust1 (col%, lyne%)
REM ** SPRITE TEST **
' Program 6-4   File: PRO0604.BAS

REM ** Initialize **
DIM kursor%(1 TO 11)
SCREEN 1: CLS : DEFINT A-Z
LINE (1, 1)-(8, 8), 1, B
GET (1, 1)-(8, 8), kursor: CLS
LOCATE 2, 2: PRINT "Press an arrow key to move the cursor"
PRINT " from letter to letter."
LOCATE 5, 2: PRINT "Press a number: 1, 2, or 3 to change"
PRINT " the color of the character."
LOCATE 8, 2: PRINT "Press the ENTER key to quit."

REM ** Put Cursor and Make Changes **
column = 2: row = 2
col = column * 8 - 8: lyne = row * 8 - 8
PUT (col, lyne), kursor, XOR
DO
  DO
    ky$ = INKEY$
  LOOP WHILE ky$ = ""
```

Program 6-4. Text Coloring

```
      PUT (col, lyne), kursor, XOR         'turn off pointer
      IF ky$ = CHR$(0) + "M" THEN
         col = col + 8                      'move pointer
         IF col > 312 THEN CALL Adjust1(col%, lyne%)
         PUT (col, lyne), kursor, XOR       'turn on pointer
      ELSEIF ky$ = CHR$(0) + "K" THEN
         col = col - 8                      'move
         IF col < 8 THEN CALL Adjust2(col%, lyne%)
         PUT (col, lyne), kursor, XOR       'turn on
      ELSEIF ky$ = CHR$(0) + "P" THEN
         lyne = lyne + 8                    'move
         IF lyne > 192 THEN CALL Adjust1(col%, lyne%)
         PUT (col, lyne), kursor, XOR       'turn on
      ELSEIF ky$ = CHR$(0) + "H" THEN
         lyne = lyne - 8                    'move
         IF lyne < 8 THEN CALL Adjust2(col%, lyne%)
         PUT (col, lyne), kursor, XOR       'turn on
      ELSEIF ky$ > "0" AND ky$ <= "3" THEN
         kolor = VAL(ky$)
         FOR poynt = col TO col + 8         'color text
            FOR tier = lyne TO lyne + 7
               IF POINT(poynt, tier) <> 0 THEN
                  PSET (poynt, tier), kolor
               END IF
            NEXT tier
         NEXT poynt
         PUT (col, lyne), kursor, XOR       'turn on
      ELSE PUT (col, lyne), kursor, XOR     'turn on
      END IF
   LOOP WHILE ky$ <> CHR$(13)
   PUT (col, lyne), kursor, XOR
   END

   SUB Adjust1 (col%, lyne%)
      DEFINT A-Z
      IF col > 312 THEN
         col = 8
         lyne = lyne + 8
      END IF
      IF lyne > 192 THEN lyne = 8
   END SUB

   SUB Adjust2 (col%, lyne%)
      DEFINT A-Z
      IF col < 8 THEN
         col = 312
         lyne = lyne - 8
      END IF
      IF lyne < 8 THEN lyne = 192
   END SUB
```

Program 6-4.   Text Coloring (*continued*)

Using Program 6-4

The LEFT and RIGHT ARROW keys allow you to move the cursor along a line of text. The UP and DOWN ARROW keys allow you to move it up and down between lines.

To change the color of the character under the cursor, press the 1, 2, or 3 key. Then use an arrow key to move the cursor to the next character you want to recolor.

Press the ENTER key when you have set the desired colors. This removes the cursor from the screen so that you can examine the result. Then press any key to end the program.

Analysis of Program 6-4

The Put Cursor and Make Changes block performs most of the work done by Program 6-4. When this block is entered, it positions the pointer below the left-most character in the first line of text, as shown in Figure 6-10. You may recognize that this placement converts text row and column values to graphic pixel values as discussed in Chapter 4. The opening lines of the block perform this conversion, as shown here:

```
column = 2: row = 2
col = column * 8 - 8: lyne = row * 8 - 8
PUT (col, lyne), kursor, XOR
```

where

> *column* and *row* are text values
>
> *col* and *lyne* are graphic values
>
> and *kursor* is the cursor array

The rest of the block consists of one large DO...LOOP. This loop is exited when you press the ENTER key after changing the color of any text that you wish.

The INKEY$ function is used with a series of IF...ELSEIF ...ELSE clauses to recognize any of the following keys that perform the following actions:

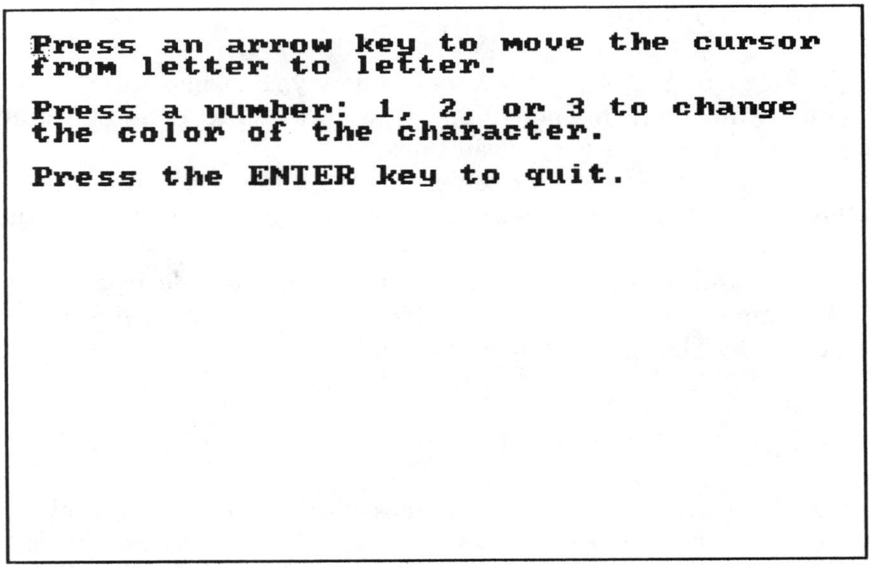

```
Press an arrow key to move the cursor
from letter to letter.

Press a number: 1, 2, or 3 to change
the color of the character.

Press the ENTER key to quit.
```

Figure 6-10.   Opening cursor position

1. The UP, DOWN, LEFT, or RIGHT ARROW key to move the pointer

2. The number key 1, 2, or 3 to change the color of the letter above the pointer

3. The ENTER key to exit the DO...LOOP

The program lets your entries "wrap around" to the next line when the pointer reaches the right edge of the screen and moves the pointer to the top line when it reaches the bottom of the screen. In addition, it does not let the pointer move above the top line or to the left of the left-most character in a line.

When a key is pressed, a PUT statement with XOR turns the pointer off. If one of the arrow keys was pressed, one of a series of four IF (or ELSEIF) clauses is satisfied. The pointer is moved one character space (or one text line) in the appropriate direction, and a PUT statement with XOR turns it back on.

When a press of the LEFT ARROW key results in a calculated column position less than the left-most character position (*col* = 8), the following subprogram (Adjust2) is called to adjust the cursor's position:

```
ELSEIF ky$ = CHR$(0) + "K" THEN
  col = col - 8
  IF col < 8 THEN CALL Adust2(col%, lyne%)
```

A similar adjustment is made when the cursor is instructed to move beyond column 312 in any given row. This time the Adjust1 subprogram is called to make the adjustments.

When a press of the UP ARROW key results in a calculated row position less than that of the first text line, the Adjust2 subprogram is called, as shown in the following listing. This subprogram moves the cursor to the bottom of the screen.

```
ELSE IF ky$ = CHR$(0) + "H" THEN
  lyne = lyne - 8
  IF lyne < 8 THEN CALL Adjust2(col%, lyne%)
```

The Adjust1 subprogram is called if a press of the DOWN ARROW key results in a calculated *lyne* value that would move any part of the pointer off the bottom of the screen.

Each of these subprograms must consider and adjust for two conditions:

Adjust1

1. If the cursor is now off the line to the right, move it to the beginning of the next line.
2. If the cursor is now off the screen at the bottom, move it to the top of the screen.

Adjust2

1. If the cursor is now off the line to the left, move it to the end of the previous line.

2. If the cursor is now off the screen at the top, move it to the bottom of the screen.

For example, the following listing shows the adjustments in Adjust1:

```
SUB Adjust1 (col%, lyne%)
   DEFINT A-Z
   IF col > 312 THEN
      col = 8                        ' move to extreme left
      lyne = lyne + 8                ' move down one line
   END IF
   IF lyne > 192 THEN lyne = 8       ' move to top
END SUB
```

If a number key (1, 2, or 3) was pressed, PSET is used to set all the pixels of the appropriate letter to the chosen color. The pointer is turned back on by a PUT statement with XOR. The pixels are set one at a time by the nested FOR...NEXT loops shown here:

```
ELSE IF ky$ > "0" and ky$ <= "3" THEN
   kolor = VAL(ky$)
   FOR poynt = col TO col + 8
      FOR tier = lyne TO lyne + 7
         IF POINT(poynt, tier) <> 0 THEN
            PSET (poynt, tier), kolor
         END IF
      NEXT tier
   NEXT poynt
   PUT (col, lyne), kursor, XOR          ' kursor on
```

The key to changing only the colors in the letter is the IF POINT statement. Since the background color is 0, the condition in the IF clause of this statement is only true when the pixel's color is different from the background color. If the condition is true, the color of the pixel is set by the PSET statement. Otherwise, nothing is changed.

When the entire pixel area has been scanned and the appropriate colors have been set, the pointer is turned back on. Since the pointer was off while the letter was scanned and colored, its colors did not interfere with the process.

If a key other than an arrow key or a number key (1, 2, or 3) is pressed, a final ELSE clause merely turns the cursor back on with a PUT statement with XOR. The pointer is not moved, and the color of the letter is not changed. This clause is shown in the following listing:

```
ELSE PUT (col, lyne), kursor, XOR        'kursor on
```

Figure 6-11 shows the word "arrow" after each character has been colored. The cursor is still on the last letter of the word.

The DO...LOOP ends after the series of IF...ELSEIF ...ELSE clauses. If the ENTER key was pressed, the loop is exited and the program ends. Otherwise, program control returns to the

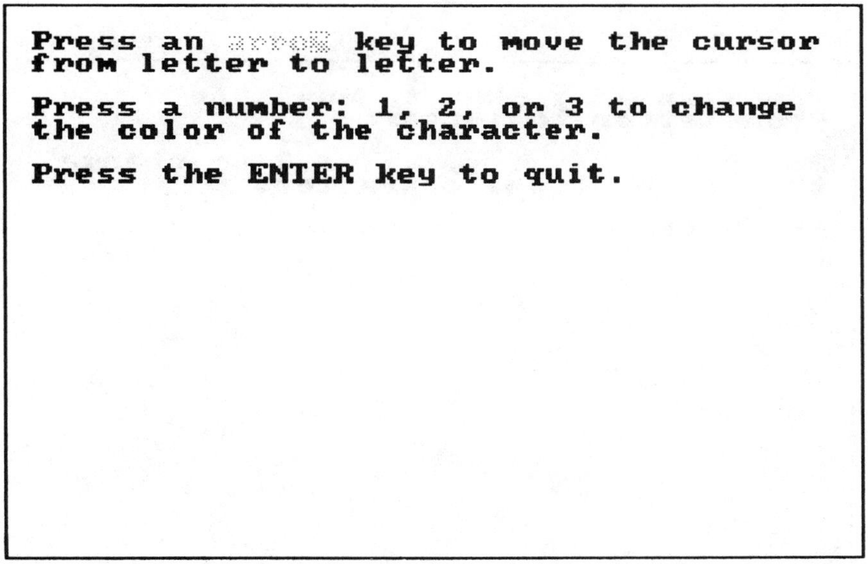

Figure 6-11.   One word colored

top of the loop. You can once again move the pointer or change the color of the letter above the pointer.

A completed session of text coloring is shown in Figure 6-12.

FLYING SAUCERS

You can make sprites move around the screen in an unpredictable manner with the computer's help. Since reports of unidentified flying objects (UFO's) often describe them as appearing to hover in mid-air and then disappear into space, you might think of Program 6-5 as a simulation of UFO flight.

The UFO is created when Program 6-1 produces the following 13-element array:

24 6 21765 4176 1024 -21846 10922 -22358 5124 16 0 0 0

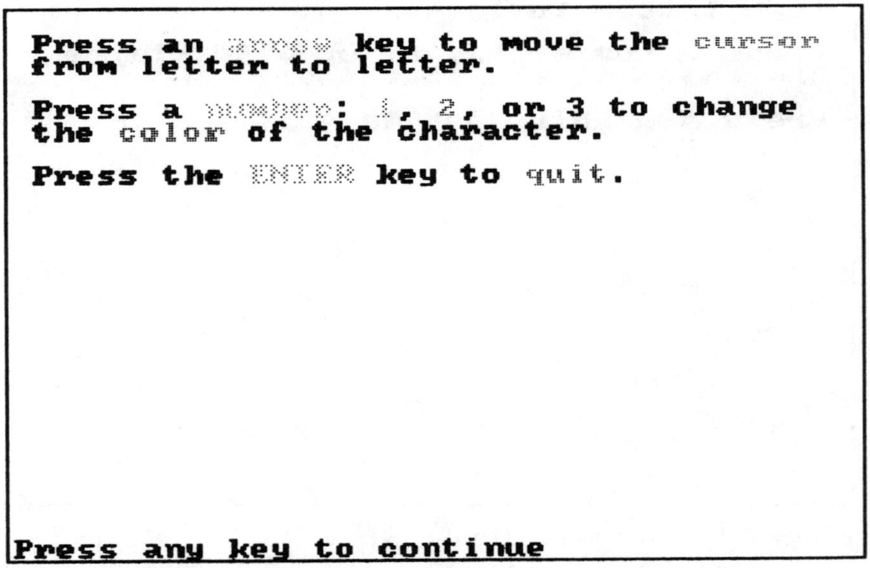

Figure 6-12.   Coloring complete

```
DECLARE SUB SpriteLoad ()
REM ** FLYING SAUCER **
' Program 6-5   File: PRO0605.BAS

REM ** Initialize **
DIM SHARED dimen AS INTEGER, sprite%(0 TO 34)
DEFINT A-Z
CALL SpriteLoad
REDIM SHARED saucer(0 TO dimen) AS INTEGER
FOR num = 0 TO dimen
  saucer(num) = sprite(num)
NEXT num
SCREEN 1: CLS : RANDOMIZE TIMER

REM ** Fly It **
here:
col = 160: row = 100
begin! = TIMER
DO UNTIL TIMER > begin! + 20
  FOR move = 1 TO 5 * RND
    xpwr = (-1) ^ (INT(RND * 2) + 1)
    ypwr = (-1) ^ (INT(RND * 2) + 1)
    xinc = 12 * RND * xpwr: yinc = 4 * RND * ypwr
    FOR num = 1 TO ABS(yinc)
      col = col + xinc: row = row + yinc
      IF col > 0 AND col < 307 THEN
        IF row > 0 AND row < 193 THEN
          PUT (col, row), saucer, XOR          ' on
          Delay! = TIMER
          DO UNTIL TIMER > Delay! + .1
          LOOP
          PUT (col, row), saucer, XOR
        ELSE
          EXIT DO
        END IF
      ELSE
        EXIT DO
      END IF
    NEXT num
    PUT (col, row), saucer, XOR
    marktime! = TIMER
    DO UNTIL TIMER > marktime! + 2 * RND
    LOOP
    PUT (col, row), saucer, XOR
  NEXT move
LOOP
CLS : LOCATE 2, 2: PRINT "Press Q to quit"
LOCATE 4, 2: PRINT "Press any other key to go again."
key$ = INPUT$(1)
IF UCASE$(key$) = "Q" THEN
  END
ELSE
```

Program 6-5.   Flying Saucer

```
     CLS : GOTO here
  END IF

  SUB SpriteLoad
     DEFINT A-Z: SCREEN 0: CLS : WIDTH 80
     INPUT "Array file name with extension"; fyle$
     INPUT "Disk drive (A, B, C, etc.)"; drive$
     fyle$ = LEFT$(drive$, 1) + ":" + fyle$
     DEF SEG = VARSEG(sprite(0))
     BLOAD fyle$, VARPTR(sprite(0))
     DEF SEG
     some = INT((sprite(0) + 7) / 8)
     dimen = INT(4 + some * sprite(1)) / 2 + 1
  END SUB
```

Program 6-5. Flying Saucer (*continued*)

The array is saved under the file name SAUCER.DAT.

Program 6-5 includes the SpriteLoad subprogram that you have used several times in this chapter. SpriteLoad is called early in the program to load the sprite array from the SAUCER.DAT file. The elements are then copied to the saucer array. Before the saucer appears, the random number generator is seeded with a RANDOMIZE TIMER statement so that the UFO will move unpredictably.

The RND function returns a single-precision random number between zero and one. It obtains this number from a generated sequence of random numbers. The same sequence of numbers is generated each time you run a program unless you initialize the random number generator with a RANDOMIZE statement. The TIMER function (which returns the number of seconds elapsed since midnight) is a convenient way to provide a number for the RANDOMIZE statement. This ensures a new series of random numbers each time you run the program.

Most UFO reports describe a single appearance, but you can make this one repeat its 20-second flight as often as you like. You can do this because of a label at the beginning and a GOTO statement at the end of the Fly It block of the main program, which are shown here:

```
REM ** Fly It **
here:
col = 160: row = 100
begin! = TIMER
DO UNTIL TIMER > begin! + 20
   .
   .
   .
LOOP
CLS: LOCATE 2, 2: PRINT "Press Q to quit"
LOCATE 4, 2: PRINT "Press any other key to go again."
key$ = INPUT$(1)
IF UCASE$(key$) = "Q" THEN
   END
ELSE
   CLS : GOTO here
END IF
```

The UFO can move in many directions by combining left, right, up, down, and zero movements. This is done by adding random increments to the PixelColumn value *pcol* and PixelRow value *prow*. The direction of the movement is determined by raising −1 to an odd or even power, in the following listing:

```
xpwr = (-1) ^ (INT(RND * 2) + 1)     'left or right
ypwr = (-1) ^ (INT(RND * 2) + 1)     'up or down
```

Possible combinations for *xpwr* and *ypwr* produce the movements shown in Table 6-2. These values are then used to calculate the column movement *xinc* and the row movement *yinc* as follows:

```
xinc = 12 * RND * xpwr: yinc = 4 * RND * ypwr
```

The column increment *xinc* can range from +12 to −12, and the row increment *yinc* can range from +4 to −4. Each increment can be zero, so that no movement may occur in either or both directions.

Table 6-2.   Column and Row Movements

xpwr	ypwr	Movement
+1	+1	Right and down
+1	−1	Right and up
−1	+1	Left and down
−1	−1	Left and up

Notice that RND produces a single-precision, floating point value. This value is multiplied by an integer (12 or 4) to produce a single-precision result. The result is then multiplied by the integer power (*xpwr* or *ypwr*), giving another single-precision result.

When QuickBASIC converts a non-integer value to an integer, the value is rounded to the nearest integer. These conversions illustrate this process:

11.333 rounds to 11	−11.333 rounds to −11
11.901 rounds to 12	−11.901 rounds to −12
3.1234 rounds to 3	−3.1234 rounds to −3
3.6002 rounds to 4	−3.6002 rounds to −4

Therefore, the range for *xinc* is 12 to −12, and the range for *yinc* is 4 to −4.

Moving the Saucer

The saucer's erratic movements are determined by nested FOR ...NEXT loops. The size of the movements are determined by the increments just discussed. These increments are added within the outer FOR...NEXT loop, as shown in the following listing:

```
DO UNTIL TIMER > begin! + 20
  FOR move = 1 to 5 * RND
    xpwr = (-1) ^ (INT(RND * 2) + 1)
    ypwr = (-1) ^ (INT(RND * 2) + 1)
    xinc = 12 * RND * xpwr: yinc = 4 * RND * ypwr
      .
      .
      .
  NEXT move
LOOP
```

The upper limit of the loop (5 * RND) has a maximum value of five and a minimum value of zero. If the upper limit is zero, the outer loop is not executed. However, if the DO...LOOP has not timed out, the outer loop is re-entered with a new upper limit.

The inner FOR...NEXT loop moves the saucer with PUT statements. The number of moves is controlled by the absolute value of the row increment *yinc*. When new column and row values are calculated, the program tests if the whole sprite can be displayed at the new position. If it can be, the saucer is moved to the new position. However, if part of the saucer would be outside the screen, the inner loop is exited, and the saucer remains in its previous position. This process is shown in the following listing:

```
FOR move = 1 TO 5 * RND
       .
       .
       .
    FOR num = 1 TO ABS(yinc)
      col = col + xinc: row = row + yinc
      IF col > 0 AND col < 307 THEN
        IF row > 0 AND row < 193 THEN
          PUT (col, row), saucer, XOR
          Delay! = TIMER
          DO UNTIL TIMER > Delay! + .1
          LOOP
          PUT (col, row), saucer, XOR
        ELSE
          EXIT DO
        END IF
      ELSE
        EXIT DO
      END IF
    NEXT num
    PUT (col, row), saucer, XOR
    marktime! = TIMER
    DO UNTIL TIMER > marktime! + 2 * RND
    LOOP
    PUT (col, row), saucer, XOR
  NEXT move
```

A time delay keeps the saucer on the screen long enough to be seen, while the second PUT statement erases the saucer between moves. If the saucer goes off the screen or the time limit (20 seconds) is reached, the saucer disappears. Press the Q key to quit or any other key to start a new flight.

Controlling Sprite Movements

Program 6-6 is similar to Program 6-5. However, it allows you to choose a heading and a speed for the saucer's flight.

```
DECLARE SUB SpriteLoad ()
REM ** CONTROLLED FLYING SAUCER **
' Program 6-6  File: PRO0606.BAS

REM ** Initialize **
DIM SHARED dimen AS INTEGER, sprite%(0 TO 34)
DEFINT A-Z
CALL SpriteLoad
REDIM SHARED saucer(0 TO dimen) AS INTEGER
FOR num = 0 TO dimen
   saucer(num) = sprite(num)
NEXT num
SCREEN 1: CLS : pi! = 3.14159: angle! = 1.5708

REM ** Get Data for Flight **
here:
LOCATE 2, 2: INPUT "Heading in degrees (0 - 359)"; HeadDeg
LOCATE 4, 2: INPUT "Speed (1-4)"; speed
CLS : HeadRad! = HeadDeg * pi! / 180
xinc = 2 * speed * COS(angle! - HeadRad!)
yinc = -2 * speed * SIN(angle! - HeadRad!)

REM ** Fly It **
col = 160: row = 100
DO
```

Program 6-6. Controlled Flying Saucer

```
   LOCATE 1, 1: PRINT "Press any key to interrupt flight"
   DO WHILE col > 0 AND col < 307 AND row > 0 AND row < 193
     PUT (col, row), saucer, XOR          ' on
     Delay! = TIMER
     DO UNTIL TIMER > Delay! + .1
     LOOP
     PUT (col, row), saucer, XOR
     col = col + xinc: row = row + yinc
     ky$ = INKEY$
     IF ky$ <> "" THEN EXIT DO
   LOOP
   IF ky$ <> "" THEN EXIT DO
   IF row < 1 THEN
     row = 188
     col = col + 300 * COS(angle! - HeadRad!)
     IF col > 302 THEN col = col - 302
   ELSEIF row > 192 THEN
     row = 1
     col = col + 300 * COS(angle! - HeadRad!)
     IF col > 302 THEN col = col - 302
   END IF
   IF col < 1 THEN
     col = 300
     row = row - 188 * SIN(angle! - HeadRad!)
     IF row < 1 THEN row = 188 + row
   ELSEIF col > 302 THEN
     col = 1
     IF row < 1 THEN row = 188 + row
   END IF
   LOOP
   CLS : LOCATE 1, 2: PRINT "Press Q to quit, R to repeat"
   key$ = INPUT$(1)
   DO WHILE INSTR("QqRr", key$) = 0
   LOOP
   IF UCASE$(key$) = "Q" THEN END ELSE GOTO here

   SUB SpriteLoad
     DEFINT A-Z
     SCREEN 0: CLS : WIDTH 80
     INPUT "Array file name with extension"; fyle$
     INPUT "Disk drive (A, B, C, etc.)"; drive$
     fyle$ = LEFT$(drive$, 1) + ":" + fyle$
     DEF SEG = VARSEG(sprite(0))
     BLOAD fyle$, VARPTR(sprite(0))
     DEF SEG
     some = INT((sprite(0) + 7) / 8)
     dimen = INT(4 + some * sprite(1)) / 2 + 1
   END SUB
```

Program 6-6.   Controlled Flying Saucer (*continued*)

After the data file for the sprite has been loaded and copied into the Saucer array, the Get Data for Flight block requests the flight data for the flying saucer. Figure 6-13 shows some typical entries.

The same block calculates the vertical and horizontal increments by multiplying the trigonometric functions of the chosen heading by a factor of the chosen speed. This calculation is shown in the following listing:

```
REM ** Get Data for Flight **
here:
LOCATE 2, 2: INPUT "Heading in degrees (0 - 359)"; HeadDeg
LOCATE 4, 2: INPUT "Speed (1-4)"; speed
CLS : HeadRad! = HeadDeg * pi! / 180
xinc = 2 * speed * COS(angle! - HeadRad!)
yinc = -2 * speed * SIN(angle! - HeadRad!)
```

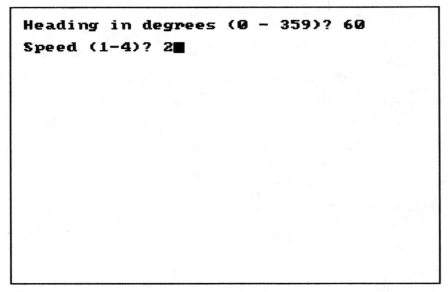

Figure 6-13.   Heading and speed entries

The Fly It block has been modified to allow the saucer to fly off the screen and return at a new location, always traveling in the same direction at a constant speed. Figure 6-14 shows possible flight paths for the saucer when it leaves and returns to the screen.

The following possibilities are shown in this figure:

1. If the saucer goes off at the top of the screen, it returns at the bottom.
2. If the saucer goes off at the bottom of the screen, it returns at the top.
3. If the saucer goes off at the left of the screen, it returns at the right.

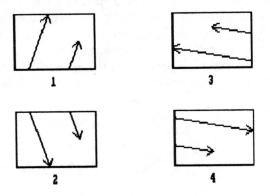

Figure 6-14.   Saucer paths

4. If the saucer goes off at the right of the screen, it returns at the left.

When the saucer leaves the screen, the location of its return is determined by IF...END IF blocks as shown here:

```
IF row < 1 THEN
   row = 188
   col = col + 300 * COS(angle! - HeadRad!)
   IF col > 302 THEN col = col - 302
ELSEIF row > 192 THEN
   row = 1
   col = col + 300 * COS(angle! - HeadRad!)
   IF col > 302 THEN col = col - 302
END IF
IF col < 1 THEN
   col = 300
   row = row - 188 * SIN(angle! - HeadRad!)
   IF row < 1 THEN row = 188 + row
ELSEIF col > 302 THEN
   col = 1
   IF row < 1 THEN row = 188 + row
END IF
```

You could modify Program 6-6 to allow the saucer to change heading and speed during the flight. You could also use a different sprite shape than the flying saucer.

After this introduction to sprite graphics, you can probably think of other uses for sprites. You can modify any of the programs to fit your own purposes or use the techniques for your own programs.

7

SCREEN
TRANSFORMATIONS

This chapter discusses screen transformations in SCREEN 1 graphics mode, which produces a graphics display 320 pixels wide by 200 pixels high. In this mode pixels are numbered, by default, from the upper left corner starting at point 0,0. Columns are numbered left to right (0 through 319), and rows are numbered from top to bottom (0 through 199).

This chapter refers to this coordinate system as the screen coordinate system. However, you probably visualize dimensions of objects from left to right and from bottom to top. Therefore, screen coordinates may be vertically inverted from your thought processes. So this chapter also discusses your option to use either the screen coordinate system or a world coordinate system.

SCALING

When you are plotting shapes on the display screen, each shape is affected by the aspect ratio of your video display and the rectangular shape of the pixels. The shapes that you create may not be the shapes you wished to produce. For example, you might expect to produce a 150-by-150 square with the following LINE statement:

```
LINE (0, 0)-(150, 150), , B
```

However, if you measure the resulting shape as displayed on a typical screen, you might get 5 inches high by 4.6 inches wide. The width of the display used here is 0.92 times its height. To make the dimensions appear equal, you can scale down the height of the display by a factor of 0.92 with the following listing:

```
SCREEN 1: CLS
scale! = .92
LINE (0, scale! * 0)-(150, scale! * 150), , B
```

Figure 7-1 compares an unscaled square and a scaled square drawn with 150-by-150 dimensions. A vertical scale factor of 0.92 was used for the scaled square.

The scale factor may vary from monitor to monitor. Therefore, you should measure the width and height of the shape produced on your own display when you try to draw a square of equal dimensions.

After you obtain your scale factor, you should use it when you draw any rectilinear figure on a display using the default coordinate system. This way you will obtain shapes that are proportional to the dimensions given in the drawing statements.

Instead of including a scale factor in each statement that draws a line, you can scale the screen with WINDOW and VIEW statements and then omit the scale factor. For example, you could produce an equivalent to the shape drawn in the previous example with the following statements:

```
SCREEN 1: CLS
scale! = .92
WINDOW SCREEN (0, 0)-(199, 199)
VIEW (0, 0)-(199, scale! * 199)
LINE (0, 0)-(150, 150), , B
```

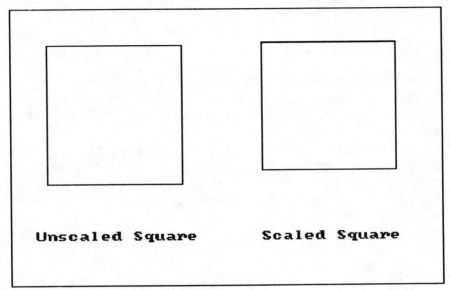

Figure 7-1.   Scaling squares

The advantages of using this form become more apparent when you must draw many straight lines to form a series of rectilinear shapes. The following sections discuss the WINDOW and VIEW statements in more detail.

WINDOW

A WINDOW statement defines the *logical dimensions* of the area displayed on the screen. It allows you to create a customized coordinate system for drawing objects that is not constrained by the screen's *physical coordinates* (columns 0 to 319 and rows 0 to 199).

The SCREEN option of the WINDOW statement allows you to choose between a screen coordinate system and a world coordinate system. You can do this with the following statements:

```
WINDOW SCREEN (0, 0)-(319, 199)      'full screen, Screen
                                      Coordinates

WINDOW (0, 0)-(319, 199)      'full screen, World Coordinates
```

Figure 7-2 shows these two systems.

If you use the WINDOW statement with no arguments, it disables any previous WINDOW statement and returns you to a full screen in the default screen coordinate mode.

WINDOW defines a *mapping* of your logical coordinate system to the physical coordinates of the screen. You can even specify logical coordinates that are greater or smaller than the default physical coordinates of the screen. Suppose you execute the following WINDOW statement:

```
WINDOW (100, 100)-(499, 499)
```

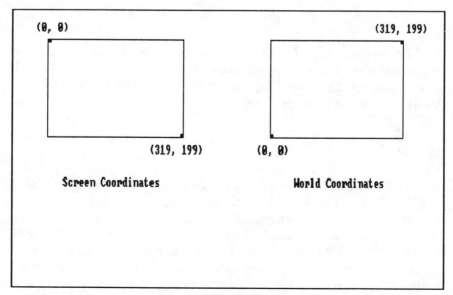

Figure 7-2.   Screen versus world coordinate systems

This statement maps the point 100,100 to the lower left corner of the display (point 0,199 in the screen coordinate system) and the point 499,499 to the upper right corner of the display (point 319,0 in the default screen coordinate system). Figure 7-3 shows the logical limits for this mapping.

The WINDOW statement lets you customize your screen to fit your needs. For example, you could use the following statement to produce the four quadrants of the *Cartesian coordinate system* with the origin at the center of the screen:

```
WINDOW (-1, -1)-(1, 1)
```

Figure 7-4 shows the axis used for this system, which was drawn by Program 7-1.

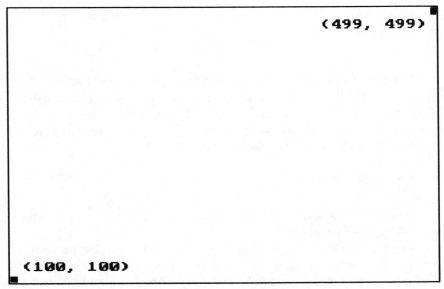

Figure 7-3.   New logical coordinate limits

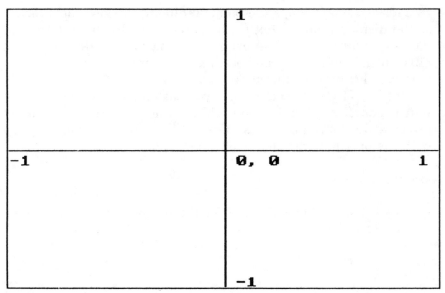

Figure 7-4.   Cartesian coordinate system

Mathematicians use the Cartesian coordinate system and its four quadrants to plot all kinds of mathematical relationships. For instance, it is ideal for plotting trigonometric relationships. The horizontal scale can be mapped to fit the cycle length of a trig function, as shown in the following listing:

```
WINDOW (2 * (-pi!), -1)-(2 * pi!, 1)
```

Program 7-2 uses this WINDOW statement to plot two complete cycles of the curve.

Figure 7-5 shows the output of Program 7-2. The magnitude of the sine wave ranges from −1 to +1 as the angle progresses from −2pi to +2pi. The origin (0,0) is located at the center of the screen. As you see, WINDOW statements can include arithmetic expressions such as 2 * (−pi!) and 2 * pi! that were used in Program 7-2.

```
REM ** CARTESIAN COORDINATES **
' Program 7-1  File: PRO0701.BAS

REM ** Define Screen **
SCREEN 1: CLS : DEFINT A-Z
WINDOW (-1, -1)-(1, 1)

REM ** Draw Axes and Label **
LINE (-1, 0)-(1, 0): LINE (0, 1)-(0, -1)
LOCATE 14, 1: PRINT "-1": LOCATE 14, 39: PRINT "1";
LOCATE 14, 22: PRINT "0, 0"
LOCATE 1, 22: PRINT "1": LOCATE 25, 22: PRINT "-1";

REM ** Press a Key to End **
ky$ = INPUT$(1)
END
```

Program 7-1.   Cartesian Coordinates

```
REM ** SINE CURVE **
' Program 7-2  File: PRO0702.BAS

REM ** Define Screen **
SCREEN 1: CLS : DEFINT A-Z
pi! = 3.14159
WINDOW (2 * -(pi!), -1)-(2 * pi!, 1)

REM ** Draw Axes and Label **
LINE (2 * -pi!, 0)-(2 * pi!, 0): LINE (0, 1)-(0, -1)
LOCATE 14, 1: PRINT "-2pi": LOCATE 14, 38: PRINT "2pi";
LOCATE 14, 22: PRINT "0, 0"
LOCATE 1, 22: PRINT "1": LOCATE 25, 22: PRINT "-1";

REM ** Draw Sine **
FOR col! = -2 * pi! TO 2 * pi! STEP .05
  PSET (col!, SIN(col!))
NEXT col!

REM ** Press a Key to End **
ky$ = INPUT$(1)
END
```

Program 7-2.   Sine Curve

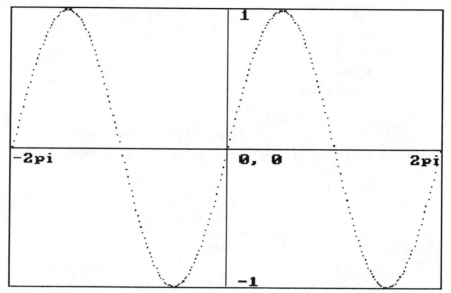

Figure 7-5.   Sine wave

CLIPPING

If a LINE statement specifies a line segment that extends beyond the defined limits of the screen, only the part of the segment within those limits is displayed. The rest of the segment is clipped off.

Program 7-3 uses the following four different maps for the screen display:

1. Lower left = (0,0) and upper right = (319, 199)
2. Lower left = (0,0) and upper right = (199, 199)
3. Lower left = (0,0) and upper right = (319, 70)
4. Lower left = (30,70) and upper right = (319, 199)

The same rectangle is drawn in each window with the following
LINE statement:

```
LINE (60, 60)-(300, 80), 1, BF        ' cyan filled
```

When you run the program, a time delay allows you to see
what is displayed in each window. The coordinates defining the
window are displayed in the lower left corner of the screen.

```
DECLARE SUB Delay ()
REM ** CHANGING WINDOWS **
' Program 7-3   FILE: PRO0703.BAS

REM ** Define Screen and Window Data **
SCREEN 1: CLS : DEFINT A-Z
DATA 0, 0,  319, 199,  0, 0,  199, 199
DATA 0, 0,  319, 65,  30, 70,  319, 199

REM ** Define 4 Windows and Draw 3 Lines **
FOR num = 1 TO 4
   READ col1, row1, col2, row2
   WINDOW (col1, row1)-(col2, row2)
   LINE (col1, row1)-(col2, row2), 3, B
   LINE (60, 60)-(300, 80), 1, BF
   LOCATE 22, 2
   PRINT col1; ","; row1; " to "; col2; ","; row2
   CALL Delay
   CLS
NEXT num
END

SUB Delay
   begin! = TIMER
   DO UNTIL TIMER > begin! + 5
   LOOP
END SUB
```

Program 7-3. Changing Windows

The rectangle is not clipped by the first window. The second window clips the right side of the rectangle. The third window clips the top of the rectangle, and the fourth window clips the bottom of the rectangle.

Figure 7-6 shows you how the second window is mapped to the display screen: point 0,0 of the window to point 0,0 of the display and point 199,199 of the window to point 319,199 of the display. Since the second window clips the right side of the rectangle, only the left portion of the rectangle is displayed on the screen. The clipped portion of the rectangle is not mapped to the image on the screen.

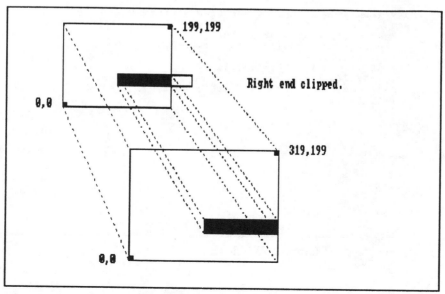

Figure 7-6.   Object mapped to image

```
REM ** ZOOM BOX **
' Program 7-4   FILE: PRO0704.BAS

REM ** Define Screen **
SCREEN 1: CLS : DEFINT A-Z

REM ** Draw Box in Changing Windows **
FOR row1 = 0 TO 72 STEP 4
   col1 = row1 * 1.6: col2 = 319 - col1: row2 = 199 - row1
   WINDOW (col1, row1)-(col2, row2)
   LINE (144, 85)-(164, 105), , B: LINE (144, 105)-(151, 115)
   LINE -(171, 115): LINE -(164, 105)
   LINE (171, 115)-(171, 95): LINE -(164, 85)
   ky$ = INPUT$(1)
NEXT row1
END
```

Program 7-4.   Zoom Box

ZOOMING

You can use WINDOW statements to zoom in on an object by enclosing the object in windows of decreasing size. Program 7-4 draws a three-dimensional box in the normal SCREEN 1 window (0,0) to (319,199).

When you run this program, the box first appears in a normal window. When you press a key, the screen is cleared and the box is redrawn in a smaller window. The lower limit of the window is increased, and the upper limit of the window is decreased. Thus, the image of the box increases in size. Figure 7-7 shows all of the boxes drawn by Program 7-4. The figure was made by removing the CLS statement from the program.

A VIEW WITHIN
THE DISPLAY

The VIEW statement also lets you define screen limits for graphics output. It defines a rectangular section of the screen into

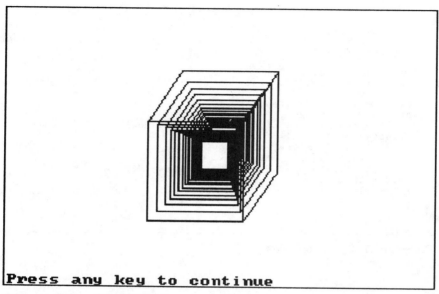

Figure 7-7. WINDOW boxes

which you may map graphics. All the coordinates that you use in a VIEW statement must be within the physical bounds of the graphics screen (0,0 to 319,199 for SCREEN 1).

You may specify a border in the VIEW statement, as well as a color for the interior of the viewport. These options are shown in the following statement:

```
VIEW (col1!, row1!)-(col2!, row2!), fill, border
```

The *border* parameter is the border color number, and the *fill* parameter is the interior color number.

The VIEW statement has a SCREEN option that performs a different function than the SCREEN option of the WINDOW statement. If you use the SCREEN option in a VIEW statement, the column and row values of graphics statements are *absolute* screen values. They are *not relative* to the border of the physical viewport defined by VIEW. This option lets you draw a figure that conforms to the absolute screen limits but lies partly, or even completely, outside the viewport. Consider the following program segment:

```
SCREEN 1: CLS
VIEW SCREEN (40, 20)-(150, 80), 2, 1
LINE (50, 30)-(140, 70), 1          ' cyan line
LINE (50, 50)-(140, 100), 3         ' white line
```

The screen (see Figure 7-8) shows the magenta viewport, cyan boundary, and two lines created by this segment. The cyan line is drawn first and is plotted in absolute screen coordinates. This line falls within the viewport limits and so is completely displayed. The white line is drawn and is also plotted in absolute screen coordinates. This line exceeds the viewport limits, so only that part of the line that lies within the viewport is displayed.

This viewport stays in effect until you execute the next VIEW statement. That is, any graphics displayed are limited to the viewport defined by the most recent VIEW statement. If you execute a new VIEW statement it redefines the limits for future graphics statements.

Program 7-5 illustrates how to redefine viewports. It begins with the same viewport and two lines shown in Figure 7-8.

After it draws the two lines in the first viewport, it executes a time delay. Then it defines a new viewport with a second VIEW SCREEN statement. When the program draws the new viewport, it overlaps the first one and obscures portions of the original two lines. The final screen is shown in Figure 7-9.

After another time delay, it redraws the same two lines. However, it reverses their colors in this viewport, as shown in Figure 7-10. It also displays only portions of the two lines in the new viewport. The missing portions remain in the first viewport.

Run Program 7-5 as it is. Then try clearing the screen before the second VIEW SCREEN statement is executed, as shown in the next listing:

```
CLS: VIEW SCREEN (70, 50)-(180, 110), 2, 1
```

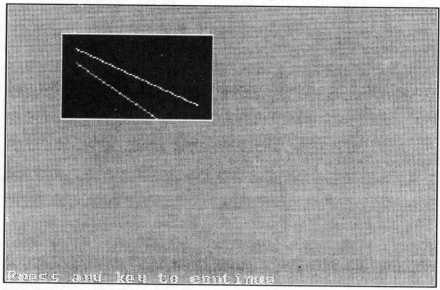

Figure 7-8. Lines in viewport

```
REM ** VIEW SCREEN DEMO **
' Program 7-5  File: PR00705.BAS

REM ** Define Screen & Viewport, Draw Two Lines **
SCREEN 1: CLS
VIEW SCREEN (40, 20)-(150, 80), 2, 1
LINE (50, 30)-(140, 70), 1
LINE (50, 50)-(140, 100), 3

REM ** Delay, Define new Viewport, Delay Again **
FOR delay = 1 TO 5000: NEXT delay
VIEW SCREEN (70, 50)-(180, 110), 2, 1
FOR delay = 1 TO 1000: NEXT delay

REM ** Draw Same Two Lines, Reverse Colors **
LINE (50, 30)-(140, 70), 3
LINE (50, 50)-(140, 100), 1
```

Program 7-5. VIEW SCREEN Demonstration

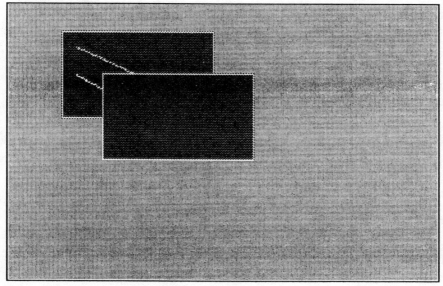

Figure 7-9.   Overlapping viewports

If you omit the SCREEN option from the VIEW statement, the column and row values of graphics statements are relative to the viewport. This means that column and row values are added to the lower bound VIEW coordinates before a point is plotted.

Next delete the keyword SCREEN from the two VIEW statements in Program 7-5 so that they read as follows:

```
VIEW (40, 20)-(150, 80), 2, 1
VIEW (70, 50)-(180, 110), 2, 1
```

Run the program with these revisions. Once again, it draws the viewport area using absolute coordinates. However, it plots the lines relative to the lower limits of the viewport. Therefore, LINE (50,30)—(140,70) is drawn with absolute coordinates of (50 + 40, 30 + 20) to (140 + 40, 70 + 20), and LINE (50,50)—(140,100) is drawn

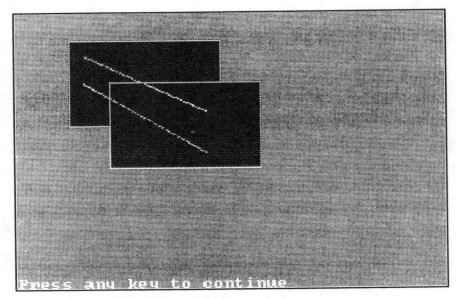

Figure 7-10. Colors reversed in new viewport

with absolute coordinates of (50 + 40, 50 + 20) to (140 + 40, 100 + 20). This puts portions of both lines outside the viewport. Therefore, as shown in Figure 7-11, the program clips the lines at the viewport boundaries.

When it draws the lines in the second viewport, as shown in Figure 7-12, it displays them in the same relative positions as in the first viewport. However, it reverses the colors of the lines.

Changing the Viewport

You can redefine the position of the current viewport within the physical screen. You can also redefine its size.

With multiple viewport definitions, you can move a viewport on the screen, expand or contract its size, remove the boundary, and draw a figure in the redefined viewport. This lets you place a

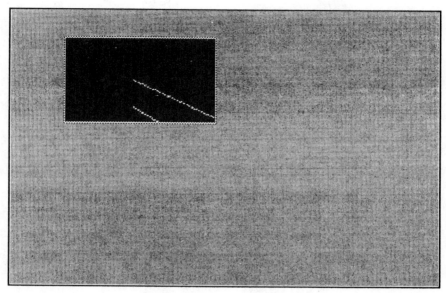

Figure 7-11.   First viewport with both lines clipped

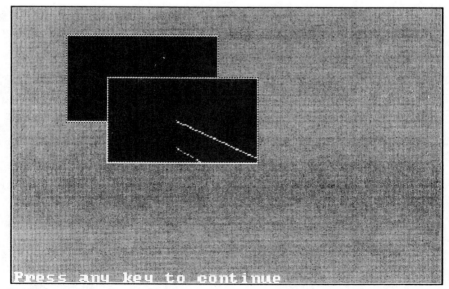

Figure 7-12.   Second viewport

```
REM ** CHANGING VIEWPORT **
' Program 7-6   File: PR00706.BAS

REM ** Define Screen & Original Viewport **
SCREEN 1: CLS
LOCATE 24, 1: PRINT "Size (+,-)   Move (L,R,U,D)";
PRINT "   Circle (C)";
col1 = 155: row1 = 95: col2 = 165: row2 = 105
VIEW SCREEN (col1, row1)-(col2, row2), , 1

REM ** Alter Viewport **
DO
  ky$ = UCASE$(INPUT$(1))
  VIEW SCREEN (col1, row1)-(col2, row2), , 0
  SELECT CASE ky$
    CASE "+"
      col1 = col1 - 5: col2 = col2 + 5
      row1 = row1 - 5: row2 = row2 + 5
    CASE "-"
      col1 = col1 + 5: col2 = col2 - 5
      row1 = row1 + 5: row2 = row2 - 5
    CASE "L"
      col1 = col1 - 5: col2 = col2 - 5
    CASE "R"
      col1 = col1 + 5: col2 = col2 + 5
    CASE "U"
      row1 = row1 - 5: row2 = row2 - 5
    CASE "D"
      row1 = row1 + 5: row2 = row2 + 5
    CASE "C"
      EXIT DO
    CASE ELSE
      ' do nothing
  END SELECT
  VIEW SCREEN (col1, row1)-(col2, row2), , 1
LOOP

REM ** Calculate and Draw Circle **
colcirc = (col1 + col2) / 2: rowcirc = (row1 + row2) / 2
radius = (col2 - col1) / 2
CIRCLE (colcirc, rowcirc), radius
END
```

Program 7-6.   Changing Viewport

graphic figure anywhere on the screen without calculating the coordinates necessary to draw the figure. Program 7-6 uses this method to allow you to determine the placement and size of a circle.

The original viewport is defined as a small cyan square at the center of the screen, as shown in the following listing:

```
col1 = 155: row1 = 95: col2 = 165: row2 = 105
VIEW SCREEN (col1, row1)-(col2, row2), , 1
```

The Alter Viewport block of the program allows you to change the size of the viewport by pressing the + key to make it bigger or the − key to make it smaller. You can move the viewport to the left by pressing the L key, to the right by pressing the R key, upward by pressing the U key, and downward by pressing the D key. When you press any of these keys, the program erases the boundaries of the previous viewport. Then it defines and draws a new viewport with the new boundaries. The following statements perform these functions:

```
VIEW SCREEN (col1, row1)-(col2, row2), , 0      ' erase

VIEW SCREEN (col1, row1)-(col2, row2), , 1      ' draw
```

When you are satisfied with the viewport's location and size, press the C key to have the program automatically calculate the center and radius of a circle that will just fit in the viewport. It calculates the column value for the center of the circle (*colcir*) by averaging the column limits of the viewport, and the row value for the center of the circle (*rowcir*) by averaging the row limits of the viewport. These two calculations center the circle in the viewport. Then it calculates the *radius* by dividing the width of the viewport by two. Finally the program draws and then ends. This process is shown in the following listing:

```
colcirc = (col1 + col2) / 2: rowcirc = (row1 + row2) / 2
radius = (col2 - col1) / 2
CIRCLE (colcirc, rowcirc), radius
```

The program decides what action to take when you press a particular key with a SELECT CASE structure in which each CASE is assigned to a given key. A CASE ELSE option provides the appropriate action if you accidentally press an inactive key.

You could easily extend the program to allow you to change the height and width of the viewport to accommodate irregular shapes. You could also make it possible to place more than one shape on the screen, or you could change the keys that invoke the various actions.

Figure 7-13 shows the boundary of the original viewport at the center of the screen and an enlarged viewport moved to the upper

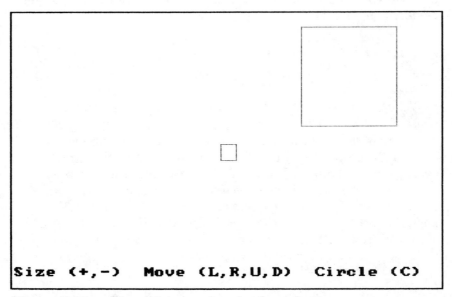

Figure 7-13.   Viewpoint moved and enlarged

right corner of the screen. When you run the program, it erases the original viewport boundary. Then it lists the active keys for moving the viewport, enlarging the viewport, and drawing the circle at the bottom of the screen. If you press the C key at this point, the program erases the viewport boundaries and draws the circle at the viewport's location.

Two Viewports in One Screen

The next two programs provide additional information on how to use the SCREEN option of the VIEW statement. Program 7-7 divides the world coordinate screen into two viewports and attempts to draw a circle and a rectangle in the viewports.

```
REM ** SPLIT SCREEN WITH VIEW SCREEN **
' Program 7-7  File: PRO0707.BAS

REM ** Define Screen **
SCREEN 1: CLS
WINDOW (0, 0)-(319, 199)

REM ** Define Lower Viewport, Draw and Wait **
VIEW SCREEN (1, 101)-(318, 198), , 2
CIRCLE (160, 50), 20
LINE (110, 130)-(209, 169), , B
ky$ = INPUT$(1)

REM ** Define Upper Viewport and Draw **
VIEW SCREEN (1, 1)-(318, 98), , 1
CIRCLE (160, 50), 20
LINE (110, 130)-(209, 169), , B

REM ** Wait for Key Press and End **
ky$ = INPUT$(1)
END
```

Program 7-7.   Split Screen with VIEW SCREEN

A world coordinate system is provided by the WINDOW statement. The first VIEW SCREEN statement specifies a viewport in the lower half of the screen, (1,100) to (318,198), with a magenta border. (These limits are absolute screen coordinates.) Then it draws a circle and a rectangle with the following statements:

```
CIRCLE (160, 50), 20
LINE (110, 130)-(209, 169), , B
```

Since the SCREEN option is used in the VIEW statement, the coordinates of the figures are absolute values. The WINDOW statement did not include a SCREEN option. Therefore, the program uses *world coordinates* ((0,0) at the lower left corner of the screen), and draws the circle within the viewport. The rectangle falls outside the viewport and so is not displayed.

At this point the computer waits for you to press a key. When you do, it executes the second VIEW SCREEN statement. This statement specifies a viewport, (1,1) to (318,99), in *screen coordinates* with a cyan border. This position lies in the upper half of the screen. The program draws a circle and a rectangle using the same coordinates as before. This time the circle falls outside the viewport, since *absolute world coordinates* are used for the figures. The rectangle lies within the viewport and is displayed. Figure 7-14 shows the final result.

Program 7-8 also divides the screen into two viewports. The only difference between this program and Program 7-7 is that this time the SCREEN option is omitted from the VIEW statements. This makes the figure coordinates *relative* to the lower limit coordinates of the viewports.

When you run this program, the lower viewport appears first. Then it displays both the circle and the rectangle. Their coordinates are relative to the lower limits of the viewport, and both figures lie within the viewport. Then the computer waits for you to press a key. When you do, the circle and the rectangle both appear in the upper viewport, since their coordinates are relative to the coordinates of that viewport's lower limit. Figure 7-15 shows the result.

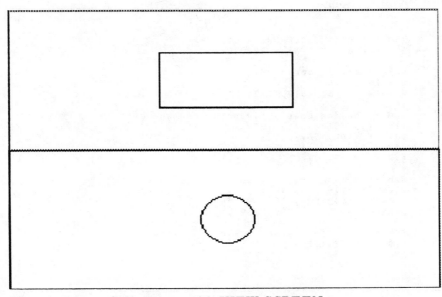

Figure 7-14.   Split screen with VIEW SCREEN

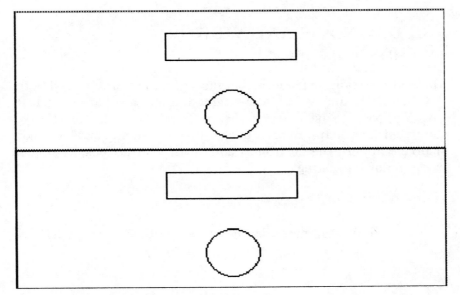

Figure 7-15.   Split screen with VIEW

```
REM ** SPLIT SCREEN WITH VIEW **
' Program 7-8  File: PRO0708.BAS

REM ** Define Screen **
SCREEN 1: CLS
WINDOW (0, 0)-(319, 199)

REM ** Define Lower Viewport, Draw and Wait **
VIEW (1, 101)-(318, 198), , 2
CIRCLE (160, 50), 20
LINE (110, 130)-(209, 169), , B
ky$ = INPUT$(1)

REM ** Define Upper Viewport and Draw **
VIEW (1, 1)-(318, 98), , 1
CIRCLE (160, 50), 20
LINE (110, 130)-(209, 169), , B

REM ** Wait for Key Press and End **
ky$ = INPUT$(1)
END
```

Program 7-8.   Split Screen with VIEW

USING WINDOW AND VIEW
TO SCALE

The scaling example from the beginning of the chapter used both
the WINDOW and VIEW statements to scale a square so that it
would appear to be a truer shape. To do this, the WINDOW
statement first maps an area to the screen with an equal number
of pixels in both the horizontal and vertical directions, as shown
in the following listing:

```
WINDOW (0, 0)-(199, 199)
```

The VIEW statement is then used without the SCREEN

option to map the figures relative to this statement's scaled coordinates. This is shown in the next listing:

```
VIEW (0, 0)-(199, scale! * 199)
```

Program 7-9 draws an unscaled "square" on the left side of the normal screen coordinate system screen (0,0 to 319,199). A WINDOW statement then reduces the screen limits to 0,0 to 199,199. This provides the same number of pixels vertically and horizontally. The VIEW statement from the last listing then scales the vertical size of the pixels to match the horizontal size so that the shape is a true square. Then the program redraws the scaled square to the right of the first rectangle.

The resulting square is shown in Figure 7-16. Both figures have specified dimensions of 70 by 70, but the unscaled square, as displayed, looks more like a rectangle.

```
REM ** SCALING WITH WINDOW AND VIEW **
' Program 7-9   File: PRO0709.BAS

REM ** Define Screen and Draw Unscaled Square **
SCREEN 1: CLS
LINE (55, 60)-(124, 129), 1, B

REM ** Redefine Screen and Draw Scaled Square **
scale! = .92
WINDOW SCREEN (0, 0)-(199, 199)
VIEW (0, 0)-(199, scale! * 199)
LINE (130, 71)-(199, 140), 2, B

REM ** Wait for Key Press and End **
ky$ = INPUT$(1)
END
```

Program 7-9. Scaling with WINDOW and VIEW

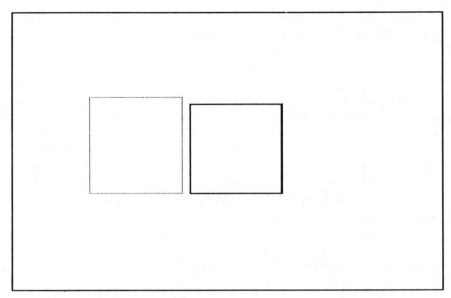

Figure 7-16. Scaling a rectangle

TRANSFORMING TWO-DIMENSIONAL OBJECTS

You can *transform* an object on the screen into an *image* that differs in shape or screen placement from the original object. A *transformation* in a two-dimensional plane involves systematically moving each point (X, Y) of the original object to a new point (XI, YI) of the image. You can animate graphic objects by periodically adding an increment to the X and Y coordinates of the object. You can do even more complex mapping of the points of an object to the points of an image by using matrix multiplication.

Matrices

A matrix is a rectangular array of numbers consisting of rows and columns. If a matrix has m rows and n columns, it is called an *m*-by-*n* or *m* × *n* matrix. For example, a 3-by-2 matrix has the following form:

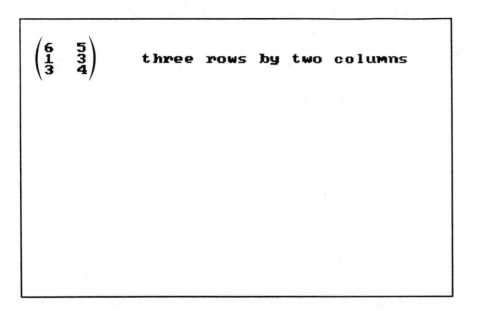

The following discussion omits the usual mathematical notations. Instead it uses a simpler notation system, one more relevant to QuickBASIC.

The medium-resolution color graphics screen (SCREEN 1) is an array of pixels with 200 rows and 320 columns. Therefore, it can be represented by a 200-by-320 matrix. You can represent each individual point on the screen by its *X*, *Y* coordinates. Therefore, you can also represent each point with a 1-by-2 matrix (*X*, *Y*).

Two coordinates (*X* and *Y*) are usually used to represent each point in a two-dimensional plane. But for transforming objects, you need to use three elements (*X*, *Y*, and 1) to represent a point. The third element of the new 1-by-3 matrix does not locate the point in the *XY* plane. The three elements used to represent a point are called the *normalized homogeneous coordinates* of the point (*X*, *Y*).

A special 3-by-3 matrix is used to multiply the normalized homogeneous coordinates of the object to obtain the normalized homogeneous coordinates for the transformed image. This special matrix is called a *transformation matrix,* and it has the following form:

$$
\begin{pmatrix}
A & B & 0 \\
C & D & 0 \\
E & F & 1
\end{pmatrix}
$$

Notice that two elements of the 3-by-3 matrix are zeros.

You multiply the normalized homogeneous coordinates of an object by the transformation matrix to obtain the normalized homogeneous coordinates of the image in the following way:

$$(X \ Y \ 1) \begin{pmatrix} A & B & 0 \\ C & D & 0 \\ E & F & 1 \end{pmatrix} = (A*X+C*Y+E \quad B*X+D*Y+F \quad 1)$$

Thus you can convert each normalized homogeneous coordinate of the original object to a normalized homogeneous coordinate of the image. Since QuickBASIC, as well as most other versions of BASIC, cannot perform matrix multiplications directly, you transform objects by performing ordinary multiplication on the individual elements of the matrices.

If you ignore the third element in the 1-by-3 matrices, you can see that each (X, Y) coordinate pair will have a corresponding (*XI*, *YI*) coordinate pair. Each screen coordinate (*XI*, *YI*) of the image will then correspond to each screen coordinate (X, Y) of the original object. Consider the following equation:

```
(XI, YI) = (A * X + C * Y + E, B * X + D * Y + F)
```

By varying the values for A, B, C, D, E, and F, you can perform different transformations. You can use Program 7-10 to demonstrate the following types of transformations:

1. Identity
2. Translation
3. Scaling
4. Reflection
5. Shear
6. Rotation

This program uses a WINDOW statement to scale the screen for the Cartesian coordinate system. Then it draws a unit square to be used as a reference with its lower left corner at the origin (0,0) of the coordinate system.

Then it asks you to enter the elements A, B, C, D, E, and F of the transformation matrix. It uses these elements to convert the reference square into a transformed image. At the end of the program, you can either perform a new transformation or quit.

Typical Transformations

Run the program using the following values for the required elements. These values will produce the six different transformation types just discussed.

1. The *identity transformation* redraws the reference square in a new color, leaving its size, shape, and location unchanged. To perform this transformation, use the following entries:

$$A = 1 \quad B = 0 \quad C = 0 \quad D = 1 \quad E = 0 \quad F = 0$$

```
REM ** TRANSFORMATIONS **
' Program 7-10  File PRO0710.BAS

REM ** Define Screen and Standard Square **
SCREEN 1: WINDOW (-3, -2)-(3, 2)
begin: CLS
LINE (0, 0)-(1, 1), 1, B

REM ** Input Matrix Elements **
LOCATE 1, 1: INPUT "A ="; A: LOCATE 1, 20: INPUT "B ="; B
LOCATE 2, 1: INPUT "C ="; C: LOCATE 2, 20: INPUT "D ="; D
LOCATE 1, 1: PRINT SPACE$(38): PRINT SPACE$(38);
LOCATE 1, 1: INPUT "E ="; E: LOCATE 1, 20: INPUT "F ="; f
LOCATE 1, 1: PRINT SPACE$(38)

REM ** Read Data and PLot **
DATA 0, 0,  1, 0,  1, 1,  0, 1,  0, 0
READ X, Y
(XI = A * X + C * Y + E: YI = B * X + D * Y + f
PSET (XI, YI)
FOR side = 1 TO 4
  READ X, Y
  (XI = A * X + C * Y + E: YI = B * X + D * Y + f
  LINE -(XI, YI), 2
NEXT side

REM ** Get Ready to Repeat **
RESTORE
LOCATE 24, 1: PRINT "Press N for new input, Q to quit";
ky$ = INPUT$(1)
IF INSTR("Nn", ky$) <> 0 THEN GOTO begin
END
```

Program 7-10. Transformations

2. The *translation transformation* moves the reference square to a new position, retaining its size and shape. Figure 7-17 shows the translation performed by the following matrix entries:

$$A = 1 \quad B = 0 \quad C = 0 \quad D = 1 \quad E = .2 \quad F = .4$$

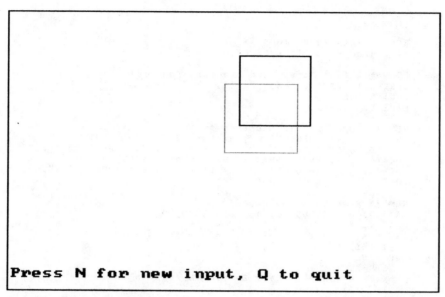

Figure 7-17.   Translation

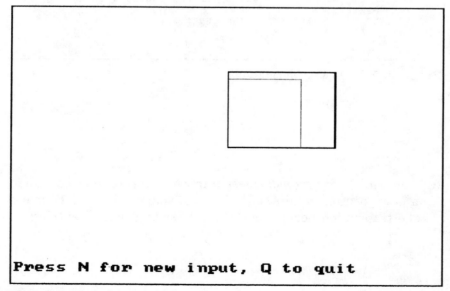

Figure 7-18.   Scaling

You may use other values for E and F to translate the object to other locations. E translates along the X axis, and F translates along the Y axis.

3. The *scaling transformation* scales the length and width of the reference square. Figure 7-18 shows the result of using scale factors of 1.2 for the height and 1.5 for the width. These scale factors are obtained from the following entries:

$$A = 1.5 \quad B = 0 \quad C = 0 \quad D = 1.1 \quad E = 0 \quad F = 0$$

Try other values for A and D. The value for A scales the X magnitude (width), and the value for B scales the Y (height) magnitude.

4. The *reflection transformation* reflects the image about the origin or one of the axes. Figure 7-19 illustrates a reflection of an image about the X axis. This image is transformed by changing the quantity assigned to D to a negative value, as in the following entries:

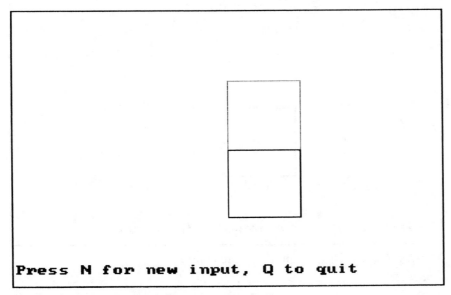

Figure 7-19.   Reflection about the X axis

$$A = 1 \quad B = 0 \quad C = 0 \quad D = -1 \quad E = 0 \quad F = 0$$

If you change A to a negative value, as in the following entries, the image is reflected about the Y axis:

$$A = -1 \quad B = 0 \quad C = 0 \quad D = 1 \quad E = 0 \quad F = 0$$

You can scale and reflect at the same time by changing the magnitudes of A and D. You could also transform the image by entering non-zero values for E or F.

Figure 7-20 illustrates an image reflected about the point of origin. This is achieved by changing both A and D to negative values, as shown in the following entries:

$$A = -1 \quad B = 0 \quad C = 0 \quad D = -1 \quad E = 0 \quad F = 0$$

5. The *shear transformation* skews the shape of the reference square so that its interior angles are not right angles. You can

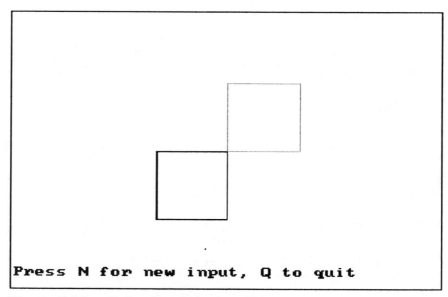

Press N for new input, Q to quit

Figure 7-20.   Reflection about the origin

shear the square along the Y axis, as shown in Figure 7-21, by entering the following values:

$A = 1$ $B = .5$ $C = 0$ $D = 1$ $E = 0$ $F = 0$

You can shear the square along the X axis by entering the following values:

$A = 1$ $B = 0$ $C = .5$ $D = 1$ $E = 0$ $F = 0$

You can also combine other transformations with shear.

6. The *rotation transformation* uses COS and SIN functions to rotate the reference square a certain number of degrees. If no translation is involved, the square is rotated counterclockwise about the origin. Figure 7-22 shows the rotation of the square 30 degrees about the origin produced by the following entries:

$A = .866$ $B = .5$ $C = -.5$ $D = .866$ $E = 0$ $F = 0$

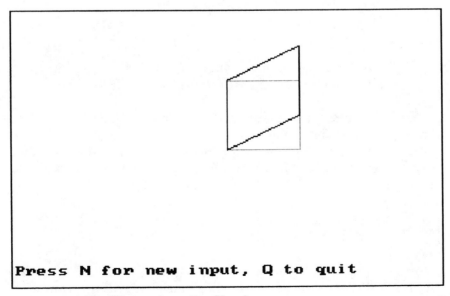

Press N for new input, Q to quit

Figure 7-21.   Shear along the Y axis

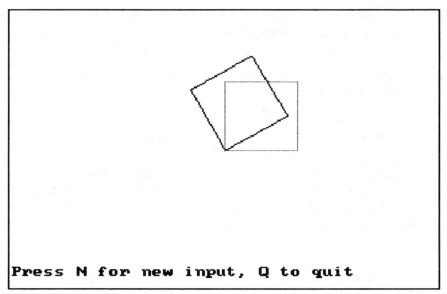

Figure 7-22.   Rotation of 30 degrees

Try other angles. For the angle of rotation, $A = \text{COS}(angle)$, $B = \text{SIN}(angle)$, $C = -\text{SIN}(angle)$, and $D = \text{COS}(angle)$.

You can obtain a variety of results by combining several of these types of transformations.

If you want to experiment with the transformations another way, move the *begin:* label from in front of the CLS statement to the next line, as shown in the following listing:

```
REM ** Define Screen and Standard Square **
SCREEN 1: WINDOW (-3, -2)-(3, 2)
CLS
begin: LINE (0, 0)-(1, 1), , b
```

Figure 7-23 shows the result of using this changed program with some experimentation.

You can extend the transformations used in this chapter to three dimensions by enlarging the transformation matrix to four

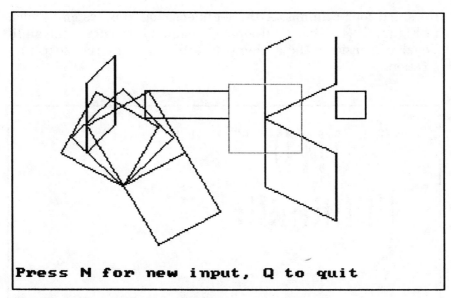

Figure 7-23.   Miscellaneous transformations

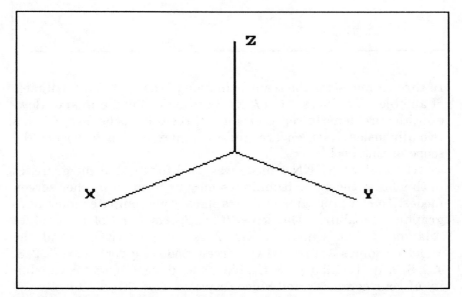

Figure 7-24.   Three-dimensional axis system

rows and four columns. A three-dimensional axis system, shown in Figure 7-24, needs additional elements to transform the additional dimension. These elements are shown in the next illustration:

$$
X \ Y \ Z \ 1 \begin{pmatrix} A & B & J & 0 \\ C & D & K & 0 \\ E & F & L & 0 \\ G & H & M & 1 \end{pmatrix} = (XI \ YI \ ZI \ 1)
$$

$$XI = A * X + C * Y + E * Z + G$$
$$YI = B * X + D * Y + F * Z + H$$
$$ZI = J * X + K * Y + H * Z + M$$

In three dimensions the transformation of the X, Y, Z coordinates of an object produces XI, YI, ZI coordinates for the image. However, the problems of representing a three-dimensional object on a two-dimensional screen are quite complex, and are beyond the scope of this book.

Although SCREEN 1 mode was used for most of the graphics in this book, the same techniques may be used with other screen modes. To run programs with graphics, your computer must have graphics capability. QuickBASIC supports the Color Graphics Adapter (CGA), Enhanced Graphics Adapter (EGA), and the Video Graphics Array (VGA). Screen modes supported are 1, 2, 3, 4, 7, 8, 9, 10, 11, 12, and 13. Usable modes depend upon the capability of your computer and video display.

8

SEARCHING AND SORTING

Searching and sorting data bases are two fundamental programming tasks. Searching and sorting routines are used in almost all data base programs, as well as in language interpreters, compilers, and operating systems. Since sorting data makes searching easier and faster, sorting is discussed first in this chapter.

SORTING

Sorting is the process of arranging data that consists of similar pieces of information into increasing or decreasing order by the specified criteria. Generally, you can sort a list of n pieces of data in increasing order as follows:

$$data(1) <= data(2) <= data(3) <= \ldots <= data(n)$$

Sorting algorithms can be separated into the following two categories:

1. Sorting arrays (in memory or in random access disk files)

2. Sorting sequential disk files

The main difference between sorting arrays and sorting sequential files is that each element of an array is always available in memory. Therefore, you may compare or exchange any element of the array with any other element at any given time. Sequential files are sorted differently because in those files only one element is available at any specific time. This chapter just discusses sorting arrays, while the following chapters discuss sorting and using disk files.

When you are sorting arrays, you use a small portion of the data as a *sort key* for making comparisons. When a comparison shows that an exchange must be made, the entire data structure (such as a complete record) is transferred. For example, you might have a simple mailing list that includes the following consecutive array entries:

Josephs, Phil, 999 Fortyniner St., Wembly, CA 99999
Jones, Trinka, 1234 Jackson Ave., Santa Park, CA 99998
Joshkin, Joe, 987 Ford St., Freos, CA 99997

If the sort key for an ascending alphabetical sort is the last name, the comparisons would find that Jones should be exchanged with Josephs. To do this, the entire records for Jones and Josephs would be exchanged. The new order would be

Jones, Trinka, 1234 Jackson Ave., Santa Park, CA 99998
Josephs, Phil, 999 Fortyniner St., Wembly, CA 99999
Joshkin, Joe, 987 Ford St., Freos, CA 99997

Classes of Sorting Algorithms

Arrays are usually sorted by the exchange, selection, or insertion method. All of these methods are described in the following section, which uses a deck of cards for purposes of illustration.

1. **Exchange**   Spread a deck of cards on a table face up. Exchange cards that are out of order until the deck is ordered correctly.

2. **Selection**   Spread the deck of cards on the table again (face up, of course). Select the lowest valued card, take it out of the deck, and hold it in your hand. Then take the lowest card from those that remain on the table. Place it in your hand behind the previously selected card. Repeat this process until you hold the entire sorted deck in your hand.

3. **Insertion**   Hold the deck in your hand. Take out a card and place it on the table. Take another card from the deck in your hand and insert it in an ordered position in the new deck being built on the table. When no cards are left in your hand, the deck on the table is completely ordered.

Judging Sorting Algorithms

Many algorithms have been developed over the years for each of the three sorting methods. The best algorithm to use will vary from situation to situation. To decide which algorithm you should use, apply the following criteria:

1. First, decide the necessary *speed* of the algorithm. The speed of a sorting algorithm is directly related to the number of comparisons it makes and the number of exchanges it requires. An exchange takes more time than a comparison. Algorithm speed varies according to how disordered the array is before it is sorted. The *best case* is when an array requires no exchanges (it is already ordered). The *worst case* array requires the maximum number of exchanges. Most cases lie somewhere between these two extremes. A sorting algorithm may perform average cases quickly, but worst cases very slowly. On the other hand, it may perform worst cases quickly and average cases slowly.

2. Second, determine whether a sorting algorithm has a *natural* or *unnatural behavior*. A natural sort works easily when the list is already in order, harder when the list is less ordered, and

hardest when the list is in inverse order. The difficulty is based on the number of comparisons and exchanges that the sort performs.

3. Third, determine whether the algorithm rearranges elements with *equal keys*. For example, you might sort the previous mailing list example by using the person's last name as a *main key*. Then you might use the ZIP code as a *sub key*. If you add a new address to the mailing list and then resort it, you want to sort primarily on the main key. You do not want it to be rearranged by sub key.

SORTING ALGORITHMS

One of the QuickBASIC distribution disks contains a program called SORTDEMO.BAS that graphically demonstrates six common sorting algorithms. The program first looks at the video adapter installed in your system. Then, depending on the installed adapter, it randomly prints 25 or 43 horizontal bars of different lengths. Next, you select one of the following six sorting routines: insertion, bubble, heap, exchange, Shell, and quick. When you select a routine, the program uses that method to sort the bars from shortest to longest.

The program incorporates SOUND statements using different pitches. These statements slow down the sort so that you can follow each step of the process. They also add to the time needed to perform the sorts. This destroys the accuracy of the execution times displayed at the end of the sort. However, by running each sort, you can get a general idea of their relative speeds for a short sort. Also remember that the time needed to complete a sort depends on the number of elements to be sorted and the amount of "scrambling" achieved by the program's random ordering.

If you are unfamiliar with one or more of these six sorting routines, load the SORTDEMO program. Each of the sorting routines is written as a separate subprogram. Use the SUBs command from the View menu to access the routines you wish to examine. Microsoft has included enough remarks to give you some idea of how the sorting routines are implemented. Discussions in this chapter are limited to the bubble, insertion, and quick sorting methods.

Bubble Sort

The *bubble sort* is probably the best known of all sorting routines because of its simplicity and its name, which creates a visual image that matches the way it works. It uses the exchange method of sorting, making comparisons and exchanging adjacent elements when necessary so the elements seem to bubble their way to the correct level in the ordering process. Even though the bubble sort is simple and well known, it sorts large numbers of elements inefficiently.

The following QuickBASIC bubble sort subprogram is used in this chapter to sort a set of randomly generated five-letter words:

```
SUB BubSort (Nayme$())
   DEFINT A-Z
   count = UBOUND(Nayme$)
   upper = count - 1
begin: flag = 0
   FOR num = 1 TO upper
      IF Nayme$(num) > Nayme$(num + 1) THEN
         SWAP Nayme$(num), Nayme$(num + 1)
         flag = num
      END IF
   NEXT num
   upper = flag
   IF flag THEN GOTO begin
END SUB
```

The bubble sort loops through this array of words, swapping the positions of words that are out of alphabetical order. The number of loop executions is controlled by a flag that is a positive number if two words are swapped during a pass through the loop. If no words are swapped, the value of the flag is zero. This ensures that every element is in its proper position at the end of the sort, even in the worst case condition.

The number of comparisons made in a bubble sort of a given array is always the same for the worst case, the average case, and the best case. The two loops always repeat the specified number of times whether the original list is ordered or not. The outer loop is performed $n-1$ times and the inner loop $n/2$ times. Multiply $n-1$ by $n/2$ to find the number of comparisons that are made.

No exchanges are made in a best case condition. In the worst case condition, $3(n-1)n/2$ exchanges are made. The average case falls midway between these two values, or $3(n-1)n/4$ exchanges. The bubble sort is very inefficient when sorting an array with a large number of elements because execution time is directly related to the number of comparisons and exchanges.

Program 8-1 demonstrates how to use a variation of the bubble sort. The main program builds a list of 100 five-letter combinations that are called words. The character codes for the letters that form the words are chosen at random by a user-defined function called DEF FNrndchr%. The words are assigned as elements of the array named *Nayme$* and are printed in five columns across the screen. A typical word list is shown in Figure 8-1.

After the word list is printed, the program prompts you to press a key to sort the list. When you do this the subprogram BubSort is called to perform the sorting. This subprogram swaps out of order names until the list is completely ordered in bubble fashion.

When the list is sorted, as shown in Figure 8-2, program control is returned to the main program, which then prints the sorted list. You may want to wrap some timing statements around the sorting routine to compare the bubble sort with other types.

Insertion Sort

The *insertion sort* is used extensively because it is also simple. This type of sort starts by sorting the first two elements in an array. It inserts the third element into its proper position relative to the first two elements. Then it inserts the fourth element into

```
DECLARE SUB BubSort (Nayme$())
REM ** WORD SCRAMBLER AND BUBBLE SORT **
' Program 8-1   File:PRO0801.BAS
' Generates random 5-letter words & invokes bubble sort

REM ** Define Function and Variables **
' FNrndchr% returns a random character code
DEF FNrndchr% = INT(RND(1) * 26 + 65)
DEFINT A-Z

REM ** Main Program **
DIM Nayme$(100)
CLS
RANDOMIZE TIMER
FOR num = 1 TO 100
  word$ = ""
  FOR addletter = 1 TO 5
    word$ = word$ + CHR$(FNrndchr%)
  NEXT addletter
  Nayme$(num) = word$
  PRINT word$,
NEXT num
PRINT
LOCATE 24, 2: PRINT "Press a key to sort the words";
ky$ = INPUT$(1)
CALL BubSort(Nayme$())
LOCATE 24, 2: PRINT SPACE$(30); : PRINT
FOR num = 1 TO 100
  PRINT Nayme$(num),
NEXT num
END

SUB BubSort (Nayme$())
  DEFINT A-Z
  count = UBOUND(Nayme$)
  upper = count - 1
begin: flag = 0
  FOR num = 1 TO upper
    IF Nayme$(num) > Nayme$(num + 1) THEN
      SWAP Nayme$(num), Nayme$(num + 1)
      flag = num
    END IF
  NEXT num
  upper = flag
  IF flag THEN GOTO begin
END SUB
```

Program 8-1.   Word Scrambler and Bubble Sort

ZWBJD	HNDTD	DXWXW	WRMIG	KWRQD
HUMGE	QAXRU	HSOQO	UXETD	JOKZT
UQRRN	QQIEA	QYLWJ	EVSCR	QUTEY
UGPEN	VRRCA	LOGOI	WUPGA	QJGKT
UAFLQ	WRCRB	MWGDG	TZQPC	YEFYR
LFZYU	UOKYE	ENWRW	ACFBH	ZTUCR
LXUUL	QKYSM	ESGJK	XHRKD	FGUDE
VYFNJ	WYVGF	EXZID	JXBYD	GJIJP
INPKM	PEUHR	UPWUN	WDCUF	YLXUP
JQJTO	EOHZC	MQWZO	HGXRP	UJJRO
LLUGD	XWWDY	EBMGJ	JZQVI	JWBXB
TPECK	VJCUL	AWUXJ	VBDFC	HPQNA
OMCIP	NQZJL	NQPNC	NKCVG	SVAXD
KTJZR	AUJQZ	QYAUN	MYKSB	XRREY
UUHBA	RTBHD	NJTDT	FUKCG	XNMDO
IGKDM	IXQET	BBLMP	MGIQZ	EHRIH
CFGDV	JSCDY	TBJLB	ABRML	WLBJJ
KBBMJ	IZZSB	NDCRS	VKUOW	XUYHU
NTLYW	CSOEZ	XSPCU	TRUWS	FUISO
EHTUR	LLMPT	NQEIZ	QCADX	HODHG

Press a key to sort the words

Figure 8-1.   Scrambled word list

ABRML	ACFBH	AUJQZ	AWUXJ	BBLMP
CFGDV	CSOEZ	DXWXW	EBMGJ	EHRIH
EHTUR	ENWRW	EOHZC	ESGJK	EVSCR
EXZID	FGUDE	FUISO	FUKCG	GJIJP
HGXRP	HNDTD	HODHG	HPQNA	HSOQO
HUMGE	IGKDM	INPKM	IXQET	IZZSB
JOKZT	JQJTO	JSCDY	JWBXB	JXBYD
JZQVI	KBBMJ	KTJZR	KWRQD	LFZYU
LLMPT	LLUGD	LOGOI	LXUUL	MGIQZ
MQWZO	MWGDG	MYKSB	NDCRS	NJTDT
NKCVG	NQEIZ	NQPNC	NQZJL	NTLYW
OMCIP	PEUHR	QAXRU	QCADX	QJGKT
QKYSM	QQIEA	QUTEY	QYAUN	QYLWJ
RTBHD	SVAXD	TBJLB	TPECK	TRUWS
TZQPC	UAFLQ	UGPEN	UJJRO	UOKYE
UQRRN	UXETD	VBDFC	VJCUL	VKUOW
UPWUN	URRCA	VUHBA	VYFNJ	WDCUF
WLBJJ	WRCRB	WRMIG	WUPGA	WYVGF
XHRKD	XNMDO	XRREY	XSPCU	XUYHU
XWWDY	YEFYR	YLXUP	ZTUCR	ZWBJD

Press any key to continue

Figure 8-2.   Words sorted by bubble sort

the list of three elements at its ordered place. It continues this process until the array is completely ordered. A version of the insertion sort is shown in the next listing.

```
SUB InsertSort (Sort$(), count%)
  DEFINT A-Z
  FOR num = 2 TO count
    top = num - 1
    starter$ = Sort$(num)
    first$ = Sort$(num)
    WHILE starter$ < Sort$(top) AND top > 0
      Sort$(top + 1) = Sort$(top)
      top = top - 1
    WEND
    Sort$(top + 1) = starter$
  NEXT num
END SUB
```

Suppose you use this listing to sort the following four randomly ordered five-letter words:

ORANJ APPUL BANAN GRAPE

After each pass of the insertion sort, the list would be rearranged as follows:

	1	2	3	4	Change
Initial order	ORANJ	APPUL	BANAN	GRAPE	
After 1 pass	APPUL	ORANJ	BANAN	GRAPE	1 & 2
After 2 passes	APPUL	BANAN	ORANJ	GRAPE	2 & 3
After 3 passes	APPUL	BANAN	GRAPE	ORANJ	3 & 4

Unlike the bubble sort, the number of comparisons made by the insertion sort depends on the degree of disorder in the original list. The number of exchanges it makes for the worst case is comparable to those made by the bubble sort, both high. The number of exchanges it makes for the average case is only slightly better than the number made by the bubble sort.

The insertion sort has two advantages over the bubble sort. The first advantage is that it behaves *naturally*. That is, it works least when the array is already sorted and most when the array is in inverse order. Therefore, it is very useful for lists that are almost in order, such as when you have added some entries to a presorted mailing list. The insertion sort would quickly reorder the list. The second advantage is that the insertion sort leaves the order of equal keys unchanged.

Program 8-2 uses the same main program as Program 8-1. However, an insertion sort subprogram has replaced the previous bubble sort subprogram. Running this program with the sample list shown in Figure 8-3 results in the ordered list shown in Figure 8-4.

Both the bubble sort and the insertion sort are called n-squared algorithms because their execution times are a multiple of the square of the number of elements in the sorted array. Figure 8-5 shows the exponential growth of the execution time as the number of array elements increases.

HEOMS	TORAM	MMAQC	WQUST	UVHNL
OKIQG	UFGVU	YSTON	WUUQM	OKOML
EEAVM	KGRMR	RASST	EIWNO	KDQSU
XTHQU	WSBRH	UXXMT	ZFIGL	DUBKL
RPVEI	ZTNJE	OHWMQ	IFFIR	DSBDC
KSCML	GUSGR	IAPAO	XRXRL	RDKGM
NJILB	PMWIH	TFGCD	YRGSL	UFVEN
ORGWZ	YYGQA	WFSCA	CIRGP	MNBPM
KKLQS	CDROA	EGWBI	DHXWS	JHTXH
NPEIA	HXFLD	ZBVNP	DYGJN	FNMCK
GSYCD	QPWPG	EFLZC	LHKLT	NBLYK
LLVQL	OIRWG	UYFRF	TXOBY	LCHBB
IJWRO	XYSDH	LPQPK	IWWAH	NMMHA
ZMXHW	UDHZK	CKSDG	FZRPK	BSGIQ
DMFOY	OBJXB	REUTX	AVADH	FHCJE
CXQXU	EOCNS	KNWFP	YPGAG	BPYYB
ROOXK	USTCG	GEXBP	ZCVKJ	ADJCC
JOFZC	OXDLJ	IQUBG	CUBMB	MNPJU
YFAJB	GGCXK	OXLEN	UYRHQ	ZGXEO
WEHPY	OHKPT	QRSRD	QUWUK	NVMPC

Press a key to sort the words

Figure 8-3.   Scrambled words for insertion sort

```
DECLARE SUB InsertSort (Sort$(), count%)
REM ** WORD SCRAMBLER AND INSERTION SORT **
' Program 8-2   File:PRO0802.BAS
' Generates random 5-letter words & invokes insertion sort

REM ** Define Function & Variables **
' FNrndchr% returns a random character code
DEF FNrndchr% = INT(RND(1) * 26 + 65)
DEFINT A-Z

REM ** Main Program **
DIM Sort$(100)
CLS
RANDOMIZE TIMER: count = 100
FOR num = 1 TO 100
  word$ = ""
  FOR addletter = 1 TO 5
    word$ = word$ + CHR$(FNrndchr%)
  NEXT addletter
  Sort$(num) = word$
  PRINT word$,
NEXT num
PRINT
LOCATE 24, 2: PRINT "Press a key to sort the words";
ky$ = INPUT$(1)
CALL InsertSort(Sort$(), count%)
LOCATE 24, 2: PRINT SPACE$(30); : PRINT
FOR num = 1 TO 100
  PRINT Sort$(num),
NEXT num
END

SUB InsertSort (Sort$(), count%)
  DEFINT A-Z
  FOR num = 2 TO count
    top = num - 1
    starter$ = Sort$(num)
    first$ = Sort$(num)
    WHILE starter$ < Sort$(top) AND top > 0
      Sort$(top + 1) = Sort$(top)
      top = top - 1
    WEND
    Sort$(top + 1) = starter$
  NEXT num
END SUB
```

Program 8-2.   Word Scrambler and Insertion Sort

```
ADJCC      AVADH      BPYYB      BSGIQ      CDROA
CIRGP      CKSDG      CUBMB      CXQXU      DHXWS
DMFOY      DSBDC      DVBKL      DYGJN      EEAVM
EFLZC      EGWBI      EIWNO      EOCMS      FHCJE
FNNCK      FZRPK      GEXBP      GGCXK      GSYCD
GUSGR      HEOMS      HXFLD      IAPAO      IFFIR
IJWRO      IQUBG      IWWAH      JHTXH      JOFZC
KDQSU      KGRNR      KKLQS      KNWFP      KSCML
LCHBB      LHKLT      LLVQL      LPQPK      MMAQC
MNBPN      MNPJV      NBLYK      NJILB      NMMHA
NPEIA      NVNPC      OBJXB      OHKPT      OHWMQ
OIRWG      OKIQG      OKOML      ORGWZ      OXDLJ
OXLEN      PMWIH      QPWPG      QRSRD      QUWUK
RASST      RDKGN      REUTX      ROOXK      RPUEI
TFGCD      TORAM      TXOBY      UDHZK      UFGVV
UFVEN      UVHNL      UYFRF      UYRHQ      VSTCG
VXXMT      WEHPY      WFSCA      WQVST      WSBRH
WVUQM      XRXRL      XTHQV      XYSDH      YFAJB
YPGAG      YRGSL      YSTON      YYGQA      ZBVNP
ZCVKJ      ZFIGL      ZGXEO      ZMXHW      ZTNJE

Press any key to continue
```

Figure 8-4.   Words sorted by insertion sort

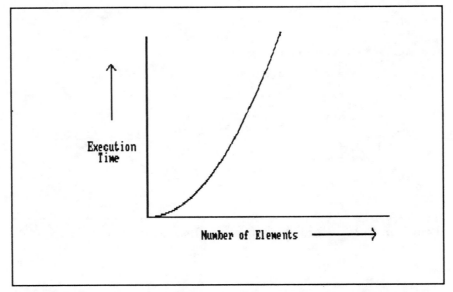

Figure 8-5.   Growth of execution time

Program 8-3 allows you to enter the number of elements for an array to be sorted. A FOR...NEXT loop containing a PRINT USING statement accepts the elements of your array. The number symbol (#) represents a digit of the entry number. Since the array has been dimensioned for 99 elements, two number symbols (##) are used to hold places for a two-digit number.

```
PRINT USING "##: "; num;
INPUT Element$(num)
```

```
DECLARE SUB InsertSort (Sort$(), count%)
REM ** ENTER ARRAY AND INSERTION SORT **
' Program 8-3   File:PRO0803.BAS

REM ** Initialize **
DIM Element$(99)
DEFINT A-Z
CLS

REM ** Get Data **
INPUT "How many elements in your list "; count
FOR num = 1 TO count
  PRINT USING "##: "; num;
  INPUT Element$(num)
NEXT num
CALL InsertSort(Element$(), count%)
FOR num = 1 TO count
  PRINT Element$(num)
NEXT num
END


SUB InsertSort (Sort$(), count%) STATIC
  DEFINT A-Z
  FOR num = 2 TO count
    top = num - 1
    starter$ = Sort$(num): Temp$ = UCASE$(Sort$(num))
    first$ = Sort$(num)
    WHILE Temp$ < UCASE$(Sort$(top)) AND top > 0
      Sort$(top + 1) = Sort$(top)
    top = top - 1
    WEND
    Sort$(top + 1) = first$
  NEXT num
END SUB
```

Program 8-3.   Enter Array and Insertion Sort

The elements of the array can be strings or numbers. You can change the DIM statement and add # characters to the PRINT USING statement to increase the size of the array.

The sort subprogram was written generically so that you may include it in a library and use it with any program. The program using the sort subprogram must pass the array and its element count when it calls the subprogram. Notice that the UCASE$ function makes the comparisons case insensitive. Therefore, it does not matter whether you enter your array elements in upper case, lower case, or a mixture of the two. The subprogram makes all comparisons in upper case, but moves the elements as they were entered, leaving their form (upper, lower, or mixed case) unchanged.

Quicksort

The *quicksort* was created and named by C.A.R. Hoare. The quicksort and bubble sort are both based on the exchange method of sorting. Yet the quicksort is generally considered the best sorting algorithm available, while the bubble sort is considered one of the worst.

The main difference between the two methods is that the quicksort process sorts the array using the concept of partitioning. The quicksort process first selects a value called the *comparand*. It then partitions the array into two parts. All the elements greater than or equal to the comparand are placed in one part, and those less than the comparand are placed in the other part. It continues this partitioning process on each part (two parts into four parts, four parts into eight parts, and so on) until the array is completely sorted.

You can use various ways to select the comparand. The ideal value is located in the middle of the range of the elements. However, this value is not easy to locate for most arrays. Even in the worst case, where an element at one end is selected, the quicksort still performs reasonably well. You can choose the comparand by averaging a small set of values selected from the array or even by choosing a random element from the array.

The process of subdividing the array in a quicksort algorithm is *recursive*. QuickBASIC versions 4.0 and 4.5 allow recursion, which is the ability of a procedure to *call itself*. Recursion is useful for solving certain problems such as sorting, especially the partitioning technique used by quicksort.

You should remember certain cautions when you are using the recursive process. Recursion must always have a terminating condition so that the computer cannot end up in an infinite loop. Recursion can also use a lot of memory, since QuickBASIC saves each set of automatic variables used in a procedure on the stack. Saving these variables allows a procedure to continue with the correct variable values after control returns from a recursive call. See Section 3.9, "Recursive Procedures," in your *Programming in BASIC* manual for a more complete discussion of recursion. This section also discusses how to adjust the size of the stack to alleviate memory space problems.

Program 8-4 uses a variation of the Microsoft Quicksort subprogram included on one of the distribution disks in your QuickBASIC package. The main program allows you to enter the

```
DECLARE SUB QuickSort (sort$(), low%, high%)
REM ** QUICKSORT DEMO **
' Program 8-4   File: PRO0804.BAS

REM ** Initialize **
DIM SHARED sort$(1 TO 50)
DEFINT A-Z: CLS

REM ** Define Function & Variables **
' FNrndchr$ returns a random character from a string
DEF FNrndchr$ (strng$) = MID$(strng$, INT(LEN(strng$)
* RND(1)) + 1, 1)
```

Program 8-4.   Quicksort Demo

```
REM ** Main Program **
' Define strings
letter$ = "ABCDEFGHIJKLMNOPQRSTUVWXYZ"
CLS
RANDOMIZE TIMER
INPUT "Number of elements"; count
FOR num = 1 TO count
  word$ = ""
  FOR addletter = 1 TO 5
    word$ = word$ + FNrndchr$(letter$)
  NEXT addletter
  sort$(num) = word$
  PRINT word$,
NEXT num
PRINT
LOCATE 24, 2: PRINT "Press a key to sort the words";
ky$ = INPUT$(1)
LOCATE 24, 2: PRINT SPACE$(30); : PRINT
CALL QuickSort(sort$(), 1, count)
PRINT
FOR num = 1 TO count
  PRINT sort$(num),
NEXT num
END

DEFINT A-Z
SUB QuickSort (sort$(), left%, right%)
  IF right > left THEN
    count1 = left - 1: count2 = right
    DO
      DO
        count1 = count1 + 1
      LOOP WHILE (sort$(count1) < sort$(right))
      DO
        count2 = count2 - 1
      LOOP WHILE (sort$(count2) > sort$(right)) AND count2 > 0
      temp$ = sort$(count1)
      sort$(count1) = sort$(count2)
      sort$(count2) = temp$
    LOOP WHILE count2 > count1
    sort$(count2) = sort$(count1)
    sort$(count1) = sort$(right)
    QuickSort sort$(), left, count1 - 1
    QuickSort sort$(), count1 + 1, right
  END IF
END SUB
```

Programs 8-4.   Quicksort Demo (*continued*)

number of elements you want in an unsorted array. The program prints this unsorted list. When you press a key, the subprogram quickly sorts the array. When control is returned to the main program, it prints the sorted array.

SEARCHING

You create an array to provide easier access to related information that you expect to use. Therefore, you will sometimes want to locate and use information from this array. You can search the array and find individual elements by providing a *key* for the search. This section discusses two searching methods. You need to use a *sequential* search to find an element of an unsorted array. You can use a *binary* search, which is much faster than a sequential search, to find an element of a sorted array.

Sequential Search

A sequential search begins by comparing the first element in the array with the search key. The search continues, element by element, until it finds a match or reaches the end of the array. A sequential search algorithm is short and easy to code. To implement the search you need only an array, the number of elements in the array, and a search key.

The following subprogram searches an array containing a known number of elements until it finds a match or reaches the end of the file. The subprogram must be passed the array, *Sort$( )*; the key for searching, *SearchKey$*; and the number of elements in the array, *count%*.

```
SUB SequenSearch (Sort$(), SearchKey$, count%)
  DEFINT A-Z
  flag = 0
  FOR num = 1 to count
    IF SearchKey$ = Sort$(num) THEN
```

```
      PRINT Sort$(num); " is item number"; num
      flag = 1: EXIT FOR
    END IF
  NEXT num
  IF flag = 0 THEN PRINT SearchKey$; " was not found"
END SUB
```

Suppose you have a program containing the following ten unordered elements in an array:

DOG BAKER INDEX ABLE HANDY GOFOR
CHARLEY JERSEY FOX EASY

Your program first requests that you enter a search key. After you enter the search key, it calls the subprogram. The subprogram begins the search by comparing your search key with the entry DOG. If your search key matches DOG, it prints the entry and its numbered position in the list and then ends. If the key does not match DOG, the subprogram compares the key with the next entry. It continues this process until it finds a match or reaches the end of the list.

The subprogram uses a flag to determine whether a match has been found. It sets the flag to zero before the search begins. If it finds a match in the IF clause of the IF...END IF structure of the subprogram, it sets the flag to one (1) after it prints the item and its number. The QuickBASIC EXIT FOR statement then passes execution control to the statement following the FOR...NEXT loop, as shown in the following listing:

```
IF flag = 0 THEN PRINT SearchKey$; " was not found"
```

If it finds a match, it sets the flag to 1. Therefore, it does not execute the THEN clause (PRINT SearchKey$; "was not found") and so ends.

If it does not find a match, it exits the FOR...NEXT loop after it compares the last element of the array with the search key. The flag is still set to zero, and the line following the loop prints the fact that your search key was not found.

A straight sequential search tests only one element of the array in the best case and tests all elements of the array in the worst case. The average case tests half the number of elements in the array. Large arrays may take a significant amount of time to search sequentially. However, for unsorted arrays, a sequential search is the only method available.

Binary Search

If the data in the array has been sorted, you can use a binary search to find an element in the array. A binary search is much faster than a sequential search because it does not search each element of the array. Instead, it tests an element in the middle of the data. This test produces one of the following three results:

1. The middle element is larger than the key. If so, the program tests the middle element of the first half of the array.
2. The middle element is less than the key. If so, the program tests the middle element of the last half of the array.
3. The middle element is the same as the search key. If so, the match has been found, and the program ends.

   If either of the first two results occur, the testing process is continued until there are no more elements to test, or the third result occurs. The following listing shows an example of a binary search subprogram:

```
SUB Binsearch (Sort$(), SearchKey$, count%, flag%) STATIC
   DEFINT A-Z
   low = 0
   high = count + 1
   WHILE ABS(low - high) > 1
      mid = INT((low + high) / 2)
      Temp$ = UCASE$(Sort$(mid))
      IF SearchKey$ > Temp$ THEN
         low = mid
      ELSEIF SearchKey$ < Temp$ THEN
         high = mid
      ELSE
         flag = INT(mid)
         low = high
      END IF
   WEND
END SUB
```

Suppose you have the ten elements used previously in the sequential search. This time the elements have been sorted as follows:

ABLE
BAKER
CHARLEY
DOG
EASY
FOX
GOFOR
HANDY
INDEX
JERSEY

If you entered CHARLEY as the search key, the binary search would be carried out in the following way:

First Test	Second Test	Third Test	
ABLE	ABLE	ABLE	
BAKER	**BAKER**	BAKER	
CHARLEY	CHARLEY	**CHARLEY**	Match in third try
DOG	DOG	DOG	
EASY	EASY	EASY	
FOX	FOX	FOX	
GOFOR	GOFOR	GOFOR	
HANDY	HANDY	HANDY	
INDEX	INDEX	INDEX	
JERSEY	JERSEY	JERSEY	

EASY is selected for the first test from the integer calculation INT((0 + 10) / 2) = 5. BAKER is selected for the second test since INT((0 + 5) / 2) = 2. CHARLEY is selected for the third test since INT((2 + 5) / 2) = 3.

In the best case situation (when you are searching for the middle element), the program makes only one test. The worst case for a binary search is log(base 2) of the number of elements. The average case lies somewhere between those two extremes.

Program 8-5 allows you to enter up to 99 elements in an array. After you have entered all of them, the following FOR...NEXT loop shuffles the array:

```
FOR num = 1 TO count
  rndindex = INT(count * RND(1)) + 1
  SWAP Element$(num), Element$(rndindex)
NEXT num
```

The program prints the shuffled array, and then asks you to press a key to sort the array. When you do so, it calls an insertion sort routine to sort the array. After sorting, the program stops again and requests that you enter a search key. After you enter the search key, the binary search subprogram is called to look for a match in the array.

If the subprogram finds a match, it prints the element and its position in the array. If it does not find a match, it prints this fact. You can then choose to search the same array again or end the program. To enter a new array, end the program and restart it.

This chapter has presented some of the most common search and sort algorithms used with arrays. Searching and sorting arrays are straightforward processes, but more complicated structures require different techniques. The next chapter discusses the techniques used to manipulate information in the structures used in data files.

```
DECLARE SUB Binsearch (Sort$(), SearchKey$, count%, flag%)
DECLARE SUB InsertSort (Sort$(), count%)
REM ** SHUFFLE, INSERTION SORT, AND BINARY SEARCH **
' Program 8-5  File:PRO0805.BAS

REM ** Initialize **
DIM Element$(99)
DEFINT A-Z
CLS
```

Program 8-5.   Shuffle, Insertion Sort, and Binary Search

```
REM ** Get Data **
INPUT "How many elements in your list "; count
FOR num = 1 TO count
  PRINT USING "##: "; num;
  INPUT "", Element$(num)
NEXT num
FOR num = 1 TO count
  rndindex = INT(count * RND(1)) + 1
  SWAP Element$(num), Element$(rndindex)
NEXT num

REM ** Print Shuffled Array, Sort, and Search **
CLS
FOR num = 1 TO count
  PRINT Element$(num),
NEXT num
LOCATE 19, 2: PRINT "Press a key to sort array";
ky$ = INPUT$(1)
CALL InsertSort(Element$(), count%)
begin: CLS
  PRINT "Enter your search key : ";
  INPUT ; "", Kee$: SearchKey$ = UCASE$(Kee$)
  flag = 0
  CALL Binsearch(Element$(), SearchKey$, count%, flag%)
  IF flag > 0 THEN
    PRINT : PRINT Kee$; " is element number "; flag
  ELSE
    PRINT : PRINT Kee$; " was not found"
  END IF
  PRINT : PRINT
  PRINT "Press Q to quit, any other key to search again."
  ky$ = INPUT$(1)
  IF INSTR("Q,q", ky$) = 0 THEN GOTO begin
END

DEFINT A-Z
SUB Binsearch (Sort$(), SearchKey$, count%, flag%) STATIC
  DEFINT A-Z
  low = 0
  high = count + 1
  WHILE ABS(low - high) > 1
    mid = INT((low + high) / 2)
    Temp$ = UCASE$(Sort$(mid))
    IF SearchKey$ > Temp$ THEN
      low = mid
    ELSEIF SearchKey$ < Temp$ THEN
      high = mid
    ELSE
      flag = INT(mid)
      low = high
```

Program 8-5.   Shuffle, Insertion Sort, and Binary Search (*continued*)

```
      END IF
   WEND
END SUB

SUB InsertSort (Sort$(), count%) STATIC
   DEFINT A-Z
   FOR num = 2 TO count
      top = num - 1
      starter$ = Sort$(num): Temp$ = UCASE$(Sort$(num))
      first$ = Sort$(num)
      WHILE Temp$ < UCASE$(Sort$(top)) AND top > 0
         Sort$(top + 1) = Sort$(top)
         top = top - 1
      WEND
      Sort$(top + 1) = first$
   NEXT num
END SUB
```

Program 8-5.   Shuffle, Insertion Sort, and Binary Search (*continued*)

9

INDEXED AND
KEYED FILES

In Chapter 8 you learned how to use various sorting and searching techniques to reorganize and access information. Since computers are routinely used to store very large amounts of data for later retrieval, this is potentially very useful information. The discussion of binary searches in the last chapter also showed you that a sorted list of information allows much more rapid information access than accessing a file one record at a time.

This and the following chapters extend sorting and searching techniques to disk files. If a disk file is small enough, you may read it into memory and treat it as an array. However, many disk files are too large to be manipulated in memory and therefore require you to use special sort and search techniques.

There are two types of disk files, sequential files and random access files. You use different methods to manipulate the data in these two types of files. Sequential files are discussed in Chapter 11. This chapter and the next discuss only random access files.

Random access files are used for most microcomputer data base applications. They have the following three advantages over sequential files:

1. They are easy to maintain. You can add, delete, and update data without copying the entire file.

2. They can be treated as a huge array on disk, which simplifies sorting and searching.

3. They do not require that both the unsorted and sorted files be stored on the disk when sorting.

INDEXED DATA FILES

A random access file usually has several fields in a record. For example, consider a mailing list data file. Each record might contain five fields such as name, street, city, state, and ZIP code. There may be thousands of records in the file.

Sorting such a large file each time you need information is unnecessary and tedious. In addition, you may need to sort data on more than one field, which requires more than one sort. But you do not want to destroy the original file. You can avoid this by maintaining sorted files of *pointers*, such as record numbers, instead of sorting the complete file. This leaves the original file undisturbed.

A list of pointers sorted on the order of the data in a particular field of the records is called an *index*. Thus, the indexed files discussed in this chapter are those random access data files for which an index has been created.

Let's use a portion of a mailing list in a data file called ADDRESS.DAT as an example. Suppose that, as each item is entered, it is assigned a record number, as shown in Table 9-1.

You can create a separate indexed file of the record numbers. Then, instead of moving records in the original file when you are sorting, you can move the corresponding record numbers. This can speed up the sorting process, especially when the files contain many fields in their records. In this example, the list of sorted index numbers would be 5, 3, 1, 2, 4.

Record Number	Name
1	Jones E
2	Smith R
3	Johnson C
4	Zebra S
5	Alpha B

Table 9-1.   Record Numbers and Names in the Sample File

Each record number acts as a place holder, pointing at the file entry that would appear in its place. Since the first record number (or index) appearing in the sorted list is 5, the fifth entry (Alpha B) would be first in an ordered list of names. The record numbers in the indexed file are called *pointers* because they point at the correct entry in the original file for sorting on the name field.

The following illustration shows the list of original entries and the sorted index numbers or pointers. Each pointer indicates the number of the original entry to be selected for a list of records ordered by the name field.

Original List	Sorted Index
Jones E	5
Smith R	3
Johnson C	1
Zebra S	2
Alpha B	4

You might refer to a new file containing the pointers as NAME.NDX. In this file name NAME is the sort field and NDX indicates that the file is an index file.

Creating an Index List

Program 9-1 illustrates the use of pointers with arrays, since they are simpler than data files. The original array is also simplified by entering only the names of the would-be records. The program allows up to 1000 name entries. For this example, five names are entered, as shown in the following listing:

```
How many elements in your list? 5
  1: ? Jones E
  2: ? Smith R
  3: ? Johnson C
  4: ? Zebra S
  5: ? Alpha B
```

As the entries are made in the Input Data and Create Index block of the program, a separate array of record numbers (*Ke%(entry)*)) is created by the FOR...NEXT loop shown in the next listing:

```
FOR entry = 1 to num
   Ke$(entry) = entry                ' Record numbers
   PRINT USING "##: "; entry;
   INPUT Nayme$(entry)               ' Name
NEXT entry
```

The names are assigned as elements of the *Nayme$* array, and the record numbers are assigned as elements of the *Ke%* array.

After all the entries have been made, the program calls the InsertKeSort subprogram. The program passes both arrays as well as the number of elements to the subprogram. Since the entries are simple and relatively few in number, an insertion sort was used in this program. However, a quicksort would be faster.

Notice that this sort compares the actual names, but only changes the order of the record numbers. It leaves the original array unchanged. This process is performed by the following program lines:

```
WHILE Temp$ < Sort$(Ke%(order)) AND order > 0
  Ke%(order + 1) = Ke%(order)
  order = order - 1
WEND
Ke%(order + 1) = Temp
```

You can also create individual indexed files for other fields of the ADDRESS.DAT file. Table 9-2 shows the example mailing list with the city entries added.

If you used the subprogram now to sort on the city field instead of the name field, the new index order would be 3, 5, 2, 1, 4. You could name this file CITY.NDX to distinguish it from the previous NAME.NDX. Once again, the original data file would remain unchanged.

You can continue to create sorted indexed files until you have the following files:

ADDRESS.DAT   The original data file containing unsorted records with fields for name, street, city, state, and ZIP code

NAME.NDX   A file of record numbers sorted by the name field

STREET.NDX   A file of record numbers sorted by the street field

CITY.NDX   A file of record numbers sorted by the city field

STATE.NDX   A file of record numbers sorted by the state field

ZIP.NDX   A file of record numbers sorted by the ZIP code field

Indexing is particularly well suited to data bases used to generate reports. The presorted indexed files make it easy to quickly generate a report with the data sorted on any field of the random access data file.

Run Program 9-1 a few times to create your own lists of names and see the indexes generated. Then change the Print Original

```
DECLARE SUB InsertKeSort (sort$(), Ke%(), num%)
REM ** Indexed Insertion Sort **
' Sort on an index, leaving the
' original data untouched.
' Program 9-1  File: PRO0901.BAS

REM ** Initialize **
DIM Nayme$(1000), Ke(1000) AS INTEGER
CLS : DEFINT A-Z

REM ** Input Data and Create Index **
INPUT "How many elements in your list "; num

REM ** Initialize Key Array **
FOR entry = 1 TO num
  Ke%(entry) = entry
  PRINT USING "##: "; entry;
  INPUT Nayme$(entry)
NEXT entry

REM ** Sort Index Array **
CALL InsertKeSort(Nayme$(), Ke%(), num%)

REM ** Print Original List; Sorted Index Numbers **
PRINT : PRINT : PRINT "Original"; TAB(23); "Sorted"
PRINT "  List"; TAB(23); "Index": PRINT
FOR order = 1 TO num
  PRINT Nayme$(order); TAB(25); Ke%(order)
NEXT order
END


SUB InsertKeSort (sort$(), Ke%(), num%) STATIC
DEFINT A-Z
FOR count = 2 TO num
    order = count - 1
    Temp$ = sort$(Ke%(count))
    Temp = Ke%(count)
    WHILE Temp$ < sort$(Ke%(order)) AND order > 0
      Ke%(order + 1) = Ke%(order)
      order = order - 1
    WEND
    Ke%(order + 1) = Temp
NEXT count
END SUB
```

Program 9-1.   Indexed Insertion Sort

Record Number	Name	City
1	Jones E	New York
2	Smith R	Chicago
3	Johnson C	Atlanta
4	Zebra S	San Jose
5	Alpha B	Berkeley

Table 9-2.   Record Numbers, Name, and Cities in the Sample File

List; Sorted Index Numbers block of the program to read as follows:

```
REM ** Print Lists: Original, Index, Final **
PRINT : PRINT : PRINT "Original"; TAB(23); "Sorted";
PRINT TAB(32); "Printed"
PRINT "  List"; TAB(23); "Index"; TAB(32); "List"
PRINT
FOR order = 1 to num
  PRINT Nayme$(order); TAB(25); Ke%(order);
  PRINT TAB(32); Nayme$(Ke%(order))
NEXT order
```

This change prints the original data list, the index list, and the names in the original list sorted by their record numbers (or indexes). The third list represents the items as they would be listed in a report.

Figure 9-1 shows the resulting printout. The index numbers in the sorted index list point to entries in the original list. The printed list shows the original list printed in alphabetical order according to the pointers. For example, the first item in the printed list, Alpha B, is entry 5 in the original list. The second item in the printed list, Clark K, is entry 8 in the original list. The third item in the printed list, Happy F, is entry 10 in the original list, and so on down the list. In this way an alphabetically ordered report is generated.

```
Original    Sorted     Printed
  List      Index        List

Jones E       5        Alpha B
Smith R       8        Clark K
Johnson C    10        Happy F
Zebra S       3        Johnson C
Alpha B       1        Jones E
Winston C     7        Moor L
Moor L        2        Smith R
Clark K       9        Turgid S
Turgid S      6        Winston C
Happy F       4        Zebra S
```

Figure 9-1.   Result of Program 9-1

Preparing a Practical Application

This section introduces a medical data base application program. This application is developed throughout the rest of this book. This section uses a program to show how information is entered in the data base. Later sections show how to index, sort, and search the data base.

Program 9-2 contains a short main program that opens a random access file, allocates buffer space for fields, initializes some values, calls a menu subprogram, closes the file, and ends. The following REM outline shows how these processes are performed:

```
REM ** MEDICAL DATA BASE ENTRY PROGRAM **
REM ** Open patient data file & allocate buffer space **
REM ** Insurance company data **
REM ** Begin main program **
SUB Display.patient.record (acct)
SUB Enter.patient.record
SUB Menu
```

```
DECLARE SUB Menu ()
DECLARE SUB Enter.patient.record ()
DECLARE SUB Display.patient.record (acct!)

REM ** MEDICAL DATA BASE ENTRY PROGRAM **
' Program 9-2   File: PRO0902.BAS
DIM SHARED ins.co$(4), ke$(2)
DIM SHARED last$, first$, dob$, account$, ins$, acctnum$

REM ** Open patient data file & allocate buffer space **
OPEN "Patient.Dat" FOR RANDOM AS #1 LEN = 50
FIELD #1, 20 AS last$, 10 AS first$, 6 AS dob$, 6 AS account$,
4 AS ins$, 4 AS null$
FIELD #1, 50 AS acctnum$
FIELD #1, 5 AS ke$(2), 37 AS null$, 4 AS ke$(1)

REM ** Insurance company data **
ins.co$(1) = "Presidential Insurance"
ins.co$(2) = "Generic Insurance"
ins.co$(3) = "Piroshki Insurance"
ins.co$(4) = "Total Disaster Insurance"

REM ** Begin main program **
CALL Menu
CLOSE #1
END

SUB Display.patient.record (acct)
  REM ** Initialize Values **
  lname$ = ""
  name$ = ""
  date.of.birth$ = ""
  CLS
  IF acct > 1 THEN
    PRINT "Patient Record "; acct
    GET #1, acct
    lname$ = last$
    name$ = first$
    date.of.birth$ = dob$
    insurance$ = ins$
  ELSE
    GET #1, 1
    acct = VAL(acctnum$) + 1
  END IF

  REM ** Prepare the screen **
  LOCATE 3, 1
  PRINT "Last Name:                  ..............."
  PRINT "First Name:                 ..........."
  PRINT "Date of birth (YYMMDD): ......"
  PRINT "Insurance Company Code: ."
  PRINT
  FOR count1 = 1 TO 4
```

Program 9-2.   Medical Data Base Entry Program

```
      LOCATE 7 + count1, 15
      PRINT USING "## &"; count1; ins.co$(count1)
   NEXT count1
   LOCATE 3, 25: PRINT lname$
   LOCATE 4, 25: PRINT name$
   LOCATE 5, 25: PRINT date.of.birth$
   LOCATE 6, 25: PRINT ins$; "  "; ins.co$(VAL(ins$))
END SUB

SUB Enter.patient.record
   DO
      GET #1, 1
      account = VAL(acctnum$)
      CALL Display.patient.record(0)
      LOCATE 1, 1
      PRINT "Patient Record "; account
      LOCATE 3, 25
      INPUT ; "", last.name$: last.name$ = UCASE$(last.name$)
      LOCATE 3, 25: PRINT last.name$
      LOCATE 4, 25
      INPUT ; "", first.name$: first.name$ = UCASE$(first.name$)
      LOCATE 4, 25: PRINT first.name$
      LOCATE 5, 25
      INPUT ; "", date.of.birth$
      LOCATE 6, 25
      INPUT ; "", inscode$
      LOCATE 6, 25
      PRINT ins.co$(VAL(inscode$))
      LOCATE 14, 1
      IF last.name$ = "" AND first.name$ = "" AND dob$ = "" AND
      inscode$ = "" THEN
         recrd$ = ""
      ELSE
         INPUT "Are these correct? (Y/N)", recrd$
      END IF
   LOOP UNTIL UCASE$(recrd$) <> "N"
   IF recrd$ <> "" THEN
      IF account < 2 THEN account = 2
      LSET last$ = last.name$
      LSET first$ = first.name$
      LSET dob$ = date.of.birth$
      LSET ins$ = inscode$
      PUT #1, account
      account = account + 1
      LSET acctnum$ = STR$(account)
      PUT #1, 1
   END IF
   CLS
END SUB
```

Program 9-2.   Medical Data Base Entry Program (*continued*)

```
SUB Menu
  REM ** Initialize **
  maxopt = 6
  CLS
  DO
     LOCATE 5, 20: PRINT "1    Enter a New Patient"
     LOCATE 6, 20: PRINT "2    View a Patient"
     LOCATE 7, 20: PRINT "3    Index a file"
     LOCATE 8, 20: PRINT "4    Key a file"
     LOCATE 9, 20: PRINT "5    Print an Insurance Report"
     LOCATE 4 + maxopt, 19: PRINT maxopt; "  Quit"
     LOCATE 12, 20: INPUT "Enter your selection"; opt
     SELECT CASE opt
        CASE 1
           CALL Enter.patient.record
        CASE 2
        CASE 3
        CASE 4
        CASE 5
        CASE 6
        CASE ELSE
           LOCATE 24, 10
           PRINT "Enter a number from 1 to "; maxopt;
     END SELECT
  LOOP UNTIL opt = maxopt
END SUB
```

Program 9-2.   Medical Data Base Entry Program (*continued*)

In this program and the following programs, only the name of the file to be accessed is specified in OPEN statements. A disk drive is not specified, so if you read to or write from a file, the program will do so on the default disk drive. If you want to use another drive, alter all I/O statements, such as OPEN statements, to include a complete pathname.

Buffer space for the random access file PATIENT.DAT is allocated with FIELD statements. You may find it more convenient to use QuickBASIC's TYPE...END TYPE statement to define variables and allocate buffer space. With the TYPE...END TYPE structure, you can mix numeric and string fields; with FIELD statements you are limited to strings.

When you are using the TYPE structure, you do not have to use the string-to-numeric and numeric-to-string conversion functions, such as MKI\$ and CVI. However, you cannot build field formatting "on the fly" as you can with FIELD statements.

The FIELD statements list the file number, field width, and string variable name. This is shown in the following listing:

```
FIELD #filenumber, fieldwidth AS stringvariable
```

The total number of bytes that you allocate in a FIELD statement must not exceed the record length you specified when opening the file. You can include any number of FIELD statements in the same file.

Be careful when you use a variable name defined as a field. Do not use such a variable name in an INPUT or assignment statement if you want the variable to remain defined as a field. Once a variable name is a field, it points to the correct place in the random access file buffer. If a subsequent INPUT or assignment statement with that variable name is executed, the variable's pointer refers to the string space, rather than to the random access buffer.

Each time QuickBASIC accesses a string, it finds a new place in string memory to hold that string. Even though it also keeps a file buffer in string memory, the location of the file buffer must not be changed. However, you can use the LSET and RSET statements to assign strings without changing their locations.

LSET moves data from memory to a random access file buffer in preparation for a PUT statement. You can also use it to left justify the value of a string in a string variable. RSET moves data the same way, but right justifies the value of a string in a string variable.

The FIELD statement offers you somewhat more flexibility than the TYPE variable. You must define the various components of a TYPE for program compilation, while you can create a FIELD buffer "on the fly" using variables to define the length of each field.

The Menu subprogram is used later to develop the application to control the operations performed by the rest of the program. Although six SELECT CASE options are listed in the menu, only the first option (Enter.patient.record) and the sixth option (Quit) are active in Program 9-2. The menu is shown in Figure 9-2.

The Enter.patient.record subprogram is called from the menu when you select item 1. The Display.patient.record is called to display the format for entering patient information as shown in Figure 9-3. Then program control returns to the Enter.patient.record subprogram, which allows you to enter patient data. Data is limited to last name, first name, date of birth, and an insurance company code to keep the demonstration relatively simple. When you have entered these four items, the program displays a prompt

```
      1     Enter a New Patient
      2     View a Patient
      3     Index a file
      4     Key a file
      5     Print an Insurance Report

      6     Quit
Enter your selection?
```

Figure 9-2.   Medical menu

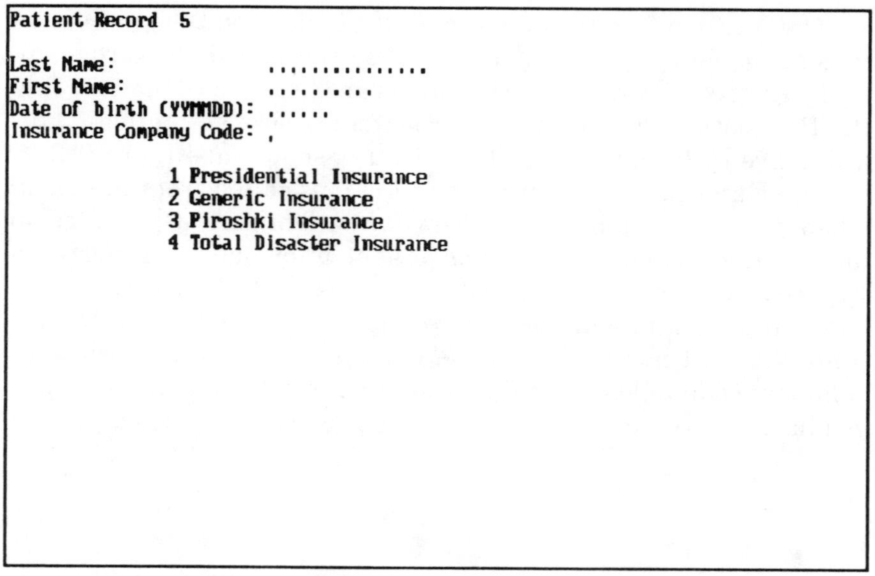

```
Patient Record  5

Last Name:              ..............
First Name:             ..........
Date of birth (YYMMDD): ......
Insurance Company Code: ,

                1 Presidential Insurance
                2 Generic Insurance
                3 Piroshki Insurance
                4 Total Disaster Insurance
```

Figure 9-3.   Enter medical data

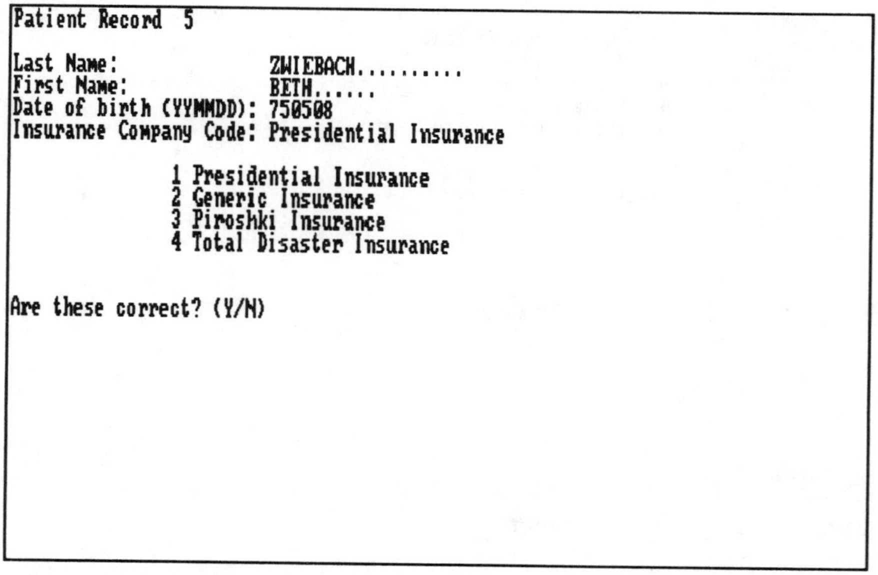

```
Patient Record  5

Last Name:              ZWIEBACH..........
First Name:             BETH......
Date of birth (YYMMDD): 750508
Insurance Company Code: Presidential Insurance

                1 Presidential Insurance
                2 Generic Insurance
                3 Piroshki Insurance
                4 Total Disaster Insurance


Are these correct? (Y/N)
```

Figure 9-4.   Record entered

to allow you to verify the entered information. A typical entry and prompt is shown in Figure 9-4.

Record 1 is not assigned to any entry; it is reserved for record keeping. Entered data records are assigned consecutive record numbers beginning with record 2. That is, the first record you enter is assigned record 2; the second record you enter is assigned record 3; the third record is assigned record 4; and so on. When you have entered all the new patients, select item 6 (Quit) from the menu to end the program.

Expanding the Application

This section expands the medical data base application to include indexing, sorting, and searching. Program 9-3 uses Program 9-2 as a base, and adds the subprograms Show.patient, Binsearch, Create.index, and Quicksort.

```
DECLARE SUB show.patient ()
DECLARE SUB binsearch (serch$, search.field!, count!, num!)
DECLARE SUB create.index ()
DECLARE SUB menu ()
DECLARE SUB enter.patient.record ()
DECLARE SUB display.patient.record (acct!)
DECLARE SUB quicksort (sort$(), left, right)

REM ** MEDICAL DATA BASE MANIPULATION **
' Program 9-3  File: PRO0903.BAS
DIM SHARED ss$(100), fld$(10), ndx(100), ins.co$(4), ke$(2)
DIM SHARED last$, first$, dob$, account$, ins$, acctnum$

REM ** Open patient data file **
OPEN "Patient.Dat" FOR RANDOM AS #1 LEN = 50
FIELD #1, 20 AS last$, 10 AS first$, 6 AS dob$, 6 AS account$,
4 AS ins$, 4 AS null$

REM ** Field layout for record 1 **
FIELD #1, 50 AS acctnum$

REM ** This field statement allows user **
```

Program 9-3.   Medical Data Base Manipulation

```
'        to specify the key or index field
FIELD #1, 30 AS fld$(1), 6 AS fld$(2), 6 AS fld$(3),
4 AS fld$(4), 4 AS null$

REM ** Layout of field for insurance key **
FIELD #1, 5 AS ke$(2), 37 AS null$, 4 AS ke$(1)

REM ** Insurance company data **
ins.co$(1) = "Presidential Insurance"
ins.co$(2) = "Generic Insurance"
ins.co$(3) = "Piroshki Insurance"
ins.co$(4) = "Total Disaster Insurance"

REM *** Begin main program
CALL menu
CLOSE #1
END

SUB binsearch (serch$, search.field, count, num) STATIC
  low = 0
  high = count + 1
  WHILE ABS(low - high) > 1
    mid = INT((low + high) / 2)
    GET #1, ndx(mid)
    IF serch$ > fld$(search.field) THEN
      low = mid
    ELSEIF serch$ < fld$(search.field) THEN
      high = mid
    ELSE
      num = INT(mid)
      low = high
    END IF
  WEND
END SUB

SUB create.index
  CLS
  INPUT "Enter field to index"; index.field
  GET #1, 1
  maxrecord = VAL(acctnum$) - 1
  FOR record = 2 TO maxrecord
    GET #1, record
    ss$(record) = fld$(index.field)
    ndx(record) = record
  NEXT record
  CALL quicksort(ss$(), 1, maxrecord)
  ndx(1) = maxrecord
  PRINT
  OPEN "O", #2, "patfld" + MID$(STR$(index.field), 2) + ".ndx"
  FOR record = 1 TO maxrecord
    PRINT #2, ndx(record)
  NEXT record
```

Program 9-3. Medical Data Base Manipulation (*continued*)

```
   DO: LOOP UNTIL INKEY$ <> ""
   CLOSE #2
END SUB

SUB display.patient.record (acct)
   REM Initialize Values
   lname$ = ""
   name$ = ""
   date.of.birth$ = ""
   CLS
   IF acct > 1 THEN
     PRINT "Patient Record "; acct
     GET #1, acct
     lname$ = last$
     name$ = first$
     date.of.birth$ = dob$
     insurance$ = ins$
   ELSE
     GET #1, 1
     acct = VAL(acctnum$) + 1
   END IF

   REM Prepare the Screen
   LOCATE 3, 1
   PRINT "Last Name:              ................"
   PRINT "First Name:             ..........."
   PRINT "Date of birth (YYMMDD): ......"
   PRINT "Insurance Company Code: ."
   PRINT
   FOR count = 1 TO 4
     LOCATE 7 + count, 15
     PRINT USING "## &"; count; ins.co$(count)
   NEXT count
   LOCATE 3, 25: PRINT lname$
   LOCATE 4, 25: PRINT name$
   LOCATE 5, 25: PRINT date.of.birth$
   LOCATE 6, 25: PRINT ins$; "   "; ins.co$(VAL(ins$))
END SUB

SUB enter.patient.record
   DO
     GET #1, 1
     account = VAL(acctnum$)
     CALL display.patient.record(0)
     LOCATE 1, 1
     PRINT "Patient Record "; account
     LOCATE 3, 25
     INPUT ; "", last.name$: last.name$ = UCASE$(last.name$)
     LOCATE 3, 25: PRINT last.name$
     LOCATE 4, 25
     INPUT ; "", first.name$: first.name$ = UCASE$(first.name$)
```

Program 9-3.   Medical Data Base Manipulation (*continued*)

```
   LOCATE 4, 25: PRINT first.name$
   LOCATE 5, 25
   INPUT ; "", date.of.birth$
   LOCATE 6, 25
   INPUT ; "", inscode$
   LOCATE 6, 25
   PRINT ins.co$(VAL(inscode$))
   LOCATE 14, 1
   IF last.name$ = "" AND first.name$ = "" AND dob$ = "" AND
   inscode$ = "" THEN
     recrd$ = ""
   ELSE
     INPUT "Are these correct? (Y/N)", recrd$
   END IF
  LOOP UNTIL UCASE$(recrd$) <> "N"
  IF recrd$ <> "" THEN
    IF account < 2 THEN account = 2
    LSET last$ = last.name$
    LSET first$ = first.name$
    LSET dob$ = date.of.birth$
    LSET ins$ = inscode$
    PUT #1, account
    account = account + 1
    LSET acctnum$ = STR$(account)
    PUT #1, 1
  END IF
  CLS
END SUB

SUB menu
  REM initialize
  maxopt = 6
  CLS
  DO
    LOCATE 5, 20: PRINT "1    Enter a New Patient"
    LOCATE 6, 20: PRINT "2    View a Patient"
    LOCATE 7, 20: PRINT "3    Index a file"
    LOCATE 8, 20: PRINT "4    Key a file"
    LOCATE 9, 20: PRINT "5    Print an Insurance Report"
    LOCATE 4 + maxopt, 19: PRINT maxopt; "  Quit"
    LOCATE 12, 20: INPUT "Enter your selection"; opt
    SELECT CASE opt
      CASE 1
        CALL enter.patient.record
      CASE 2
        CALL show.patient
      CASE 3
        CALL create.index
        CLS
      CASE 4
      CASE 5
      CASE 6
      CASE ELSE
        LOCATE 24, 10
```

Program 9-3.   Medical Data Base Manipulation (*continued*)

```
        PRINT "Enter a number from 1 to "; maxopt;
    END SELECT
  LOOP UNTIL opt = maxopt
END SUB

SUB quicksort (sort$(), left, right)
  IF right > left THEN
    count1 = left - 1: count2 = right
    DO
      DO
        count1 = count1 + 1
      LOOP WHILE (sort$(count1) < sort$(right))
      DO
        count2 = count2 - 1
      LOOP WHILE (sort$(count2) > sort$(right)) AND (count2 > 0)
        temp$ = sort$(count1): temp = ndx(count1)
        sort$(count1) = sort$(count2): ndx(count1) = ndx(count2)
        sort$(count2) = temp$: ndx(count2) = temp
    LOOP WHILE count2 > count1
    sort$(count2) = sort$(count1): ndx(count2) = ndx(count1)
    sort$(count1) = sort$(right): ndx(count1) = ndx(right)
    sort$(right) = temp$: ndx(right) = temp
    quicksort sort$(), left, count1 - 1
    quicksort sort$(), count1 + 1, right
  END IF
END SUB

SUB show.patient
  CLS
  LINE INPUT "Patient record or last name, first name: ", serch$
  IF VAL(serch$) > 0 THEN
    acct = VAL(serch$)
  ELSE
    comma = INSTR(serch$, ",")
    LSET last$ = LEFT$(serch$, comma - 1)
    LSET first$ = MID$(serch$, comma + 1)
    serch$ = UCASE$(fld$(1))
    CLS
    PRINT "Searching for "; serch$
    GET #1, 1
    maxrecord = VAL(acctnum$) - 1
    OPEN "patfld1.ndx" FOR INPUT AS #2
    FOR num = 1 TO maxrecord
      INPUT #2, ndx(num)
    NEXT num
    CLOSE #2
    CALL binsearch(serch$, 1, maxrecord, acct!)
  END IF
  CALL display.patient.record(acct)
  LOCATE 24, 1: PRINT "hit any key to continue";
  DO: LOOP UNTIL INKEY$ <> ""
  CLS
END SUB
```

Program 9-3.   Medical Data Base Manipulation (*continued*)

The following four items are now active on the menu:

1. Enter a New Patient
2. View a Patient
3. Index a File
6. Quit

You have already used the Enter a New Patient menu selection to enter new patient records in Program 9-1. You entered three patient records from that program: Ernest Jones, Roberta Smith, and Clifford Johnson. You can view these patient records by selecting item 2, View a Patient, from the menu. When you enter 2, the program displays the following prompt:

```
Patient record or last name, first name : _
```

```
Patient Record  2

Last Name:             JONES
First Name:            ERNEST
Date of birth (YYMMDD): 771122
Insurance Company Code: 2     Generic Insurance

              1 Presidential Insurance
              2 Generic Insurance
              3 Piroshki Insurance
              4 Total Disaster Insurance













hit any key to continue
```

Figure 9-5.   Medical record #2

Since none of the fields have been indexed yet, you can only search the file by the patient's record number. Remember that the record numbers start with 2: record 2 is Jones, record 3 is Smith, and record 4 is Johnson. Figure 9-5 shows the result of viewing record 2.

You can add patient records by selecting item 1 from the menu. Table 9-3 shows the original medical data on Jones, Smith, and Johnson, as well as patient information added after choosing the Enter a New Patient menu item.

To create an indexed file for one of the fields, select item 3, Index a File, from the menu. The program displays the following prompt:

```
Enter field to index  _
```

Enter the number of the field for which you want to create the indexed file. Field 1 is last name, field 2 is date of birth, field 3 is record number, and field 4 is insurance company.

Last Name	First Name	Record Number	Date of Birth	Insurance Code
Jones	Ernest	2	771122	2
Smith	Roberta	3	661111	3
Johnson	Clifford	4	440303	2
Zwiebach	Beth	5	750508	1
Arnold	Baker	6	800315	4
Winston	Carl	7	220930	2
Moor	Laura	8	350103	2
Clark	Kendra	9	420210	3
Turgid	Bill	10	841007	2
Happy	Flora	11	721220	1

Table 9-3.   Medical Entries

The indexed file shown in Table 9-4 is created from the ten-record PATIENT.DAT file if you index it on field 1. This file holds ll pieces of information. The first value in the indexed file named PATFLD1.NDX is the number of the last record entered. This value is followed by record numbers pointing to the last names in the PATIENT.DAT file in alphabetical order. If the records were pulled out in the order listed in the indexed file, they would appear in alphabetical order by the last names of the patients. You can see this from the comments on the right side of the indexed file table.

Table 9-5 shows the indexed files created for all four fields. The original medical data file contained ten entries, but since the record numbers started with 2, the last file entered was number 11. This number appears at the head of each of the indexed files.

You have now completed the indexed files for the sample data in the PATIENT.DAT file. The next section discusses how to use indexed files to search for records.

Indexed File PATFLD1.NDX	Explanation of Numbers
11	Number of the last record entered
6	Pointer to Arnold, Baker
9	Pointer to Clark, Kendra
11	Pointer to Happy, Flora
4	Pointer to Johnson, Clifford
2	Pointer to Jones, Ernest
8	Pointer to Moor, Laura
3	Pointer to Smith, Roberta
10	Pointer to Turgid, Bill
7	Pointer to Winston, Carl
5	Pointer to Zwiebach, Beth

Table 9-4.   Indexed File PATFLD1.NDX

Field 1 PATFLD1.NDX	Field 2 PATFLD2.NDX	Field 3 PATFLD3.NDX	Field 4 PATFLD4.NDX
11	11	11	11
6	7	2	5
9	8	8	11
11	9	7	10
4	4	9	7
2	3	10	8
8	11	11	2
3	5	3	4
10	2	6	3
7	6	4	9
5	10	5	6

Table 9-5.   Indexed File for Four Fields

Searching by Index

You searched the PATIENT.DAT file earlier by the patient's account number. Since all the fields have now been indexed, you can search the file on field 1, the patient's name.

You begin a search by choosing item 2, View a Patient, from the menu. This selection executes CASE 2 (CALL Show.patient) of the SELECT CASE structure. Then the Show.patient subprogram clears the display and prompts you to choose one of the following two options:

1. Enter a patient record number.
2. Enter a name in the form: last name, first name.

```
LINE INPUT "Patient record or last name, first name: ", Serch$
```

If you enter a number, the program interprets your entry as a patient record and assigns it to the variable *acct*. If you enter alphabetic characters, it interprets them as a patient name. The program determines the type of your entry with the VAL function, as shown in this listing:

```
IF VAL(serch$) > 0 THEN
   acct = VAL(serch$)
ELSE
   .
   .
   .
   OPEN "patfld1.ndx" FOR INPUT AS #2
   .
   .
   .
```

The VAL function returns the numeric value of a string. The function stops reading the string at the first character that it cannot recognize as part of a number. Thus, if your entry is a number, the value of that number is assigned to the variable *acct* in the THEN clause of the IF...END IF structure.

If your entry is a patient's name, the VAL function stops at the first character of the name and returns a value of zero. Then the program executes the ELSE clause of the IF...END IF structure of the Show.patient subprogram.

After you select item 2 (View a Patient) from the main menu, the program opens the indexed file for field 1 (PATFLD1.NDX) so it can be searched. You search this file on the patient's name by entering the last name, a comma, and the first name. Be sure the comma immediately follows the last name, and the first name immediately follows the comma, as in the following example:

```
Patient record or last name, first name: Winston,Carl
```

Figure 9-6 shows the results of your search.

KEYED DATA FILES

A keyed file is similar to an indexed file. However, a keyed file uses two pieces of information from a record, rather than one piece like an indexed file.

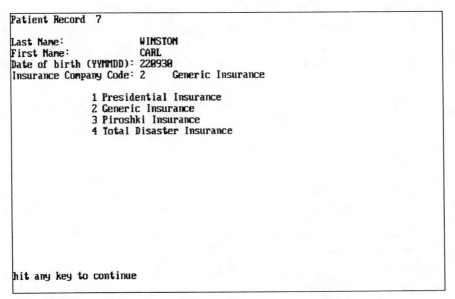

```
Patient Record  7

Last Name:            WINSTON
First Name:           CARL
Date of birth (YYMMDD): 220938
Insurance Company Code: 2      Generic Insurance

              1 Presidential Insurance
              2 Generic Insurance
              3 Piroshki Insurance
              4 Total Disaster Insurance
```

```
hit any key to continue
```

Figure 9-6.   Search on patient name

For example, one of the indexed files you created earlier (PATFLD4.NDX) was based on the insurance code field. The file contains record numbers pointing to the insurance codes in sorted order.

When you create a keyed file, it takes information from two or more fields and joins them. The information might be the first five letters from the last name field and the patient's insurance code. In this case the keyed file forms groups of last names based on the insurance codes. If you created such a keyed file with data from the PATIENT.DAT file used previously, it would group together the insurance codes and patient names as shown in Table 9-6. In this file, each insurance code carries with it the first five letters of the patient's last name. You can see a unique feature of this pairing of insurance codes and names when you sort the keyed file.

Insurance Code	First Five Letters from Name
1	HAPPY
1	ZWIEB
2	JOHNS
2	JONES
2	MOOR
2	TURGI
2	WINST
3	CLARK
3	SMITH
4	ARNOL

Table 9-6.   Data from PATINS.KEY File

The codes and names are joined in the file so that the name follows the insurance code. Therefore, when you sort this file, the insurance company dictates the order of a group and the name dictates the order of the entries within a particular group. Thus the data is sorted on both pieces of information.

Indexed files are ideal for printing reports because they access one record at a time. Keyed files are better for searching as they group related items together. Keyed files are easier to maintain, but they use more memory. For simple applications and small data bases, you can use either type of file, but there is usually no reason to use both types at the same time. Situations are either suited to the use of indexed files or to the use of keyed files.

Program 9-4 is the same as Program 9-3 except for the addition of two subprograms. One of the added subprograms (Create.key) allows you to create a keyed file (PATINS.KEY). The other new subprogram (Print.report) prints the information from the PATIENT.DAT file in the format provided by the keyed file (PATINS.KEY).

```
DECLARE SUB print.report ()
DECLARE SUB print.record ()
DECLARE SUB create.key ()
DECLARE SUB show.patient ()
DECLARE SUB binsearch (serch$, search.field!, N!, f!)
DECLARE SUB create.index ()
DECLARE SUB menu ()
DECLARE SUB enter.patient.record ()
DECLARE SUB display.patient.record (acct!)
DECLARE SUB quicksort (sort$(), left, right)

REM ** MEDICAL DATA BASE - INDEXED & KEYED **
' Program 9-4   File: PRO0904.BAS
DIM SHARED ss$(100), fld$(10), ndx(100), ins.co$(4), ke$(2)
DIM SHARED last$, first$, dob$, account$, ins$, acctnum$

REM ** Open patient data file **
OPEN "Patient.Dat" FOR RANDOM AS #1 LEN = 50
FIELD #1, 20 AS last$, 10 AS first$, 6 AS dob$, 6 AS account$,
4 AS ins$, 4 AS null$

REM ** Field layout for record 1 **
FIELD #1, 50 AS acctnum$

REM ** This field statement allows user **
'       to specify the key or index field
FIELD #1, 30 AS fld$(1), 6 AS fld$(2), 6 AS fld$(3),
4 AS fld$(4), 4 AS null$

REM ** Layout of field for insurance key **
FIELD #1, 5 AS ke$(2), 37 AS null$, 4 AS ke$(1)

REM ** Insurance company data **
ins.co$(1) = "Presidential Insurance"
ins.co$(2) = "Generic Insurance"
ins.co$(3) = "Piroshki Insurance"
ins.co$(4) = "Total Disaster Insurance"

REM *** Begin main program
CALL menu
CLOSE #1
END

SUB binsearch (serch$, search.field, count, num) STATIC
  low = 0
  high = count - 1
  WHILE low <= high
    mid = INT((low + high) / 2)
    GET #1, ndx(mid)
    IF serch$ > fld$(search.field) THEN
```

Program 9-4.   Medical Data Base—Indexed & Keyed

```
        low = mid + 1
        IF low = count THEN num = ndx(count)
      ELSEIF serch$ < fld$(search.field) THEN
        high = mid - 1
      ELSE
        num = ndx(mid)
        low = high + 1
      END IF
    WEND
END SUB

SUB create.index
  CLS
  INPUT "Enter field to index"; index.field
  GET #1, 1
  maxrecord = VAL(acctnum$) - 1
  FOR record = 2 TO maxrecord
    GET #1, record
    ss$(record) = fld$(index.field)
    ndx(record) = record
  NEXT record
  CALL quicksort(ss$(), 1, maxrecord)
  ndx(1) = maxrecord
  PRINT
  OPEN "O", #2, "patfld" + MID$(STR$(index.field), 2) + ".ndx"
  FOR record = 1 TO maxrecord
    PRINT #2, ndx(record)
  NEXT record
  CLOSE #2
END SUB

SUB create.key
  CLS
  GET #1, 1
  maxrecord = VAL(acctnum$) - 1
  FOR record = 2 TO maxrecord
    GET #1, record
    ss$(record) = ke$(1) + ke$(2)
    ndx(record) = record
  NEXT record
  CALL quicksort(ss$(), 1, maxrecord)
  ndx(1) = maxrecord
  PRINT
  OPEN "patins.key" FOR RANDOM AS #1
  FIELD #2, 9 AS inskey$, 4 AS pntr$
  FOR record = 1 TO maxrecord
    LSET inskey$ = ss$(record)
    LSET pntr$ = MKI$(ndx(record))
    PUT #2, record
  NEXT record
```

Program 9-4.   Medical Data Base—Indexed & Keyed (*continued*)

```
    CLOSE #2
  END SUB

SUB display.patient.record (acct)
  REM Initialize Values
  lname$ = ""
  name$ = ""
  date.of.birth$ = ""
  CLS
  IF acct > 1 THEN
    PRINT "Patient Record "; acct
    GET #1, acct
    lname$ = last$
    name$ = first$
    date.of.birth$ = dob$
    insurance$ = ins$
  ELSE
    GET #1, 1
    acct = VAL(acctnum$) + 1
  END IF

  REM Prepare the Screen
  LOCATE 3, 1
  PRINT "Last Name:              ................"
  PRINT "First Name:          ..........."
  PRINT "Date of birth (YYMMDD): ......"
  PRINT "Insurance Company Code: ."
  PRINT
  FOR count = 1 TO 4
    LOCATE 7 + count, 15
    PRINT USING "## &"; count; ins.co$(count)
  NEXT count
  LOCATE 3, 25: PRINT lname$
  LOCATE 4, 25: PRINT name$
  LOCATE 5, 25: PRINT date.of.birth$
  LOCATE 6, 25: PRINT ins$; "   "; ins.co$(VAL(ins$))
END SUB

SUB enter.patient.record
  DO
    GET #1, 1
    account = VAL(acctnum$)
    CALL display.patient.record(0)
    LOCATE 1, 1
    PRINT "Patient Record "; account
    LOCATE 3, 25
    INPUT ; "", last.name$: last.name$ = UCASE$(last.name$)
    LOCATE 3, 25: PRINT last.name$
    LOCATE 4, 25
    INPUT ; "", first.name$: first.name$ = UCASE$(first.name$)
```

Program 9-4.   Medical Data Base—Indexed & Keyed (*continued*)

```
      LOCATE 4, 25: PRINT first.name$
      LOCATE 5, 25
      INPUT ; "", date.of.birth$
      LOCATE 6, 25
      INPUT ; "", inscode$
      LOCATE 6, 25
      PRINT ins.co$(VAL(inscode$))
      LOCATE 14, 1
      IF last.name$ = "" AND first.name$ = "" AND dob$ = "" AND
      inscode$ = "" THEN
        recrd$ = ""
      ELSE
        INPUT "Are these correct? (Y/N)", recrd$
      END IF
   LOOP UNTIL UCASE$(recrd$) <> "N"
   IF recrd$ <> "" THEN
      IF account < 2 THEN account = 2
      LSET last$ = last.name$
      LSET first$ = first.name$
      LSET dob$ = date.of.birth$
      LSET ins$ = inscode$
      PUT #1, account
      account = account + 1
      LSET acctnum$ = STR$(account)
      PUT #1, 1
   END IF
   CLS
END SUB

SUB menu
   REM initialize
   maxopt = 6
   CLS
   DO
      LOCATE 5, 20: PRINT "1   Enter a New Patient"
      LOCATE 6, 20: PRINT "2   View a Patient"
      LOCATE 7, 20: PRINT "3   Index a file"
      LOCATE 8, 20: PRINT "4   Key a file"
      LOCATE 9, 20: PRINT "5   Print an Insurance Report"
      LOCATE 4 + maxopt, 19: PRINT maxopt; "  Quit"
      LOCATE 12, 20: INPUT "Enter your selection"; opt
      SELECT CASE opt
         CASE 1
           CALL enter.patient.record
         CASE 2
           CALL show.patient
         CASE 3
           CALL create.index
           CLS
         CASE 4
           CALL create.key
         CASE 5
           CALL print.report
         CASE 6
```

Program 9-4.   Medical Data Base—Indexed & Keyed (*continued*)

```
        CASE ELSE
          LOCATE 24, 10
          PRINT "Enter a number from 1 to "; maxopt;
      END SELECT
    LOOP UNTIL opt = maxopt
END SUB

SUB print.report
    OPEN "patins.key" FOR RANDOM AS #2
    FIELD #2, 9 AS inskey$, 4 AS pntr$
    record = 2
    GET #1, 1
    maxrecord = VAL(acctnum$) - 1
    ins.code = 0
    CLS
    DO
      GET #2, record
      GET #1, CVI(pntr$)
      IF VAL(inskey$) > ins.code THEN
        PRINT
        ins.code = ins.code + 1
        PRINT ins.co$(ins.code)
      END IF
      PRINT "     "; ins.code; ": "; last$; first$, CVI(pntr$), ins$
      record = record + 1
    LOOP UNTIL record > maxrecord
    LOCATE 24, 1: PRINT "hit any key to continue";
    DO: LOOP UNTIL INKEY$ <> ""
    CLOSE #2
    CLS
END SUB

SUB quicksort (sort$(), left, right)
    IF right > left THEN
      count1 = left - 1: count2 = right
      DO
        DO
          count1 = count1 + 1
        LOOP WHILE (sort$(count1) < sort$(right))
        DO
          count2 = count2 - 1
        LOOP WHILE (sort$(count2) > sort$(right)) AND (count2 > 0)
          temp$ = sort$(count1): temp = ndx(count1)
          sort$(count1) = sort$(count2): ndx(count1) = ndx(count2)
          sort$(count2) = temp$: ndx(count2) = temp
      LOOP WHILE count2 > count1
      sort$(count2) = sort$(count1): ndx(count2) = ndx(count1)
      sort$(count1) = sort$(right): ndx(count1) = ndx(right)
      sort$(right) = temp$: ndx(right) = temp
      quicksort sort$(), left, count1 - 1
      quicksort sort$(), count1 + 1, right
    END IF
END SUB
```

Program 9-4.   Medical Data Base—Indexed & Keyed (*continued*)

```
SUB show.patient
  CLS
  LINE INPUT "Patient record or last name, first name: ", serch$
  IF VAL(serch$) > 0 THEN
    acct = VAL(serch$)
  ELSE
    comma = INSTR(serch$, ",")
    LSET last$ = LEFT$(serch$, comma - 1)
    LSET first$ = MID$(serch$, comma + 1)
    serch$ = UCASE$(fld$(1))
    CLS
    PRINT "Searching for "; serch$
    GET #1, 1
    maxrecord = VAL(acctnum$) - 1
    OPEN "patfld1.ndx" FOR INPUT AS #2
    FOR num = 1 TO maxrecord
      INPUT #2, ndx(num)
    NEXT num
    CLOSE #2
    CALL binsearch(serch$, 1, maxrecord, acct!)
  END IF
  CALL display.patient.record(acct)
  LOCATE 24, 1: PRINT "hit any key to continue";
  DO: LOOP UNTIL INKEY$ <> ""
  CLS
END SUB
```

Program 9-4. Medical Data Base—Indexed & Keyed (*continued*)

Several statements have been added to CASEs 4 and 5 of the SELECT CASE structure in the menu subprogram to provide access to these two new subprograms. These statements are shown in the following listing:

```
CASE 4
  CALL create.key
CASE 5
  CALL print.report
```

The Create.key subprogram is very similar to the Create.index subprogram. The main difference between them is how the records for the two files are created.

In the Create.index subprogram, a record is created from one field as follows:

```
ss$(record) = fld$(index.field)    ' data from one field
```

In the Create.key subprogram, a record is created by joining two fields as follows:

```
ss$(record) = ke$(1) + ke$(2)    ' join data from two fields
```

To create a keyed file, select item 4, Key a File, from the menu. The program creates the file automatically.

The Print.report subprogram uses data from the keyed file to print the insurance code, patient name, record number, and insurance company. The report is sorted by insurance companies and by patient last name within each company. Figure 9-7 shows a printed report for the PATIENT.DAT file used in previous examples. The program generates the reports when you select item 5, Print an Insurance Report, from the menu.

```
Presidential Insurance
    1 : HAPPY              FLORA        11        1
    1 : ZWIEBACH           BETH          5        1

Generic Insurance
    2 : JOHNSON            CLIFFORD      4        2
    2 : JONES              ERNEST        2        2
    2 : MOOR               LAURA         8        2
    2 : TURGID             BILL         10        2
    2 : WINSTON            CARL          7        2

Piroshki Insurance
    3 : CLARK              KENDRA        9        3
    3 : SMITH              ROBERTA       3        3

Total Disaster Insurance
    4 : ARNOLD             BAKER         6        4




hit any key to continue
```

Figure 9-7.   Printed insurance report

10

RELATIONAL FILES

To use a patient data file such as the one presented in Chapter 9, you need to be able to keep track of all transactions that occur for each patient. However, keeping this type of data in the patient data file itself would be cumbersome and inefficient. Some patients may have only one transaction over a period of time, while other patients may have many transactions in the same time period. Therefore, a fixed area of memory in the patient file for each patient would not work, since this method wastes space reserved for the infrequently visiting patient and does not provide enough space for the frequently visiting patient. You can solve this problem by using relational files.

Relational files, as the name suggests, are files that are related (or connected) in some way. That is, information in one file is directly related to information in another. Related information is connected between files by pointers. Individually, the files are meaningless. But when connected by pointers, the files let you efficiently access individual pieces of information from a large amount of data.

CONNECTING
RELATIONAL FILES

This chapter uses the patient data file from Chapter 9 as a model for discussions. In this chapter Program 9-4 is modified to accommodate a relational patient transaction file. Then pointers are established to relate patient information in the patient data file to transaction information in the transaction file. The transaction file also connects all the items of information that it contains for a given patient.

The illustration below shows an example of the relationships between the two files and those within the transaction file:

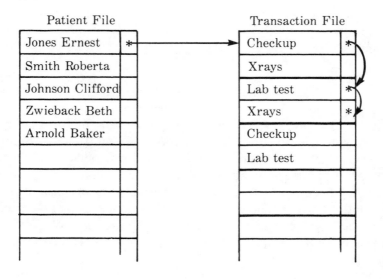

Pointer 1 connects the data on Ernest Jones in the patient file to his first transaction in the transaction file, which was a checkup. Jones' next transaction is a lab test. Therefore, an internal pointer (pointer 2) points from the checkup to the lab test. Later, Jones came in for X-rays. Pointer 3 points from his lab test transaction to his X-ray transaction. Jones' transaction trail, or series of transactions, ends there.

For each patient transaction, the program adds a new transaction record. Then it adds a pointer connecting the previous transaction to the new one. The next illustration shows the beginning of a transaction trail for two other patients, Roberta Smith and Clifford Johnson:

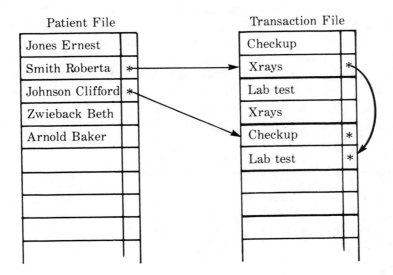

Smith's trail now shows X-rays and a lab test, and ends there. Johnson has had only one transaction, a checkup, so his transaction trail ends at the checkup.

In summary, a patient record is entered in the patient data file when the patient first visits. The program attaches a pointer to the patient's record, relating that record to the patient's first transaction. Any given patient transaction points to the next transaction for that patient. Thus the transaction file builds a patient's medical history. The patient is entered in the original patient data file only once, when the patient comes in for the first visit and initiates the first transaction.

MODIFYING THE PROGRAM

Since Program 10-1 is based on Program 9-4, this section only discusses the modifications that have been made to the program. The Binary Search, Create Key, and Quicksort subprograms are unchanged.

In the listing of Program 10-1, three program lines wrap around to the next line. QuickBASIC allows long program lines, but the width of this book's pages requires that these long lines be printed in two parts. When you enter these program lines, type them as a single line. QuickBASIC 4.5 does not include the line continuation character used in some earlier versions. Comments in the program mark these three lines.

```
DECLARE SUB binsearch (serch$, search.field%, count%, num%)
DECLARE SUB create.key ()
DECLARE SUB create.index ()
DECLARE SUB display.patient.record (acct%)
DECLARE SUB enter.patient.record ()
DECLARE SUB enter.transaction (acct%)
DECLARE SUB find.patient (acct%)
DECLARE SUB hit.any.key ()
DECLARE SUB maintain.ins.key ()
DECLARE SUB menu ()
DECLARE SUB print.report ()
DECLARE SUB quicksort (sort$(), left%, right%)
DECLARE SUB show.patient ()

REM ** MEDICAL DATA BASE MAINTENANCE PROGRAM **
' Program 10-1  File: PRO1001
DEFINT A-Z
DIM SHARED ss$(100), fld$(10), ndx(100), ins.co$(4)
DIM SHARED ke$(2), last$, first$, dob$, account$
DIM SHARED ins$, acctnum$, trns$              'add new field

REM ** Open patient data file **
OPEN "Patient.Dat" FOR RANDOM AS #1 LEN = 50
```

Program 10-1.   Medical Data Base Maintenance Program

```
REM ** Field Statements **
' Field statement to trns$
' Note the change of the null$ at the end
FIELD #1, 20 AS last$, 10 AS first$, 6 AS dob$, 6 AS account$,
4 AS ins$, 4 AS trns$         'enter FIELD statement as 1 line
' Field layout for record 1
FIELD #1, 50 AS acctnum$
' This field statement allows the
' user to specify the key or index field
FIELD #1, 30 AS fld$(1), 6 AS fld$(2), 6 AS fld$(3),
4 AS fld$(4), 4 AS null$       'enter FIELD statement as 1 line
' Layout of field for insurance key
FIELD #1, 5 AS ke$(2), 37 AS null$, 4 AS ke$(1)

REM ** Insurance Company Data **
ins.co$(1) = "Presidential Insurance"
ins.co$(2) = "Generic Insurance"
ins.co$(3) = "Piroshki Insurance"
ins.co$(4) = "Total Disaster Insurance"

REM *** begin main program
CALL menu
CLOSE #1
END

SUB binsearch (serch$, search.field%, count%, num%) STATIC
  DEFINT A-Z
  low = 0
  high = count - 1
  WHILE low <= high
    mid = INT((low + high) / 2)
    GET #1, ndx(mid)
    IF serch$ > fld$(search.field) THEN
      low = mid + 1
      IF low = count THEN num = ndx(count)
    ELSEIF serch$ < fld$(search.field) THEN
      high = mid - 1
    ELSE
      num = ndx(mid)
      low = high + 1
    END IF
  WEND
END SUB

SUB create.index STATIC
  CLS : DEFINT A-Z
  INPUT "Enter field to index"; index.field
  GET #1, 1
```

Program 10-1.   Medical Data Base Maintenance Program (*continued*)

```
   maxrecord = VAL(acctnum$) - 1
   FOR record = 2 TO maxrecord
     GET #1, record
     ss$(record) = fld$(index.field)
     ndx(record) = record
   NEXT record
   CALL quicksort(ss$(), 1, maxrecord)
   FOR record = 1 TO maxrecord
     PRINT USING "## &"; ndx(record); ss$(record)
   NEXT record
   CALL hit.any.key
   ndx(1) = maxrecord
   PRINT
   OPEN "O", #2, "patfld" + MID$(STR$(index.field), 2) + ".ndx"
   FOR record = 1 TO maxrecord
     PRINT #2, ndx(record)
   NEXT record
   CLOSE #2
END SUB

SUB create.key STATIC
   CLS : DEFINT A-Z
   GET #1, 1
   maxrecord = VAL(acctnum$) - 1
   FOR record = 2 TO maxrecord
     GET #1, record
     ss$(record) = ke$(1) + ke$(2)
     ndx(record) = record
   NEXT record
   CALL quicksort(ss$(), 1, maxrecord)
   ndx(1) = maxrecord
   PRINT
   OPEN "patins.key" FOR RANDOM AS #2
   FIELD #2, 9 AS inskey$, 4 AS pntr$
   FOR record = 1 TO maxrecord
     LSET inskey$ = ss$(record)
     LSET pntr$ = MKI$(ndx(record))
     PUT #2, record
   NEXT record
   CLOSE #2
END SUB

SUB display.patient.record (acct%) STATIC
   DEFINT A-Z
   REM ** Initialize Values **
   lname$ = ""
   name$ = ""
   date.of.birth$ = ""
   CLS
   IF acct > 1 THEN
```

Program 10-1.   Medical Data Base Maintenance Program (*continued*)

```
   PRINT "Patient Record "; acct
   GET #1, acct
   lname$ = last$
   name$ = first$
   date.of.birth$ = dob$
ELSE
   GET #1, 1
   acct = VAL(acctnum$) + 1
END IF

REM **Prepare the Screen **
LOCATE 3, 1
PRINT "Last Name:              ..............."
PRINT "First Name:             ..........."
PRINT "Date of birth (YYMMDD): ......."
PRINT "Insurance Company Code: ."
PRINT
FOR count = 1 TO 4
   LOCATE 7 + count, 15
   PRINT USING "## &"; count; ins.co$(count)
NEXT count
LOCATE 3, 25: PRINT lname$
LOCATE 4, 25: PRINT name$
LOCATE 5, 25: PRINT date.of.birth$
LOCATE 6, 25: PRINT ins$; "  "; ins.co$(VAL(ins$))
LOCATE 15, 1: PRINT "Transactions"
OPEN "transact.dat" FOR RANDOM AS #2 LEN = 44
FIELD #2, 40 AS procedure$, 4 AS trns.pntr$
GET #1, acct
IF LEN(trns$) = 0 THEN trns$ = MKI$(1)
IF CVI(trns$) > 1 THEN
   trns.rec = CVI(trns$)
   DO
      GET #2, trns.rec
      PRINT TAB(5); procedure$
      old.trns.rec = trns.rec
      trns.rec = CVI(trns.pntr$)
   LOOP UNTIL trns.rec < 2
ELSE
   PRINT TAB(5); "No transactions"
END IF
CLOSE #2
END SUB

SUB enter.patient.record STATIC
   DEFINT A-Z
   DO
      GET #1, 1
      account = VAL(acctnum$)
      CALL display.patient.record(0)
```

Program 10-1.   Medical Data Base Maintenance Program (*continued*)

```
      LOCATE 1, 1
      PRINT "Patient Record "; account
      LOCATE 3, 25
      INPUT ; "", last.name$: last.name$ = UCASE$(last.name$)
      LOCATE 3, 25: PRINT last.name$
      LOCATE 4, 25
      INPUT ; "", first.name$: first.name$ = UCASE$(first.name$)
      LOCATE 4, 25: PRINT first.name$
      LOCATE 5, 25
      INPUT ; "", date.of.birth$
      LOCATE 6, 25
      INPUT ; "", inscode$
      LOCATE 6, 25
      PRINT ins.co$(VAL(inscode$))
      LOCATE 14, 1
      IF last.name$ = "" AND first.name$ = "" AND dob$ = ""
      AND inscode$ = "" THEN      'enter IF-THEN as a single line
        recrd$ = ""
      ELSE
        INPUT "Are these correct? (Y/N)", recrd$
      END IF
    LOOP UNTIL UCASE$(recrd$) <> "N"
    IF recrd$ <> "" THEN
      IF account < 2 THEN account = 2
      LSET last$ = last.name$
      LSET first$ = first.name$
      LSET dob$ = date.of.birth$
      LSET ins$ = inscode$
      PUT #1, account
      CALL enter.transaction(account)
      account = account + 1
      LSET acctnum$ = STR$(account)
      PUT #1, 1
    END IF
    CLS
END SUB

SUB enter.transaction (acct%) STATIC
  DEFINT A-Z
  OPEN "transact.dat" FOR RANDOM AS #2 LEN = 44
  FIELD #2, 40 AS procedure$, 4 AS trns.pntr$
  GET #1, acct
  GET #2, 1
  last.trans = CVI(trns.pntr$)
  IF last.trans < 2 THEN last.trans = 2
  IF LEN(trns$) = 0 THEN trns$ = MKI$(-1)     'set flag(MKI$(-1)
  IF CVI(trns$) < 2 THEN
    LSET trns$ = MKI$(last.trans)
    PUT #1, acct
  ELSE
    trns.rec = CVI(trns$)
    DO
      GET #2, trns.rec
      old.trns.rec = trns.rec
      trns.rec = CVI(trns.pntr$)
```

Program 10-1. Medical Data Base Maintenance Program (*continued*)

```
      LOOP UNTIL trns.rec < 2
      LSET trns.pntr$ = MKI$(last.trans)
      PUT #2, old.trns.rec
   END IF
   LOCATE 22, 1
   INPUT ; "Procedure: "; pro$
   LSET procedure$ = pro$
   LSET trns.pntr$ = MKI$(0)
   PUT #2, last.trans
   last.trans = last.trans + 1
   LSET procedure$ = " "
   LSET trns.pntr$ = MKI$(last.trans)
   PUT #2, 1
   CLOSE #2
END SUB

SUB find.patient (acct%) STATIC
   CLS : DEFINT A-Z
   LINE INPUT "Patient record or last name, first name: ", serch$
   IF VAL(serch$) > 0 THEN
     acct = VAL(serch$)
   ELSE
     comma = INSTR(serch$, ",")
     LSET last$ = LEFT$(serch$, comma - 1)
     LSET first$ = LTRIM$(MID$(serch$, comma + 1))
     serch$ = UCASE$(fld$(1))
     CLS
     PRINT "Searching for "; serch$
     GET #1, 1
     maxrecord = VAL(acctnum$) - 1
     OPEN "I", #2, "patfld1.ndx"
     FOR num = 1 TO maxrecord
       INPUT #2, ndx(num)
     NEXT num
     CLOSE #2
     CALL binsearch(serch$, 1, maxrecord%, acct%)
   END IF
END SUB

SUB hit.any.key
   LOCATE 24, 1
   PRINT "hit any key to continue";
   DO: LOOP UNTIL INKEY$ <> ""
   LOCATE 24, 1
   PRINT "                           ";
END SUB

SUB menu
   REM initialize
   DEFINT A-Z: maxopt = 7
   CLS
   DO
     LOCATE 5, 20: PRINT "1   Enter a New Patient"
     LOCATE 6, 20: PRINT "2   View a Patient"
```

Program 10-1.   Medical Data Base Maintenance Program (*continued*)

```
       LOCATE 7, 20: PRINT "3    Index a file"
       LOCATE 8, 20: PRINT "4    Key a file"
       LOCATE 9, 20: PRINT "5    Print an Insurance Report"
       LOCATE 10, 20: PRINT "6    Enter a Transaction"
       LOCATE 4 + maxopt, 19: PRINT maxopt; "  Quit"
       LOCATE 15, 20: INPUT "Enter your selection"; opt
       SELECT CASE opt
         CASE 1
           CALL enter.patient.record
         CASE 2
           CALL show.patient
         CASE 3
           CALL create.index
           CLS
         CASE 4
           CALL create.key
         CASE 5
           CALL print.report
         CASE 6
           acct = 0
           CALL find.patient(acct%)
           CALL enter.transaction(acct%)
           CLS
         CASE 7
         CASE ELSE
           LOCATE 24, 10
           PRINT "Enter a number from 1 to "; maxopt;
       END SELECT
     LOOP UNTIL opt = maxopt
   END SUB

   SUB print.report STATIC
     DEFINT A-Z
     OPEN "patins.key" FOR RANDOM AS #2
     FIELD #2, 9 AS inskey$, 4 AS pntr$
     record = 2
     GET #1, 1
     maxrecord = VAL(acctnum$) - 1
     ins.code = 0
     CLS
     DO
       GET #2, record
       GET #1, CVI(pntr$)
       IF VAL(inskey$) > ins.code THEN
         IF ins.code > 0 THEN CALL hit.any.key
         CLS
         PRINT
         ins.code = ins.code + 1
         PRINT ins.co$(ins.code)
       END IF
       PRINT "    "; ins.code; ": "; last$; first$, dob$
       GET #1, CVI(pntr$)
       IF LEN(trns$) <> 0 THEN
```

Program 10-1.   Medical Data Base Maintenance Program (*continued*)

```
        OPEN "transact.dat" FOR RANDOM AS #3 LEN = 44
        FIELD #3, 40 AS procedure$, 4 AS trns.pntr$
        IF CVI(trns$) > 1 THEN
          trns.rec = CVI(trns$)
          DO
            GET #3, trns.rec
            PRINT TAB(15); procedure$
            old.trns.rec = trns.rec
            trns.rec = CVI(trns.pntr$)
          LOOP UNTIL trns.rec < 2
        ELSE
          PRINT TAB(5); "No transactions"
        END IF
        CLOSE #3
      END IF
      record = record + 1
    LOOP UNTIL record > maxrecord
    CALL hit.any.key
    CLOSE #2
    CLS
END SUB

SUB quicksort (sort$(), left%, right%) STATIC
    DEFINT A-Z
    IF right > left THEN
      count1 = left - 1: count2 = right
      DO
        DO
          count1 = count1 + 1
        LOOP WHILE (sort$(count1) < sort$(right))
        DO
          count2 = count2 - 1
        LOOP WHILE (sort$(count2) > sort$(right)) AND (count2 > 0)
        temp$ = sort$(count1): temp = ndx(count1)
        sort$(count1) = sort$(count2): ndx(count1) = ndx(count2)
        sort$(count2) = temp$: ndx(count2) = temp
      LOOP WHILE count2 > count1
      sort$(count2) = sort$(count1): ndx(count2) = ndx(count1)
      sort$(count1) = sort$(right): ndx(count1) = ndx(right)
      sort$(right) = temp$: ndx(right) = temp
      quicksort sort$(), left, count1 - 1
      quicksort sort$(), count1 + 1, right
    END IF
END SUB

SUB show.patient STATIC
    DEFINT A-Z
    acct = 0
    CALL find.patient(acct)
    CALL display.patient.record(acct)
    CALL hit.any.key
    CLS
END SUB
```

Program 10-1.   Medical Data Base Maintenance Program (*continued*)

The Main Program

The main program contains only two modifications. Since a pointer is needed from the main data file to the transaction file, the null field in the PATIENT.DAT file has been replaced by a transaction field. Also, a value has been added to one of the DIM statements. This statement is shown in the following listing:

```
DIM SHARED last$, first$, dob$, account$, ins$, acctnum$, trans$
```

The DIM statement now allows the *trns$* value to be passed between subprograms. The FIELD statement changes the blank area of Program 9-4 (4 AS null) to hold the value of *trns$*. These two modifications are the only changes to the main program.

Two of the previously mentioned long program lines occur in the FIELD statements of the main program. Be sure to enter them as single lines.

The Create Index Subprogram

The create.index subprogram has been modified so that you can see the order of record numbers after the file is sorted on the desired field. The following lines have been added after the call to the Quicksort subprogram:

```
FOR record = 1 TO maxrecord
  PRINT USING "## &"; ndx(record); ss$(record)
NEXT record
CALL hit.any.key
```

If you created an indexed file on field 4 (the insurance codes), the resulting file is printed as shown in Figure 10-1. The insurance code is printed to the right of each record number for the indexed file record. This information stays on the screen until you press a key because of the new call to the hit.any.key subprogram. When you press a key, the value of *maxrecord* is assigned to the first index record (*ndx(1)*). The insurance code is not set to the indexed file in the latter part of the subprogram.

```
Enter field to index? 4
 8
 5 1
11 1
18 2
 7 2
 8 2
 2 2
 4 2
 3 3
 9 3
 6 4




hit any key to continue
```

Figure 10-1.   Create index result

The Display Patient Record Subprogram

A new section of code has been added to the end of the display.pa-tient.record subprogram. After a patient's record has been found and displayed, this new section of code prints the title "Transactions" near the center of the screen. Then it opens the transaction file. The FIELD statement in the following listing shows you that in this file 40 spaces in a record are reserved for the procedure (if there is one) and 4 spaces are reserved for the transaction pointer (*trns.pntr$*):

```
LOCATE 15,1: PRINT "Transactions"
OPEN "transact.dat" FOR RANDOM AS #2 LEN = 44
FIELD #2, 40 AS procedure$, 4 AS trns.pntr$
```

The GET statement then reads the record specified by the patient account number (*acct*). The next statement tests to see if the patient file points to a transaction. If the length of the transaction (LEN (*trns$*)) is zero, the value of *trns$* is set to 1 by the MKI$ (Make the interger a string) function. Otherwise, no action is taken. These two statements are shown in the following listing:

```
GET #1, acct
IF LEN(trns$) = 0 THEN trns$ = MKI$(1)
```

Then the value of *trns$* is tested to see if it is greater than one (the value is determined by CVI(*trns$*)). This test produces one of the following two results:

1. A transaction record exists (*trns$* is greater than one).
2. A transaction record does not exist (*trns$* is not greater than one).

When transactions do exist, the following lines of code are executed.

```
IF CVI(trns$) > 1 THEN
  trns.rec = CVI(trns$)
  DO
    GET #2, trns.rec
    PRINT TAB(5); procedure$
    old.trns.rec = trns.rec
    trns.rec = CVI(trns.pntr$)
  LOOP UNTIL trns.rec < 2
```

The DO...LOOP UNTIL block prints all the transactions for the patient from the TRANS.REC file with the GET #2 statement. For each transaction it prints the procedure and then accesses the next transaction record with the transaction pointer (*trns.pntr$*). When the subprogram reaches the end of the patient's transaction trail, the *trns.rec* variable returns a value less than 2, and the subprogram exits from the loop.

When no transactions exist, the program displays the message "No transactions." When processing is completed for either result, the subprogram closes the file and ends.

Figure 10-2 shows the transaction record for Ernest Jones that was discussed earlier in the chapter. You can display this record by selecting item 2 (View a Patient) from the menu and then entering the patient account number or name at the following prompt:

```
Patient record or last name, first name: _
```

Three transactions have now been entered for Jones. They are displayed in the lower left portion of the screen under the title "Transactions."

The Enter Patient Record Subprogram

Only one line has been added to the enter.patient.record subprogram. This line, which calls the enter.transaction subprogram, is

```
Patient Record  2

Last Name:            JONES
First Name:           ERNEST
Date of birth (YYMMDD): 771122
Insurance Company Code: 2      Generic Insurance

                 1 Presidential Insurance
                 2 Generic Insurance
                 3 Piroshki Insurance
                 4 Total Disaster Insurance




Transactions
    checkup
    lab test
    Xrays






hit any key to continue
```

Figure 10-2.   Transaction record for Ernest Jones

discussed in the next section of this chapter. The following listing shows this added line:

```
CALL enter.transaction(account)
```

This call enables you to enter the first transaction for a new patient. A new patient record is always entered with an initial transaction. Figure 10-3 shows the display at the time of Ernest Jones' first visit. His patient record is entered at the top of the screen and verified near the middle of the screen. No transactions have been entered yet, but the prompt at the bottom of the screen requests you to enter the name of the first transaction.

One of the previously mentioned long program lines occurs in an IF...THEN statement in this subprogram. Be sure to enter it as a single long line.

```
Patient Record  0

Last Name:           JONES..........
First Name:          ERNEST....
Date of birth (YYMMDD): 771122
Insurance Company Code: Generic Insurance

               1 Presidential Insurance
               2 Generic Insurance
               3 Piroshki Insurance
               4 Total Disaster Insurance


Are these correct? (Y/N)y
Transactions
    No transactions




Procedure: ?
```

Figure 10-3.   Patient entry

The Enter Transaction
Subprogram

The enter.transaction subprogram has been added to the original program. This subprogram opens a file for the transaction data and uses the following FIELD statement to describe the format of the data:

```
OPEN "transact.dat" FOR RANDOM AS #2 LEN = 44
FIELD #2, 40 AS procedure$, 4 AS trns.pntr$
```

The two fields created by this statement include the name of the procedure and the transaction pointer. The patient data file points to the procedure, and the transaction pointer points to the next transaction for the patient (if one exists).

The next listing shows how this subprogram accesses the account number from one file (#1) and the first record from the transaction file (#2). Then it searches for the last transaction for this patient.

If no previous transaction exists, the value of *last.trans* is less than 2. The subprogram then sets this value to 2 for the first transaction of this patient. Then it checks the pointer (*trns$*). If the pointer is less than 2, the subprogram resets it to the next available record (*last.trans*) in the transaction file. Then it puts that record number back into the patient file. Thus the patient file now points to the correct place in the transaction file for the patient's first transaction.

```
GET #1, acct
GET #2, 1
last.trans = CVI(trns.pntr$)
IF last.trans < 2 THEN last.trans = 2
IF LEN(trns$) = 0 THEN trns$ = MKI$(-1)   'set flag MKI$(-1)
IF CVI(trns$) < 2 THEN
  LSET trns$ = MKI$(last.trans)
  PUT #1, acct
```

If previous transactions exits, the subprogram executes the ELSE block of the IF...END IF block. It sets the value of *trns.rec* to the value of the pointer (*trns*). The DO...LOOP follows the transaction trail to its end. Then the subprogram sets the pointer to the next record to be used in the transaction file and puts that value into the old record. This process is shown in the following listing:

```
ELSE
  trns.rec = CVI(trns$)
  DO
    GET #2, trns.rec
    old.trns.rec = trns.rec
    trns.rec = CVI(trns.pntr$)
  LOOP UNTIL trns.rec < 2
  LSET trns.pntr$ = MKI$(last.trans)
  PUT #2, old.trns.rec
END IF
```

When the subprogram exits from the IF...END IF block, it prompts you to enter the procedure for the new transaction. You can enter up to 40 characters (as reserved in the earlier FIELD statement) for the procedure. The subprogram places this information in the file, and then places a zero in the transaction pointer area to denote the end of the record. Finally it puts the transaction in the transaction file. These functions are accomplished with the following program lines:

```
LOCATE 22,1
INPUT ; "Procedure: "; pro$
LSET procedure$ = pro$
LSET trns.pntr$ = MKI$(0)
PUT #2, last.trans
```

The subprogram increments the end of the transaction file, closes the file, and ends. This is shown in the following listing:

```
last.trans = last.trans + 1
LSET procedure$ = " "
LSET trns.pntr$ = MKI$(last.trans)
PUT #2, 1
CLOSE #2
```

Figure 10-3, which was discussed previously, displays the prompt the program uses to ask you to enter an initial transaction procedure. If you are entering a subsequent transaction, the program displays only the record number or name of the search at the top of the screen and the following prompt near the bottom of the screen:

```
Procedure:  ?_
```

The Find Patient
Subprogram

The find.patient subprogram has a new name, but the statements are taken from the show.patient subprogram of Program 9-4. That subprogram was broken into two parts to give you more flexibility in displaying the patient information. You can use this subprogram to access a patient's record by record number or by patient name.

No new statements have been added to this subprogram. However, the last four lines of the show.patient subprogram of Program 9-4 have been removed. Their functions are performed by other statements in the new program. The find.patient subprogram is called from the menu when you choose item 6, Enter a Transaction. It is also called from the show.patient subprogram when you choose item 2, View a Patient, from the menu.

The Hit Any Key
Subprogram

This section of code was added as a subprogram because the prompt it prints is used many times in the program. The statement that prints this prompt is shown in the following listing:

```
PRINT "hit any key to continue"
```

The subprogram was added to avoid repeating lines of code throughout the program. You can see the prompt displayed at the bottom of the screen in Figures 10-1 and 10-2.

The Menu Subprogram

The menu subprogram has been modified to accommodate seven menu items. The following lines reflect these changes:

```
maxopt = 7
    .
    .
    .
LOCATE 10,20: PRINT "6    Enter a transaction"
    .
    .
    .
LOCATE 15, 20: INPUT "Enter your selection"; opt
```

CASE 6 of the SELECT CASE block was empty in Program 9-4. It now contains the lines of code shown in the next listing. An empty CASE 7 has been added for the Quit selection from the menu.

```
CASE 6
   acct = 0
   CALL find.patient(acct%)
   CALL enter.transaction(acct%)
   CLS
CASE 7
```

CASE 6 now calls the find.patient subprogram to select a patient. Then it calls the enter.transaction subprogram to enter the transaction for the selected patient. Select this option to enter a subsequent transaction for a patient who has been previously entered. This entry allows you to enter a transaction without entering new patient information. Figure 10-4 shows the revised menu.

The Print Report Subprogram

The print.report subprogram has been changed to print a report on the patient file. This subprogram is executed when you select item 5, Print an Insurance Report, from the menu.

```
1    Enter a New Patient
2    View a Patient
3    Index a file
4    Key a file
5    Print an Insurance Report
6    Enter a Transaction
7    Quit



Enter your selection?
```

Figure 10-4.   Menu

The subprogram separates the records into blocks, based on insurance company. It prints the name of the insurance company at the top of every block. Below this title it lists information on each patient using the company. The first line of information includes the insurance company code and the patient's name and birthdate. The title and first line of information are printed by the following statements:

```
  PRINT ins.co$(ins.code)
END IF
PRINT "     "; ins.code; ": "; last$, first$, dob$
```

Directly beneath the line of patient information, the subprogram prints a list of the patient's transactions. This is done by the inner DO...LOOP shown here:

```
DO
  GET #3, "trns.rec"
  PRINT TAB(15); procedure$
  old.trns.rec = trns.rec
  trns.rec = CVI(trns.pntr$)
LOOP UNTIL trns.rec < 2
```

The program then returns to search for another patient using the current insurance company, as controlled by the LOOP UNTIL statement of the outer DO...LOOP. This is shown in the following listing:

```
DO
  .
  .
  .
LOOP UNTIL record > maxrecord
```

After the subprogram displays all patient data for a particular insurance company, it prints a prompt asking you to press a key. When you press a key, it displays data for the patients using the next insurance company. Figure 10-5 shows an insurance report for all patients using insurance company 2, Generic Insurance.

After the subprogram displays data for all insurance companies, it closes the file and clears the screen. The subprogram ends, and you are returned to the menu.

The Show Patient Subprogram

The show.patient subprogram calls three other subprograms that were discussed previously. This subprogram is executed when you select item 2, View a Patient, from the menu. The first CALL is to the find.patient subprogram to find a patient by record number or name. The second CALL is to the display.patient.record subprogram. The third CALL is to the hit.any.key subprogram. Figure 10-6 shows the display for patient 3 after the subprogram has executed all three calls.

When you press a key, the subprogram clears the screen and ends. You are returned to the menu.

```
Generic Insurance
      2 : JOHNSON          CLIFFORD      440303
                check up
      2 : JONES            ERNEST        771122
                check up
                lab test
                Xrays
```

```
hit any key to continue
```

Figure 10-5. Insurance report block

```
Patient Record  3

Last Name:          SMITH
First Name:         ROBERTA
Date of birth (YYMMDD): 661111
Insurance Company Code: 3     Piroshki Insurance

                1 Presidential Insurance
                2 Generic Insurance
                3 Piroshki Insurance
                4 Total Disaster Insurance




Transactions
    Xrays
    lab test
```

```
hit any key to continue
```

Figure 10-6. Record of patient 3

SUMMING UP

Even though Program 10-1 seems large and cumbersome at first, it produces quick and efficient results. A professional medical relational data base program would contain more features, more safeguards, and more detail. This program was simplified to clearly demonstrate the concept of relational files.

QuickBASIC structures simplify the problem of breaking a large program into smaller portions that are more manageable and easier to understand, debug, and maintain. In the same way, you can divide a large data base file into smaller files and then link those files with pointers so that you can move between them efficiently. You can also use pointers within a file to link out-of-order records.

This chapter has shown how you can easily expand a small program such as Program 9-4 to provide more features when that program is written in functional blocks of code. QuickBASIC's procedures, such as the subprogram, make programs more structured.

This chapter has also shown you how relational files eliminate the necessity of sorting records. Instead, the organization of records is established by the pointers.

11

UNSTRUCTURED FILES

This chapter teaches you about long string processing and unstructured sequential files. Long string processing lets you access up to 32,767 bytes of information from a file in a single read operation, thus minimizing file access time. Unstructured sequential files let you store large amounts of randomly entered information as efficiently as possible. This chapter shows you how to

- Pack and unpack a long string variable containing several different fields
- Use the QuickBASIC SEEK function and SEEK statement
- Write an index file for sequential unstructured files
- Write relational sequential records

UNSTRUCTURED SEQUENTIAL FILES

Most of the file processing you have done so far has involved random files. In this chapter, you will create data bases using unstructured sequential files. As mentioned before, storing data in unstructured sequential files lets you use your disk space with a minimum of waste. In addition, since string variables can be up to 32,767 bytes long, you can use long string variables to load entire sequential data files with just a few READ statements.

An unstructured sequential file is a sequential file in which information is stored as it is entered. Both the fields and records can vary in length in an unstructured sequential file. Any number of the fields within a record can be repeated, and these fields can occur in any sequence. In addition, if no data pertaining to a given field exists, then that field is not written to the file. The term *unstructured*, then, indicates that the file contains randomly entered records with an unknown number of fields. The file's only structure is provided by the records the file contains, and by the fields that can be identified by their delimiters.

When you store information in a random file, the computer allocates the same number of bytes for each record, regardless of the actual number of bytes used by your data. For example, in Chapter 9, "Indexed and Keyed Files," you wrote a program to enter patient information. In this program, the space allocated for the patient's first name was 10 bytes, and for the last name 20 bytes. The program would use the same number of bytes to store Jo Smith's name as it would to store Andreas Popadopoulos' name. In an unstructured sequential file, however, each record uses only the number of bytes needed to store the actual data—Jo Smith would require 7 bytes and Andreas Popadopoulos would require 19 bytes. By storing these two names in a sequential file, then, you could save as many as 34 bytes.

Delimited Fields

A random file consists of fixed length records that contain fixed length fields. In the patient file you created in Chapter 9, each record contains the following four fixed length fields: first name (10 bytes), last name (20 bytes), insurance company ID (4 bytes), and date of birth (6 bytes). An unstructured sequential file consists of variable length records that contain variable length fields. A field only uses as many bytes as the actual data stored in that field. Since the length of each field aries, you cannot use a constant field length to determine the start of a field. However, to determine where a variable length field within a record begins and ends, simply append a delimiter to each field. A delimiter, as its name implies, delimits one item from another. A delimiter can be any unique combination of characters that identifies the end of a field. The following example shows a record that uses a one-character delimiter.

```
Name!Address@City#Telephone$
```

In this example, !, @, #, and $ are field delimiters. The first field (Name) ends with an exclamation point (!), the second field (Address) ends with an at sign (@), the third field (City) ends with a number sign (#), and the fourth field (Telephone) ends with a dollar sign ($).

The following example shows a record that uses two-character delimiters.

```
PATIENT ID^aINSURANCE COMPANY^bPROCEDURE^cDATE^dFEE^e
PAYMENT AMOUNT^fPAYMENT DATE^gDISALLOWEDAMOUNT^h
DISALLOWED DATE^i
```

In this record, ^a, ^b, ^c, ^d, ^e, ^f, ^g, ^h, and ^i are all field delimiters. The delimiter ^a marks the end of the first field, ^b marks the end of the second field, ^c marks the end of the third field, and so on. You could, of course, choose any characters to be delimiters, but they must be unique. Also note that a delimiter must never occur within a field; if this happened, you would never be sure where the end of the field was.

Unstructured Records

An unstructured sequential file consists of any number of variable length, delimited field unstructured records. An unstructured record is a record that contains any number of variable length fields entered in any order. As an example, consider the following delimited patient transaction record:

```
ppppp^aPROCEDURE^bDATE^cDOCTOR^dNURSE^eEQUIPMENT^f
```

This record stores the pointer to the next transaction for this patient (ppppp), the procedure or treatment performed, the date of the procedure, and so on. However, for a given patient, some of these fields may be needed more than once, and others not needed at all. For instance, assume that a patient is treated with procedures 4527, B72, and P97 on the same day. Two doctors and one nurse assisted in this treatment, using three different pieces of equipment. When you create a record to store this information, the unstructured record will consist of as many fields as necessary to record all of this related information, but no more. The patient record for this example might look like the following listing:

```
331^a4527^b051588^cSMITH^dB72^bJONES^dP97^bPAVLESKI^e
```

The delimiter for the end of the record is a return character (ASCII 13). The field that contains no information (EQUIPMENT) is not written to the record. The first field is the pointer to the next transaction record; if this is the last transaction for this patient, the next pointer is −1. Thus this unstructured sequential file is also a relational file. Relational files were described in Chapter 10.

An unstructured record can contain any number of fields, and thus might become very long. You can use long string variables to pack and retrieve these unstructured records. Later in this chapter, you will learn how to pack and unpack an unstructured record with long string variables.

Long String Processing

In an unstructured sequential file, a single record consisting of delimited, variable length fields can be very long. A string variable can be from 1 to 32,767 bytes long. So a long string variable (say, 10,000 bytes) provides enough space for any unstructured record you might create. Also, with a long string variable, you can read several thousand bytes of a sequential file into memory with only one read operation. Such a long string has to be parsed into individual records, but since this parsing is done in memory, it is very fast. And, if you create an indexed file that includes the position of each new record in the file, you can access a single record in a sequential file just as fast as a record in a random file.

The unstructured patient transaction record in the last example can contain one or several procedures that used from none to several pieces of equipment. One record may contain only one doctor and one procedure; another record may contain three procedures, two nurses, and three doctors. The records may contain any number of pieces of equipment. Since a record may be short (e.g., one doctor and one procedure), or very long (e.g., three procedures and seven doctors), you can effectively use a long string variable (10,000 bytes) to store and retrieve the patient transactions.

Packing an Unstructured Record

As you enter data for each field, the data and the appropriate delimiter are appended to the long string variable that is accumulating the data record. The process of appending fields to a string is called *packing*. Program 11-1 packs a patient transaction while building up the data record in the string *pro$*.

As you enter each field, this program appends the data entered and its delimiter to *pro$*. If you do not enter data for a given field, then the program appends neither the field nor its delimiter.

Parsing an Unstructured Record

You parse an unstructured record by locating a field delimiter and then slicing that field off of the string containing the entire

```
REM ** BUILD A DATA RECORD **
' Program 11-1  File: PRO1101.BAS

REM ** Initialize **
CLS : DEFINT A-Z

REM ** Field Descriptions (tr.type$) **
tr.type$(1) = "Procedure"
tr.type$(2) = "Date"
tr.type$(3) = "Doctor"
tr.type$(4) = "Nurse"
tr.type$(5) = "Equipment"
tr.max = 5

REM ** INPUT for Each Field **
pro$ = ""
FOR num = 1 TO tr.max
  PRINT tr.type$(num); ": ";
  INPUT ; entry$
  PRINT
  IF entry$ <> "" THEN
    pro$ = pro$ + "^" + LTRIM$(STR$(num)) + entry$
  END IF
NEXT num
pro$ = pro$ + "^"
```

Program 11-1.   Building an Unstructured Record

record. You have finished parsing when no more delimiters exist in the record. Program 11-2 illustrates this process.

In this program, *pos.hat* is the position of the next closest field delimiter; *old.pos.hat* is the position of the next field delimiter after *pos.hat*. The variable *tr.type* identifies the type of the current field. This field, then, begins at position *old.pos.hat* and is *pos.hat* minus *old.pos.hat* long.

An Index to a Sequential File

You can index a sequential file in much the same way as you did a random file. An indexed file created from a random file contains

```
REM ** PARSING A RECORD **
' Program 11-2   File: PRO1102.BAS

REM ** Initialize **
CLS : DEFINT A-Z

REM ** pro$ Contains a Patient Transaction Record **
pos.hat = INSTR(pro$, "^")
DO
   old.pos.hat = pos.hat + 2
   pos.hat = INSTR(pos.hat + 1, pro$, "^")
   tr.type = VAL(MID$(pro$, old.pos.hat - 1, 1))
   PRINT TAB(5); tr.type$(tr.type); ": ";
   PRINT MID$(pro$, old.pos.hat, pos.hat - old.pos.hat)
LOOP UNTIL pos.hat = LEN(pro$)
```

Program 11-2.   Parsing an Unstructured Record

pointers that are record numbers; an indexed file created from a sequential file contains pointers that are the beginning byte of the record in the file. In the following listing, the indexed file to the sequential file (TRANSACT.DAT) contains the beginning position of each patient's first transaction record. All other transaction records are located with the relational pointer contained in each record.

```
SUB enter.transaction (acct)
   GET #1, acct
   LOCATE 18, 1
   pro$ = ""
   FOR i = 1 TO tr.max
     PRINT tr.type$(i); ": ";
     INPUT ; entry$
     PRINT
     IF entry$ <> "" THEN
       pro$ = pro$ + "^" + CHR$(i + 64) + entry$
     END IF
   NEXT i
   pro$ = pro$ + "^"
   IF pro$ <> "^" THEN
     trns.ptr$ = "-1      "
     IF CVL(trns$) < 1 THEN
       OPEN "A", #2, "transact.dat"
       LSET trns$ = MKL$(LOF(2) + 1)
       PUT #1, acct
     ELSE
```

```
      trns.ptr = CVL(trns$)
      OPEN "I", #2, "transact.dat"
      DO
         SEEK #2, trns.ptr
         LINE INPUT #2, trns.rec$
         old.trns.ptr = trns.ptr
         trns.ptr = VAL(LEFT$(trns.rec$, 6))
      LOOP UNTIL trns.ptr <= 0
      trns.ptr = LOF(2) + 1
      trns.rec$ = LEFT$(LTRIM$(STR$(trns.ptr)) + "          ", 6)
+ MID$(trns.rec$, 7)
      CLOSE #2
      OPEN "A", #2, "transact.dat"

      REM *** update the previous record
      SEEK #2, old.trns.ptr
      PRINT #2, trns.rec$

      REM *** move filepointer to end-of-file
      SEEK #2, LOF(2) + 1
    END IF
    PRINT #2, trns.ptr$ + pro$
    CLOSE #2
  END IF
END SUB
```

This program updates the indexed file if you add a new patient, and updates the relational pointers for each new transaction for a given patient. Since each record in the transaction file contains the position of the next transaction record, this example also illustrates how you can use the SEEK statement with an indexed file to access a record in the sequential file.

The SEEK Statement and the SEEK Function

You can use the SEEK statement to position the file pointer to any byte in a sequential file. The only restriction is that you cannot move the SEEK statement more than 2,147,483,647 bytes at once. The preceding example uses the SEEK statement to position the file pointer to the first byte of the first transaction record for a given patient.

The following statement positions the file pointer of file #2 (TRANSACT.DAT) *trns.ptr* bytes into the file:

```
SEEK #2, TRNS.PTR
```

Since *trns.ptr* is the beginning position of this record, the following LINE INPUT statement loads the entire next transaction record, except for the return that delimits the end of the record:

```
LINE INPUT #2, trns.rec$
```

The SEEK function returns the current position of the file pointer. An example of this is shown in the following listing.

```
SEEK(2)
```

This statement returns the position of the file pointer for file #2.

A Medical Data Base Maintenance Program

Program 11-3 is a medical data base maintenance program that uses the techniques discussed in this chapter. Study the following highlights in this example

- The use of the index to a sequential file
- The use of the SEEK statement to move the file pointer to the beginning of the desired record
- The efficient packing in the enter.transaction procedure
- The simple and elegant parsing in the print.report procedure

The concepts presented in this chapter introduced you to an elegant and graceful way of programming. This style uses fewer lines of code, and is easier to write, read, modify, and maintain than other programming styles. Since it also packs to disk and core more tightly and executes faster, this style has every advantage over the old fixed field convention. Fixed fields are mindlessly derived from a dim ancestral root in COBOL which used punched card decks, IBM 407s, Hollerith census machines, and baked clay cuneiform accounts.

Let's conclude with this analogy: consider that those beautiful brassy baroque post office boxes lined up in formal rectilinear arrays correspond to fixed field data bases. Your box may be empty or stuffed to overflowing, but even if it is usually empty, you pay for it. In contrast, those mail bags flowing in and out of the loading dock are unstructured data bases. They hold no extra space, but can expand to whatever size is necessary, within limits. The classification of the data is neatly tagged on each letter (record), and this information always accompanies the letter. A fixed field post office box has no way to accommodate whatever information is being sent; an unstructured mail bag can expand or contract to fit the information being sent.

```
DECLARE SUB binsearch (serch$, search.field!, n!, f!)
DECLARE SUB create.key ()
DECLARE SUB create.index ()
DECLARE SUB display.patient.record (acct!)
DECLARE SUB enter.patient.record ()
DECLARE SUB enter.transaction (acct!)
DECLARE SUB find.patient (acct!)
DECLARE SUB hit.any.key ()
DECLARE SUB maintain.ins.key ()
DECLARE SUB menu ()
DECLARE SUB print.report ()
DECLARE SUB quicksort (sort$(), left, right)
DECLARE SUB show.patient ()

REM ** UNSTRUCTURED MEDICAL DATA BASE MAINTENANCE PROGRAM **
' Program 11-3  File: PRO1103.BAS

DIM SHARED ss$(100), fld$(10), ndx(100), ins.co$(4), key$(2)
DIM SHARED last$, first$, dob$, account$, ins$, acctnum$, trns$
DIM SHARED tr.type$(10), tr.max

REM ** Open patient data file **
OPEN "R", #1, "Patient.Dat", 50

REM ** Field Statements **
' Note the change of the null$ at the end of the
' Field statement to trns$
FIELD #1, 20 AS last$, 10 AS first$, 6 AS dob$, 6 AS account$,
4 AS ins$, 4 AS trns$
' Field layout for record 1
```

Program 11-3.   Medical Data Base Maintenance Program

```
FIELD #1, 50 AS acctnum$
' This field statement allows the
' user to specify the key or index field
FIELD #1, 30 AS fld$(1), 6 AS fld$(2), 6 AS fld$(3), 4 AS fld$(4),
4 AS null$
' Layout of field for insurance key
FIELD #1, 5 AS key$(2), 37 AS null$, 4 AS key$(1)

REM ** Insurance Company Data **
ins.co$(1) = "Presidential Insurance"
ins.co$(2) = "Generic Insurance"
ins.co$(3) = "Piroshki Insurance"
ins.co$(4) = "Total Disaster Insurance"

REM ** Transaction Data Types
tr.type$(1) = "Procedure"
tr.type$(2) = "Date"
tr.type$(3) = "Doctor"
tr.type$(4) = "Nurse"
tr.type$(5) = "Equipment"
tr.max = 5

REM ** Begin Main Program **
CALL menu
CLOSE #1
END

SUB binsearch (serch$, search.field, n, f) STATIC
  low = 0
  high = n - 1
  WHILE low <= high
    mid = INT((low + high) / 2)
    GET #1, ndx(mid)
    IF serch$ > fld$(search.field) THEN
      low = mid + 1
    ELSEIF serch$ < fld$(search.field) THEN
      high = mid - 1
    ELSE
      f = ndx(mid)
      low = high + 1
    END IF
  WEND
END SUB

SUB create.index
  CLS
  INPUT "Enter field to index"; index.field
  GET #1, 1
```

Program 11-3.   Medical Data Base Maintenance
Program (*continued*)

```
   maxrecord = VAL(acctnum$) - 1
   FOR record = 2 TO maxrecord
     GET #1, record
     ss$(record) = fld$(index.field)
     ndx(record) = record
   NEXT record
   CALL quicksort(ss$(), 1, maxrecord)
   FOR i = 1 TO maxrecord
     PRINT USING "## &"; ndx(i); ss$(i)
   NEXT i
   CALL hit.any.key
   ndx(1) = maxrecord
   PRINT
   OPEN "O", #2, "patfld" + MID$(STR$(index.field), 2) + ".ndx"
   FOR record = 1 TO maxrecord
     PRINT #2, ndx(record)
   NEXT record
   CLOSE #2
END SUB

SUB create.key
   CLS
   GET #1, 1
   maxrecord = VAL(acctnum$) - 1
   FOR record = 2 TO maxrecord
     GET #1, record
     ss$(record) = key$(1) + key$(2)
     ndx(record) = record
   NEXT record
   CALL quicksort(ss$(), 1, maxrecord)
   ndx(1) = maxrecord
   PRINT
   OPEN "R", #2, "patins.key"
   FIELD #2, 9 AS inskey$, 4 AS pntr$
   FOR record = 1 TO maxrecord
     LSET inskey$ = ss$(record)
     LSET pntr$ = MKL$(ndx(record))
     PUT #2, record
   NEXT record
   CLOSE #2
END SUB

SUB display.patient.record (acct)
   REM ** Initialize Values **
   lname$ = ""
   name$ = ""
   date.of.birth$ = ""
   new.acct = (acct = 0)
   CLS

   IF acct > 1 THEN
```

Program 11-3.   Medical Data Base Maintenance
Program (*continued*)

```
   PRINT "Patient Record "; acct
   GET #1, acct
   lname$ = last$
   name$ = first$
   date.of.birth$ = dob$
   insurance$ = ins$
ELSE
   GET #1, 1
   acct = VAL(acctnum$) + 1
END IF

REM ** Prepare the Screen **
LOCATE 3, 1
PRINT "Last Name:              ................"
PRINT "First Name:         ........."
PRINT "Date of birth (YYMMDD): ......"
PRINT "Insurance Company Code: ."
PRINT
IF new.acct THEN
   FOR i = 1 TO 4
      LOCATE 7 + i, 15
      PRINT USING "## &"; i; ins.co$(i)
   NEXT i
END IF
LOCATE 3, 25: PRINT lname$
LOCATE 4, 25: PRINT name$
LOCATE 5, 25: PRINT date.of.birth$
LOCATE 6, 25: PRINT ins$; "  "; ins.co$(VAL(ins$))
IF new.acct THEN
   LOCATE 14, 1
ELSE
   LOCATE 8, 1
END IF
GET #1, acct
trns.ptr$ = trns$
IF new.acct THEN trns.ptr$ = MKL$(-1)
IF CVL(trns.ptr$) > 0 THEN
   trns.ptr = CVL(trns.ptr$)
   OPEN "I", #2, "transact.dat"
   trans.count = 1
   DO
      PRINT "Transaction #"; trans.count
      SEEK #2, trns.ptr
      INPUT #2, transact$
      trns.ptr$ = LEFT$(transact$, 6)
      procedure$ = MID$(transact$, 7)
      pos.hat = INSTR(procedure$, "^")
      DO
         old.pos.hat = pos.hat + 2
         pos.hat = INSTR(pos.hat + 1, procedure$, "^")
         tr.type = ASC(MID$(procedure$, old.pos.hat - 1, 1))
         - 64
```

Program 11-3.   Medical Data Base Maintenance
Program (*continued*)

```
            PRINT TAB(5); tr.type$(tr.type); ": ";
            PRINT MID$(procedure$, old.pos.hat,
            pos.hat - old.pos.hat)
        LOOP UNTIL pos.hat = LEN(procedure$)
        old.trns.ptr = trns.ptr
        trns.ptr = VAL(trns.ptr$)
        trans.count = trans.count + 1
      LOOP UNTIL trns.ptr < 0
      CLOSE #2
    ELSE
      IF new.acct = 0 THEN
        PRINT "No transactions"
      END IF
    END IF
END SUB

SUB enter.patient.record
    DO
      GET #1, 1
      account = VAL(acctnum$)
      CALL display.patient.record(0)
      LOCATE 1, 1
      PRINT "Patient Record "; account
      LOCATE 3, 25
      INPUT ; "", last.name$: last.name$ = UCASE$(last.name$)
      LOCATE 3, 25: PRINT last.name$
      LOCATE 4, 25
      INPUT ; "", first.name$: first.name$ = UCASE$(first.name$)
      LOCATE 4, 25: PRINT first.name$
      LOCATE 5, 25
      INPUT ; "", date.of.birth$
      LOCATE 6, 25
      INPUT ; "", inscode$
      LOCATE 6, 25
      PRINT ins.co$(VAL(inscode$))
      LOCATE 14, 1
      IF last.name$ = "" AND first.name$ = "" AND dob$ = ""
      AND inscode$ = "" THEN
        r$ = ""
      ELSE
        INPUT "Are these correct? (Y/N)", r$
      END IF
    LOOP UNTIL UCASE$(r$) <> "N"
    IF r$ <> "" THEN
      IF account < 2 THEN account = 2
      LSET last$ = last.name$
      LSET first$ = first.name$
      LSET dob$ = date.of.birth$
      LSET ins$ = inscode$
      LSET trns$ = MKL$(-1)
      PUT #1, account
      CALL enter.transaction(account)
```

Program 11-3.   Medical Data Base Maintenance
Program (*continued*)

```
      account = account + 1
      LSET acctnum$ = STR$(account)
      PUT #1, 1
   END IF
   CLS
END SUB

SUB enter.transaction (acct)
   GET #1, acct
   LOCATE 18, 1
   pro$ = ""
   FOR i = 1 TO tr.max
      PRINT tr.type$(i); ": ";
      INPUT ; entry$
      PRINT
      IF entry$ <> "" THEN
         pro$ = pro$ + "^" + CHR$(i + 64) + entry$
      END IF
   NEXT i
   pro$ = pro$ + "^"
   IF pro$ <> "^" THEN
      trns.ptr$ = "-1    "
      IF CVL(trns$) < 1 THEN
         OPEN "A", #2, "transact.dat"
         LSET trns$ = MKL$(LOF(2) + 1)
         PUT #1, acct
      ELSE
         trns.ptr = CVL(trns$)
         OPEN "I", #2, "transact.dat"
         DO
            SEEK #2, trns.ptr
            LINE INPUT #2, trns.rec$
            old.trns.ptr = trns.ptr
            trns.ptr = VAL(LEFT$(trns.rec$, 6))
         LOOP UNTIL trns.ptr <= 0
         trns.ptr = LOF(2) + 1
         trns.rec$ = LEFT$(LTRIM$(STR$(trns.ptr)) + "         ", 6) +
MID$(trns.rec$, 7)
         CLOSE #2
         OPEN "A", #2, "transact.dat"

         REM *** update the previous record
         SEEK #2, old.trns.ptr
         PRINT #2, trns.rec$

         REM *** move filepointer to end-of-file
         SEEK #2, LOF(2) + 1
      END IF
      PRINT #2, trns.ptr$ + pro$
      CLOSE #2
   END IF
END SUB
```

Program 11-3.   Medical Data Base Maintenance
Program (*continued*)

```
SUB find.patient (acct)
  CLS
  LINE INPUT "Patient record or last name, first name: ", serch$
  IF VAL(serch$) > 0 THEN
    acct = VAL(serch$)
  ELSE
    comma = INSTR(serch$, ",")
    LSET last$ = LEFT$(serch$, comma - 1)
    LSET first$ = MID$(serch$, comma + 1)
    serch$ = UCASE$(fld$(1))
    CLS
    PRINT "Searching for "; serch$
    GET #1, 1
    maxrecord = VAL(acctnum$) - 1
    OPEN "I", #2, "patfld1.ndx"
    FOR i = 1 TO maxrecord
      INPUT #2, ndx(i)
    NEXT i
    CLOSE #2
    CALL binsearch(serch$, 1, maxrecord, acct!)
  END IF
END SUB

SUB hit.any.key
  LOCATE 24, 1
  PRINT "hit any key to continue";
  DO: LOOP UNTIL INKEY$ <> ""
  LOCATE 24, 1
  PRINT "                          ";
END SUB

SUB menu
  REM ** Initialize **
  maxopt = 7
  CLS

  DO
    LOCATE 5, 20: PRINT "1   Enter a New Patient"
    LOCATE 6, 20: PRINT "2   View a Patient"
    LOCATE 7, 20: PRINT "3   Index a file"
    LOCATE 8, 20: PRINT "4   Key a file"
    LOCATE 9, 20: PRINT "5   Print an Insurance Report"
    LOCATE 10, 20: PRINT "6   Enter a Transaction"
    LOCATE 5 + maxopt, 19: PRINT maxopt; "  Quit"
    LOCATE 15, 20: INPUT "Enter your selection"; opt
    SELECT CASE opt
      CASE 1
        CALL enter.patient.record
      CASE 2
        CALL show.patient
      CASE 3
        CALL create.index
        CLS
      CASE 4
        CALL create.key
```

Program 11-3.   Medical Data Base Maintenance
Program (*continued*)

```
      CASE 5
        CALL print.report
      CASE 6
        acct = 0
        CALL find.patient(acct)
        CALL enter.transaction(acct)
        CLS
      CASE 7
      CASE ELSE
        LOCATE 24, 10
        PRINT "Enter a number from 1 to "; maxopt;
    END SELECT
  LOOP UNTIL opt = maxopt
END SUB

SUB print.report
  OPEN "R", #2, "patins.key"
  FIELD #2, 9 AS inskey$, 4 AS pntr$
  record = 2
  GET #1, 1
  maxrecord = VAL(acctnum$) - 1
  ins.code = 0
  CLS
  DO
    GET #2, record
    GET #1, CVL(pntr$)
    IF VAL(inskey$) > ins.code THEN
      IF ins.code > 0 THEN CALL hit.any.key
      CLS
      PRINT
      ins.code = ins.code + 1
      PRINT ins.co$(ins.code)
    END IF
    PRINT last$; first$, dob$
    GET #1, CVL(pntr$)
    IF LEN(trns$) <> 0 THEN
      OPEN "I", #3, "transact.dat"
      IF CVL(trns$) >= 0 THEN
        trns.rec = CVL(trns$)
        trns.count = 1
        DO
          SEEK #3, trns.rec
          INPUT #3, transact$
          PRINT "Transaction: "; trns.count
trns.ptr$ = LEFT$(transact$, 6)
procedure$ = MID$(transact$, 7)
pos.hat = INSTR(procedure$, "^")
DO
  old.pos.hat = pos.hat + 2
  pos.hat = INSTR(pos.hat + 1, procedure$, "^")
  tr.type = ASC(MID$(procedure$, old.pos.hat - 1, 1)) - 64
  PRINT TAB(5); tr.type$(tr.type); ": ";
  PRINT MID$(procedure$, old.pos.hat, pos.hat - old.pos.hat)
LOOP UNTIL pos.hat = LEN(procedure$)
old.trns.rec = trns.rec
```

Program 11-3.   Medical Data Base Maintenance
Program (*continued*)

```
            trns.rec = VAL(trns.ptr$)
            trns.count = trns.count + 1
            PRINT
          LOOP UNTIL trns.rec < 0
        ELSE
          PRINT TAB(5); "No transactions"
        END IF
        CLOSE #3
      END IF
      record = record + 1
    LOOP UNTIL record > maxrecord
    CALL hit.any.key
    CLOSE #2
    CLS
END SUB

SUB quicksort (sort$(), left, right)
  IF right > left THEN
    i = left - 1: j = right
    DO
      DO
        i = i + 1
      LOOP WHILE (sort$(i) < sort$(right))
      DO
        j = j - 1
      LOOP WHILE (sort$(j) > sort$(right)) AND (j > 0)
      t$ = sort$(i): t = ndx(i)
      sort$(i) = sort$(j): ndx(i) = ndx(j)
      sort$(j) = t$: ndx(j) = t
    LOOP WHILE j > i
    sort$(j) = sort$(i): ndx(j) = ndx(i)
    sort$(i) = sort$(right): ndx(i) = ndx(right)
    sort$(right) = t$: ndx(right) = t
    quicksort sort$(), left, i - 1
    quicksort sort$(), i + 1, right
  END IF
END SUB

SUB show.patient
  acct = 0
  CALL find.patient(acct)
  CALL display.patient.record(acct)
  CALL hit.any.key
  CLS
END SUB
```

Program 11-3.   Medical Data Base
                     Maintenance Program (*continued*)

A

QuickBASIC 4.5 RESERVED WORDS

The following words are reserved in QuickBASIC Version 4.5. They may not be used as labels or as names of variables or procedures.

ABS	CALL	COM	DECLARE	ENVIRON
ACCESS	CALLS	COMMAND$	DEF	ENVIRON$
ALIAS	CASE	COMMON	DEFDBL	EOF
AND	CDBL	CONST	DEFINT	EQV
ANY	CDECL	COS	DEFLNG	ERASE
APPEND	CHAIN	CSNG	DEFSNG	ERDEV
AS	CHDIR	CSRLIN	DEFSTR	ERDEV$
ASC	CHR$	CVD	DIM	ERL
ATN	CINT	CVDMBF	DO	ERR
BASE	CIRCLE	CVI	DOUBLE	ERROR
BEEP	CLEAR	CVL	DRAW	EXIT
BINARY	CLNG	CVS	ELSE	EXP
BLOAD	CLOSE	CVSMBF	ELSEIF	FIELD
BSAVE	CLS	DATA	END	FILEATTR
BYVAL	COLOR	DATE$	ENDIF	FILES

FIX	LIST	OPTION	RND	SUB
FOR	LOC	OR	RSET	SWAP
FRE	LOCAL	OUT	RTRIM$	SYSTEM
FREEFILE	LOCATE	OUTPUT	RUN	TAB
FUNCTION	LOCK	PAINT	SADD	TAN
GET	LOF	PALETTE	SCREEN	THEN
GOSUB	LOG	PCOPY	SEEK	TIME$
GOTO	LONG	PEEK	SEG	TIMER
HEX$	LOOP	PEN	SELECT	TO
IF	LPOS	PLAY	SETMEM	TROFF
IMP	LPRINT	PMAP	SGN	TRON
INKEY$	LSET	POINT	SHARED	TYPE
INP	LTRIM$	POKE	SHELL	UBOUND
INPUT	MID$	POS	SIGNAL	UCASE$
INPUT$	MKD$	PRESET	SIN	UEVENT
INSTR	MKDIR	PRINT	SINGLE	UNLOCK
INT	MKDMBF$	PSET	SLEEP	UNTIL
INTEGER	MKI$	PUT	SOUND	USING
IOCTL	MKL$	RANDOM	SPACE$	VAL
IOCTL$	MKS$	RANDOMIZE	SPC	VARPTR
IS	MKSMBF$	READ	SQR	VARPTR$
KEY	MOD	REDIM	STATIC	VARSEG
KILL	NAME	REM	STEP	VIEW
LBOUND	NEXT	RESET	STICK	WAIT
LCASE$	NOT	RESTORE	STOP	WEND
LEFT$	OCT$	RESUME	STR$	WHILE
LEN	OFF	RETURN	STRIG	WIDTH
LET	ON	RIGHT$	STRING	WINDOW
LINE	OPEN	RMDIR	STRING$	WRITE
				XOR

B

ASCII CODES

Decimal Value	Hexadecimal Value	Control Character	Character
0	00	NUL	Null
1	01	SOH	☺
2	02	STX	●
3	03	ETX	♥
4	04	EOT	♦
5	05	ENQ	♣
6	06	ACK	♠
7	07	BEL	Beep
8	08	BS	◘
9	09	HT	Tab
10	0A	LF	Line-feed
11	0B	VT	Cursor home
12	0C	FF	Form-feed
13	0D	CR	Enter

Table B-1. ASCII Codes for the PC

Decimal Value	Hexadecimal Value	Control Character	Character
14	0E	SO	
15	0F	SI	
16	10	DLE	
17	11	DC1	
18	12	DC2	
19	13	DC3	
20	14	DC4	
21	15	NAK	
22	16	SYN	
23	17	ETB	
24	18	CAN	↑
25	19	EM	↓
26	1A	SUB	→
27	1B	ESC	←
28	1C	FS	Cursor right
29	1D	GS	Cursor left
30	1E	RS	Cursor up
31	1F	US	Cursor down
32	20	SP	Space
33	21		!
34	22		,,
35	23		#
36	24		$
37	25		%
38	26		&
39	27		'
40	28		(
41	29		)
42	2A		*
43	2B		+
44	2C		,
45	2D		-
46	2E		.
47	2F		/
48	30		0
49	31		1
50	32		2
51	33		3
52	34		4

Table B-1. ASCII Codes for the PC (*continued*)

Decimal Value	Hexadecimal Value	Control Character	Character
53	35		5
54	36		6
55	37		7
56	38		8
57	39		9
58	3A		:
59	3B		;
60	3C		<
61	3D		=
62	3E		>
63	3F		?
64	40		@
65	41		A
66	42		B
67	43		C
68	44		D
69	45		E
70	46		F
71	47		G
72	48		H
73	49		I
74	4A		J
75	4B		K
76	4C		L
77	4D		M
78	4E		N
79	4F		O
80	50		P
81	51		Q
82	52		R
83	53		S
84	54		T
85	55		U
86	56		V
87	57		W
88	58		X
89	59		Y
90	5A		Z
91	5B		[

Table B-1.   ASCII Codes for the PC (*continued*)

Decimal Value	Hexadecimal Value	Control Character	Character
92	5C		\
93	5D		]
94	5E		^
95	5F		—
96	60		'
97	61		a
98	62		b
99	63		c
100	64		d
101	65		e
102	66		f
103	67		g
104	68		h
105	69		i
106	6A		j
107	6B		k
108	6C		l
109	6D		m
110	6E		n
111	6F		o
112	70		p
113	71		q
114	72		r
115	73		s
116	74		t
117	75		u
118	76		v
119	77		w
120	78		x
121	79		y
122	7A		z
123	7B		{
124	7C			
125	7D		}
126	7E		~
127	7F	DEL	⌂
128	80		Ç
129	81		ü
130	82		é

Table B-1. ASCII Codes for the PC (*continued*)

Decimal Value	Hexadecimal Value	Control Character	Character
131	83		â
132	84		ä
133	85		à
134	86		å
135	87		ç
136	88		ê
137	89		ë
138	8A		è
139	8B		ï
140	8C		î
141	8D		ì
142	8E		Ä
143	8F		Å
144	90		É
145	91		æ
146	92		Æ
147	93		ô
148	94		ö
149	95		ò
150	96		û
151	97		ù
152	98		ÿ
153	99		Ö
154	9A		Ü
155	9B		¢
156	9C		£
157	9D		¥
158	9E		Pt
159	9F		ƒ
160	A0		á
161	A1		í
162	A2		ó
163	A3		ú
164	A4		ñ
165	A5		Ñ
166	A6		ª
167	A7		º
168	A8		¿
169	A9		⌐

Table B-1.   ASCII Codes for the PC (*continued*)

Decimal Value	Hexadecimal Value	Control Character	Character
170	AA		¬
171	AB		½
172	AC		¼
173	AD		¡
174	AE		«
175	AF		»
176	B0		░
177	B1		▒
178	B2		▓
179	B3		│
180	B4		┤
181	B5		╡
182	B6		╢
183	B7		╖
184	B8		╕
185	B9		╣
186	BA		║
187	BB		╗
188	BC		╝
189	BD		╜
190	BE		╛
191	BF		┐
192	C0		└
193	C1		┴
194	C2		┬
195	C3		├
196	C4		─
197	C5		┼
198	C6		╞
199	C7		╟
200	C8		╚
201	C9		╔
202	CA		╩
203	CB		╦
204	CC		╠
205	CD		═
206	CE		╬
207	CF		╧
208	D0		╨

Table B-1. ASCII Codes for the PC (*continued*)

Decimal Value	Hexadecimal Value	Control Character	Character
209	D1		$=$
210	D2		π
211	D3		⊫
212	D4		⊨
213	D5		⊧
214	D6		⫟
215	D7		╫
216	D8		╪
217	D9		⌐
218	DA		⌐
219	DB		█
220	DC		▄
221	DD		▌
222	DE		▐
223	DF		▀
224	E0		α
225	E1		β
226	E2		Γ
227	E3		π
228	E4		Σ
229	E5		σ
230	E6		μ
231	E7		τ
232	E8		Φ
233	E9		θ
234	EA		Ω
235	EB		δ
236	EC		∞
237	ED		$\varnothing$
238	EE		ϵ
239	EF		$\cap$
240	F0		$\equiv$
241	F1		$\pm$
242	F2		$\geq$
243	F3		$\leq$
244	F4		$\lceil$
245	F5		$\rfloor$
246	F6		$\div$
247	F7		$\approx$

Table B-1. ASCII Codes for the PC (*continued*)

Decimal Value	Hexadecimal Value	Control Character	Character
248	F8		°
249	F9		•
250	FA		·
251	FB		$\sqrt{}$
252	FC		^{n}
253	FD		^{2}
254	FE		■
255	FF		(blank)

Table B-1.   ASCII Codes for the PC (*continued*)

TRADEMARKS

INDEX

The manuscript for this book was prepared and submitted to Osborne/McGraw-Hill in electronic form.

The acquisitions editor for this project was Jeffrey Pepper, the technical reviewer was Ethan Winer, and the project editor was Fran Haselsteiner.

Text design uses Century Expanded for text body and display.

Cover art by Bay Graphics Design Associates. Cover separation and cover supplier, Phoenix Color Corp. Screens produced with InSet, from InSet Systems, Inc. Book printed and bound by R.R. Donnelley & Sons Company, Crawfordsville, Indiana.

Introducing
Microsoft® QuickC™.
The best reason to go to C.

Microsoft QuickC is a powerful first step into C programming. It compiles at the blazing speed of 10,000 lines per minute.

Its full-featured debugger lets you animate, single step, and watch the value of variables change as you execute.

And its seamlessly integrated environment means you can edit, use the in-memory MAKE utility, compile, debug, and execute your program without switching between tools.

New QuickC from Microsoft.

It's everything you need to make your programs run at top speed.

For the name of your nearest Microsoft dealer, call (800) 541-1261, Dept. D70.